THE GRAPH OF DESIRE

THE GRAPH OF DESIRE
Using the Work
of Jacques Lacan

Alfredo Eidelsztein

Translated with notes by *Florencia F.C. Shanahan*
Translation reviewed by *Philip Malone*
General editor *Florencia Eidelsztein*

Routledge
Taylor & Francis Group
LONDON AND NEW YORK

First published 2009 by Karnac Books Ltd.

Published 2018 by Routledge
2 Park Square, Milton Park, Abingdon, Oxon OX14 4RN
711 Third Avenue, New York, NY 10017, USA

Routledge is an imprint of the Taylor & Francis Group, an informa business

British Library Cataloguing in Publication Data

A C.I.P. for this book is available from the British Library

ISBN-13: 9781855756106 (pbk)

Typeset by Vikatan Publishing Solutions (P) Ltd., Chennai, India

The First Complete Edition in English of *Ecrits*, by Bruce Fink had not been
published at the time of the translation of this book, in 2004. Sheridan's
translation, especially that of "The Subversion of the Subject and Dialectic of
Desire", required several comments and notes which would perhaps have
not been necessary if we had then availed of Fink's version.

CONTENTS

INTRODUCTION   vii

CHAPTER ONE
Graph of desire and topology   1

CHAPTER TWO
Object *a* and mathematical graph and nets theory   19

CHAPTER THREE
The structure of language: Need, demand and desire   45

CHAPTER FOUR
Graph one   71

CHAPTER FIVE
Questions and answers: The impossible—neurosis
and psychosis   89

CHAPTER SIX
Ideal (*I*)—ego (*m*)—ideal (*i*): Graph 2   103

CHAPTER SEVEN
Graph 3: The question   125

CHAPTER EIGHT
Desire and *fantasme*: A pathway (I)—the symptom   143

CHAPTER NINE
Desire and *fantasme*: A pathway (II)   167

CHAPTER TEN
The formula of the *fantasme*: Introduction to the drive   183

CHAPTER ELEVEN
The drive (I)   205

CHAPTER TWELVE
The drive (II)   225

CHAPTER THIRTEEN
S(Ⱥ): Being, *jouissance* and desire   235

CHAPTER FOURTEEN
S(Ⱥ): "Being (Res), *jouissance* and desire" (II)   253

CHAPTER FIFTEEN
The castration complex in Lacan's teaching   267

REFERENCES   279

INDEX   283

INTRODUCTION

This book gathers the lectures of the Post-Graduate Course entitled *The Graph of Desire and the Psychoanalytic Clinic*, held in 1993 within the framework of the *Updating Program on Lacanian Psychoanalysis* (Post-Graduate Secretary, Faculty of Psychology, University of Buenos Aires).

Although the subject of the course was the graph of desire and its articulation with the psychoanalytical practice, the reader will find here that Lacan's article *The subversion of the subject and the dialectic of desire in the Freudian unconscious* has been intensively looked over, being paraphrased and quoted in almost every class of the course. Considering that the Spanish translation has some problems, I have translated myself certain terms and paragraphs from the original French version, in order to try to understand what Lacan affirms.

The recordings of the course lectures constitute the basis for this book; they have been barely modified, for their colloquial style will not interfere with the reading.

I would like to thank all those who collaborated, in different ways, with this book, which aims at reviving and going into Jacques Lacan's teaching in depth. This gratitude is particularly addressed to the students who made it possible to maintain a permanent interest and enthusiasm during the coursework.

CHAPTER ONE

Graph of desire and topology

I shall dedicate this class to the introduction of the subject of the course, beginning with some points that we will need to master if we want to benefit from what Lacan proposes through the graph of desire.[1]

In Lacan's teaching, the series built with models, schemata, graphs, topologic surfaces and knots takes an exclusive place and significance. There is no other psychoanalyst who has given such importance, given so much time and consideration to this problem of representations in psychoanalysis. This seems to be however very reasonable, taking into account that Lacan was the psychoanalyst who, more than anyone, studied and developed a theory of the representation of the human being.[2]

Within that series, graphs represent the first systematic inclusion of topology into psychoanalysis. I am careful and I say "the first 'systematic' inclusion of topology" because, strictly speaking, there are topological issues already involved in the models and schemata; but systematically speaking, the graph of desire constitutes the first entrance of topology in Lacan's teaching. This point has not been evident and it will be clarified and developed in later chapters.

I will start with a very important historical issue which can be related to a structural dimension: the first study on graphs was carried out by Euler (1707–1783), one of the most prolific mathematicians in history; that study on graphs by Euler is the basis of topology. This means that topology not only enters psychoanalysis via the graphs, but it enters mathematics by the same route.

This opens perhaps a new question: Why should we be interested in the fact that the graphs constitute the systematic entrance of topology into Lacan's teaching and, therefore, into psychoanalysis?

Following this line, I will include a clinical consideration. If our departure point is the structure of the Real, the Symbolic and the Imaginary and if we aim to demonstrate the subject with which Lacanian psychoanalysis operates, then it becomes necessary to depart from the same structural perspective. In other words, if the structure is real, symbolic and imaginary, a real, symbolic and imaginary structure is required to explain the subject of psychoanalysis.

Although this is not, strictly speaking, a theoretical argument, I propose it as the foundation of Lacanian psychoanalytical practice: its specificity. To be precise: theoretical elaborations in psychoanalysis, interventions of the psychoanalyst and the direction of the treatment are governed by the structure of the Real, the Symbolic and the Imaginary.

I will try to show you the difficulties that appear when we do not operate in this way. Let's start from what I consider a structural reading of the optical model. The argument is that this model responds to Lacan's theory of the topography of the unconscious. How does Lacan conceive the topography of the unconscious? The structure that corresponds to the unconscious, according to Lacan, is that of the Real, the Symbolic and the Imaginary (instead of Unconscious, Preconscious and Consciousness). Although it is true that psychoanalysis started with the latter, Lacan proposes us to continue with the former triad.

What is topography in psychoanalysis? And particularly, what is a Freudian topography? It is a spatial relation between instances,[3] between systems. This means that between the Unconscious and Consciousness there is and there will always be the Preconscious. The spatial metaphor is constituted by this 'between'.

And this is Lacan's spatial metaphor in the optical model:

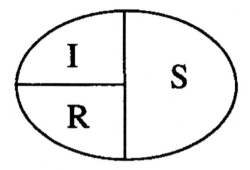

Schema 1.

Imaginary is in this schema where the image that deceives the subject is produced; real is the inaccessible body for the subject, and symbolic is the virtual space.

To visualize the problem a little bit better I propose you to move the letters an anticlockwise quarter turn:

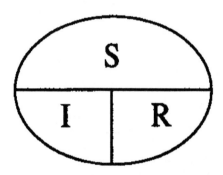

Schema 2.

This is Lacan's proposal: the Symbolic determines the Imaginary and the Real, and at the same time (this is a quotation) 'the Imaginary and the Real are at the same level'. This seems to be a mysterious phrase; are the Imaginary and the Real at the same level? What does "at the same level" mean here? It means that they have an equivalent topical relationship with the Symbolic. And what sort of equivalence is this? Precisely, the fact that both are determined by the Symbolic. But the problem is that Lacan informs us how the

Imaginary and the Real are equally determined by the Symbolic through a model whose own structure is imaginary; namely, in the optical model and because of its imaginary structure, what is trying to be affirmed through its use is denied.

I will give you two examples. The first sense in which we are going to understand "imaginary" is the analogy. In the context of the optical model, where do analogies work? There are two evident dimensions. Firstly, that the "mirror stage" is represented by a mirror. That is an obvious analogy. It is not me who says that, Lacan himself says that this is a simple analogy. And there is another one, more obvious, which is that also the Symbolic order, the A,[4] is represented by a mirror. The problem is that it is impossible to maintain the dimension of the analogy in the symbolic field, because the signifier (this is an elementary axiom) is pure difference. There is no possible analogy at the level of the signifier. So how are we going to support the notion that the signifier is the determinant, if we are using an imaginary instrument to account for it? The model, its structure, denies that which is being affirmed at the level of the content.

To say it in psychoanalytical terminology: this proceeding is a denial. We say that the Symbolic is what determines, but in the way of saying it, we annul what we are saying.

There is a very interesting example regarding this point. Lacan says that it is not in the mirror, but in the mother's look when turning around, where the child finds the captivated image ("mother" is a function that could be fulfilled by the father or the grand-mother,[5] a function as the "father" is). But, what is a "captivated look?" The first thing we notice is that the fascinated look requires symbolic determination because it has to do with the question of desire. But by explaining this with mirrors, we are doing no more than denying it.

Up to here I have only justified that it is necessary for the conceptual structure of psychoanalysis to agree with what psychoanalysis states as the structure of the subject; I have not yet said why topology is an appropriate means for doing so. Actually, I have only affirmed that Lacan's solution to this problem is topology, but I have not said why. In order that we may begin to consider this problem, I will now present you with some of the necessary elements.

The benefit derived from using a topological conception of the Imaginary, the Symbolic and the Real leads to the implication that we must consider at least five dimensions. *The first one* is that in topology, shape is not taken into account; that is to say, shapes do not perform any function in topology. That is why it is metaphorically called the geometry of the rubber sheet: because although a surface can be stretched, folded and squeezed, its shape would change but not its structure. This is very important because it allows us to rectify our conceptual notion of clinical structure. Until Lacan, we used to work using "clinical forms"; that is diagnosing according to appearances (and those who have clinical experience have surely discovered how often the obsessional appearance conceals a hysterical structure, for instance). In psychoanalysis, shapes or forms do not perform a determinant function; that is why the Imaginary cannot have a determining role in what we choose for representing the structure.

The second one: in topology no measurable function of distance or size is considered. In psychoanalysis, we apply these properties to time and space. My proposal is to articulate the fact that quantifiable functions of distance and size do not carry out any function, to articulate this within the psychoanalytical conception of time and space. You know that sometimes an instant never ends, and other times several years pass in a moment; therefore those dimensions of time do not match with any measurable category: an instant can be longer than many years. Regarding space it is even easier to notice this problem. In psychoanalysis the dimension of space does not work according to a measure. I am not saying that we psychoanalysts do not take spatial or temporal dimensions into account: I am saying that (as it happens in topology) we cannot account for them through measurement. Who would not question the clinical salience (even without being a psychoanalyst) of the separation between a father and a son who have a troubled relationship, if that separation is due to the fact that the son emigrates abroad? This means that thousands of kilometers may not have any function. The problem is that considering separation in its spatial dimension (its measure in kilometers for example) does not solve the conflict, as is the case in topology. The structures, that topology works with are not determined by measurable dimensions.

The third: topology allows us to work using a new relation between exterior and interior. Again—as happens with time and space—I am not saying that the categories of interior and exterior are not applied. What I am saying is that they are connected in a way that runs counter to our intuitive (common sense) perception. This dimension will be more difficult to explain; the graph will be a good way to approach this problem. The imaginary categories (which we all possess) of interior and exterior, and their mutual relation, do not accord us any insight into certain fundamental Lacanian statements, for instance, that the unconscious is at the same time the discourse of the Other and the subject's most personal and internal thing. How could it be the most internal thing if it is what the subject receives from the Other? Perhaps you have not considered it in this way, but what remains a problem is the structure of the analytic experience itself. Why is an analyst required for someone to be analyzed? The concept of individual (which should be recalled in opposition to the notion of subject) means "indivisible"; but do not forget that it is founded on the opposition between interior and exterior. The individual is an undivided body, but entirely divided from the inside/outside perspective (he is divided in relation to the world). Because, what would the notion of individual mean if we said there is nothing to distinguish the interior from the exterior?

The forth: topology turns upside down the usual concept of the object/subject relation; the universal, most known and with which we normally operate: *res extensa/res cogitans* (extended substance/thinking substance). It is from this Cartesian opposition that the idea of *res extensa* being three-dimensional is established (if something is *res extensa*, then it is three-dimensional, *parts extra parts*, and each of them is exterior regarding the others). On the other hand, *res cogitans*—thinking—is "non-dimensional", the well known "knowledge is no load to carry". At this point topology becomes relevant, since it works with two-dimensional objects and surfaces. This means that it is not universally true that the object is three-dimensional; there exist objects, things that are two-dimensional. And this is useful to us because Lacanian psychoanalysis maintains that the subject and the object a[6] are two-dimensional. Thus, thanks to and through the articulation between psychoanalysis and topology, we move from the pair three-dimensionality/non-dimensionality towards the two-dimensional object and subject.

You have probably already noticed that the drive's so-called satisfaction-object does not exactly agree with the Lacanian notion of a two-dimensional object. Let us take, for instance, the flowers within the optical model.[7] To embrace the flowers in the same way a body embraces its object (via the erogenous zone): is this Lacan's notion of the object *a*? No, because the flowers are three-dimensional, and the object *a* is two-dimensional. This is not a theoretical confusion; it is the subject's confusion: we permanently want to make the two-dimensional object *a* three-dimensional. Why? In order to find it in the real world. Thus, the Lacanian direction of the cure will attack the conception of the object as three-dimensional.

The fifth (and last): topology operates with the notion of invariants.[8] Invariants are structural properties.

I do not know if you have the same feeling, but it seems that the more we say the more everything begins to vanish. There is no shape, no size. Everything vanishes, except invariants; that is the structure. Why do we need invariants? Where do we find structural invariants in Lacan's teaching? That "the unconscious is structured like a language" is an invariant in Lacan. Despite the problem of shape, size, distance and subjective variability (taking subjects one by one), something invariant remains: for instance, the fact that the unconscious is structured like a language, which is true for every subject.

I know I am not explaining all the phrases that I am introducing. These are precisely the phrases we are going to work with through the graph of desire's elaboration. But at this stage we should not forget (and that is why I take as an example 'the unconscious is structured like a language') the fact that not only psychoanalysts borrow the notion of invariants from topology: linguists do too. Roman Jakobson, for instance. He states that every language in the world—known or to be known—has the same structure. Saying that the unconscious is structured like a language implies exactly the same: any unconscious that any psychoanalyst must face in his or her practice will have the same structure. Beyond any subject, it will always be an unconscious structured like a language. *Invariants* is the notion that will allow us to connect "the clinic of the case by case"[9] with the structural properties.

To conclude this initial approach, let us establish the first important point about the graph of desire: it is the channel by which topology is systematically included into psychoanalysis. But we have not yet said why the graph of desire is topological.

I first supposed (this was some time ago) that the graph of desire was not topological, that topology was the Möbius strip, the torus, the cross-cap and Klein's bottle—the four topological surfaces—. I imagine that some of you might still be in that position. It is therefore necessary to explore the articulation between the well-known basis of topology and the graph of desire.

The second point that makes the graph of desire a crucial elaboration within Lacan's teaching is that it marks the strong entrance of the notion of the letter; it is the first systematic inclusion (I am careful once again) of the notion of the letter into Lacanian psychoanalysis—and also into psychoanalysis in general. This means that there were antecedents. We find them in Freud, for example, related to the problem of the double inscription. In Lacan's work we can establish a series starting from "The Purloined Letter",[10] around *Seminar 2*.[11]

A sort of arch can be drawn in Lacan's teaching from *Seminar 2, The Ego in Freud's Theory and in the Technique of Psychoanalysis* (by 1954) to "The Instance of the Letter ..."[12] (simultaneously with *Seminar 5* in 1957/58). "The Instance of the Letter ..." is one of Lacan's less understood writings, one of the most read and least understood. I have always supposed that it was the main Lacanian text on linguistics: if we want to see how linguistics is introduced into Lacan's teaching, we have to read "The Instance of the Letter ..." It is the text where concepts such as phonemes, signifier, metaphor, metonymy, etc., appear; it is a writing full of references to Saussure and Jakobson: there are plenty of linguistic references. But it seems clear to me that even from the title the problem is being anticipated by Lacan; if this had been his main linguistic writing, he would have written "The Instance of the Signifier in the Unconscious"; he does not name it like that, but he chooses "The Instance of the Letter in the Unconscious".

This series, which begins with "The Purloined Letter" and continues with "The Instance of the Letter ..." may be closed with "The Subversion of the Subject ..." (contemporaneous with *Seminar 7, The Ethics of Psychoanalysis* and *Seminar 8, Transference*). Undoubtedly the consideration of the function and consequences of the notion of the letter in Lacan's teaching does not cease in the '60s. To the contrary, it will become progressively more important. What I am proposing to you is that the graph of desire is an ideal tool for opposing signifier and letter, that is, for opposing (for articulating and differentiating) linguistics and psychoanalysis. Thus, we have signifier and linguistics on one side, letter and psychoanalysis on the other.

To justify what I have just said, let us advance to *Seminar 17, The Reverse of Psychoanalysis.*[13] A basic but extremely important opposition appears there: the signifier is listened to, and the letter is read. Because, actually, the problem is how we understand S_1 and S_2; this is one of the aspects of the problem of the opposition between linguistics and psychoanalysis, between letter and signifier.

It is important to notice that whenever Lacan is transmitting something, he considers that the content he is transmitting has to be also present in the device he chooses for transmitting it. Lacan never talks about the thing. He always talks around the thing. S_1 and S_2: signifier 1 and signifier 2. S_1: master signifier; S_2: knowledge or set of signifying articulations. But when Lacan says this, he is considering us as subjects. What I am saying is that Lacan does not write the word 'signifier': he already writes a letter, 'S', which you read as 'signifier' and which you believe is a signifier, but which is in fact a letter with a sub-index, a number.

We are not discussing simple things; in fact we are affirming that the graph of desire is the way in which the function of the letter is, for the first time, systematically introduced into Lacanian psychoanalysis, and even into psychoanalysis itself.

We will analyze now the graph corresponding to schema number 3.

This is a schematic version, it is not the complete graph; it is the graph I need to work on this problem. We must notice that there are letters and words there. There are words such as *"jouissance"* (which I leave in French) or "signifier" (which I translate). *"Jouissance"*, which means "enjoyment", is used by Lacan taking advantage of the homophony "I hear", "I listen", "I hear sense[14]"; that is why I consider we must keep it in French, to maintain the polysemy.[15] So we have the word "enjoyment", the word "castration", the word "voice" and the word "signifier". Do you notice that they have a peculiar position in the graph? They are in the middle of a line. There is a line with an arrow (a vector, we would naively say, without knowledge of the theory of graphs), and in the middle are words. We must also notice that the intersection points are letters, and the arrival and the departure points of the vector that crosses the four intersection points are letters too. Why is it, then, that there are letters on the one hand, and words on the other?

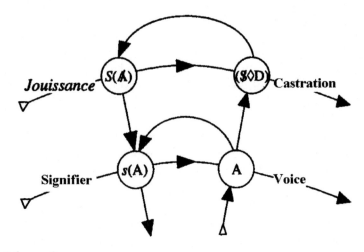

Schema 3.

S(A̸) is to be read: the signifier of a lack in the Other. What is not easy to understand is why in a certain place of the graph Lacan writes "signifier" with an "S" and in another place of the same graph he writes it with the word "signifier". Considering that the author is Lacan, we must take seriously his not being systematic. However, generally, we do not notice these details. Why? Because we are speaking beings.[16] This is precisely what he is working on through the graph: the opposition between the signifier we listen to and the letter, which has to be read.

I do not know how close to your own practice might these questions be, but if yours is actually an analytical practice, you should face the problem of distinguishing between listening and reading every day. A psychoanalyst, properly speaking, does not listen, he or she reads.

A good theoretical device is required, in order to oppose signifier and letter, and the graph of desire is such a device.

Finally, the last argument in favour of the graph of desire (the most controversial I will present to you) is that the graph of desire is the introduction of the object *a* in Lacan's teaching. But this does not fit easily. Several objections may be made to this statement. Firstly, because the object *a*—as such—is not written in the graph of desire (the function of the letter small "*a*" in brackets beside the small "*i*", *i(a)*; or the one it takes when written as a part of the formula ($̸◊a) will be discussed later on). Let us say for the moment that the former corresponds to the other's image and the latter to the *fantasme*.[17] This is not the object *a* as cause of desire. Despite that, I propose to consider that the graph of desire's structure is the object *a*. This will require several arguments as, for instance, dates do not match. You have probably studied many commentators of Lacan's work who assert that the object *a* is incorporated in Lacan's teaching around *Seminar 7*, but the graph of desire is in fact previous.

But if the object *a*'s function as cause of desire is not the fundamental structure of the graph of desire, why is this graph named 'graph of desire' then? To complicate things a little bit more: in the context of the "psychical functions" which Lacan inscribes in the graph (desire, phantasy, drive, imaginary ideal, symbolic ideal), desire is only a letter among others. Why is it then "the graph of desire" instead of "Lacan's graph" or "the graph of psychical functions" or "the graph of desire, drive, phantasy, etc."? I suggest to you that this is because through this graph the object *a*, as cause of desire, is introduced, because the fundamental structure of the graph is the object *a*. I will try to demonstrate it.

Now we have to do some work which might be boring for some of you and fun for others, but it has to be done anyway if we want to get into Lacan's teaching: namely, to study the mathematical theory of graphs and nets.

Let us begin with "the bridges of Königsberg". The following would be an approximate map of them:

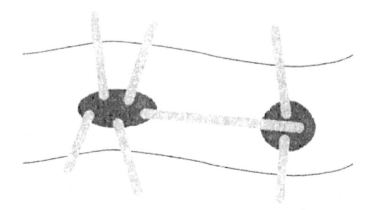

Schema 4.

We have said that it was in connection with Euler's work that topology was developed. Specifically, Euler's works on graphs are connected with the problem of the bridges of Königsberg.

Königsberg was the name of a German university city (nowadays named Kaliningrad), bisected by the Preguel river. There were two islands in the river, connected with both of its banks as well as between them, by seven bridges. The question the inhabitants used to pose to themselves was: can somebody from Königsberg leave her or his home, crossing only once each of the seven bridges and get back home? Until Euler, there was no answer to this problem. Departing from this entertainment the theory of graphs, first, and topology, later, were born.

Euler finds the answer because he transforms the map into a graph. The following is Euler's work with some clarifications added by me.

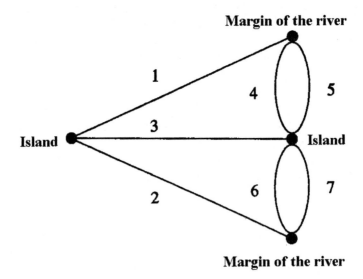

Schema 5.

Why is it difficult to understand the transformation from map to graph? Any of you would have probably accepted that the islands were represented by two circles. It is clear that their shape and size do not really matter for this system of bridges. What you would probably have not accepted so easily were the banks of the river being represented by points. Why can the riversides be represented by a point? Because there is continuity among the three arrival points (the three bridges facing the north bank, for instance).

We are going to number each of the bridges: the first one up on the left which goes from the left island to the superior bank will be 1; the one below 1 in the left island which goes down will be 2; 3 will be the one linking both islands; the first in the other island that goes up will be 4; its neighbor will be 5; below 4 will be 6, and below 5 number 7.

The graph is composed of four circles that represent respectively the four surfaces (two islands and two banks). And they are all equally represented, because the river divides the land surface in two (one point being the "north hemisphere", like an island). For problems of this kind it does not matter whether the distance between two bridges is 1 kilometer or 1 millimeter.

Notice how size and shape have disappeared as functions. An isle and a hemisphere are represented equally. Size and shape are no longer relevant and, consequently, the elements of the graph do not represent the bridges' actual dimensions.

The question is: can one cross this graph completely without passing twice over the same point and without raising the pencil? Having a graph, the question can now be formal and rigorously answered, as science demands. The necessary mathematical premises to answer this question will be developed in our next class.

We will find an experimental solution using what I have called the "school graph":

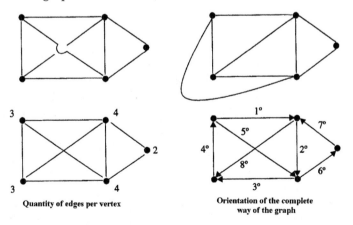

Quantity of edges per vertex   Orientation of the complete
                                       way of the graph

Schema 6.

I called this graph the "school graph" because I used to play with it at school. Can the graph be completely crossed without passing twice over the same point and without raising the pencil?

In order to answer this question we will need to progress a little into the mathematical theory of graphs. Circles will be called vertices and lines edges. The overlapping point of diagonals is a false intersection point, that is, it is not a vertex. The upper vertex on the left has three edges coming and going out of it; the one below too; the upper vertex on the right has four; the one below that has four too; and the one further to the right has two. Which is the right way of 'traveling' this graph? To depart from a vertex, which has an even number of, edges, in this case, three. That is why I wrote "1st"over the edge that goes from 3 to 4. The rest is clear: first cross the rectangle's perimeter, and then take a diagonal; after that both sides of the triangle, and finally go back along the other diagonal. I want you to notice that although we could make it complete, we could not do so and return to the point of departure. I will remind you of the question: Can somebody from Königsberg leave her or his home, cross only once each of the seven bridges and get back home? If the structure of the bridges of Königsberg was that of the "school graph" the answer would be: "No. He or she can travel the complete circuit but will not return to the departure point". Please observe that in this 'school graph' we departed from a vertex with an even number of edges (3) and we arrived to another vertex, also with an even number of edges (3).

I will propose some definitions. We can say that the graph is a tripartite structure—like the structure we are working with: Real, Symbolic and Imaginary. The graph's structure implies vertices, edges and a relation. Each "E" (edge) element is associated to a pair of "V" (vertex) elements; each edge is the union of two vertices. There exists no edge, which connects a vertex with nothing: that is impossible. The mathematical formula for this: G: (V, E, φ), where "V" is vertex, "E" is edge and "φ" is the relation. Notice that φ is a symbol frequently used in mathematics; we also use it, following Lacan's teaching.

A vertex can be represented as a "point" (also called a "node"); edges can be represented by "lines" or "arches". And it is important to remember that the overlapping of two edges (like the diagonals in the 'school graph') is not a vertex.

So we have two questions: Can the bridges of Königsberg be crossed as implied by the problem? And, what are those edges that come from nowhere and go nowhere in the graph of desire? These questions will remain unanswered for the moment.

There is a Freudian assertion repeatedly and frequently quoted by Lacan. I will say it in German because it was in German that the problem was posed: '*Wo Es war, soll Ich werden*'. Lacan's translation is: 'Where id was, there the subject shall be'.[18] Why does he translate "*Ich*" as "subject" and not as "ego"? Would Lacan (whose teaching began by emphasizing the opposition of subject and ego) misunderstand the translation of the German "*Ich*"?

For finding a rational answer to this problem I propose that you consider a quotation from Freud (1895) and its schema (Schema 7). It was posited in his "Project for a scientific psychology":

"Let us picture the ego as a network of cathected neurones well facilitated in relation to one another, thus: [see Fig. 14]. If we suppose that a $Q\tilde{n}$ enters a neurone a from outside (ϕ), then, if it were uninfluenced, it would pass to neurone b; but it is so much influenced by the side-cathexis a "that" it gives off only a quotient to b and may even perhaps not reach b at all. Therefore, if an ego exists, it must *inhibit* psychical primary processes (p. 323)."

Freud is proposing us to picture the "ego as a network of cathected [invested] neurones".

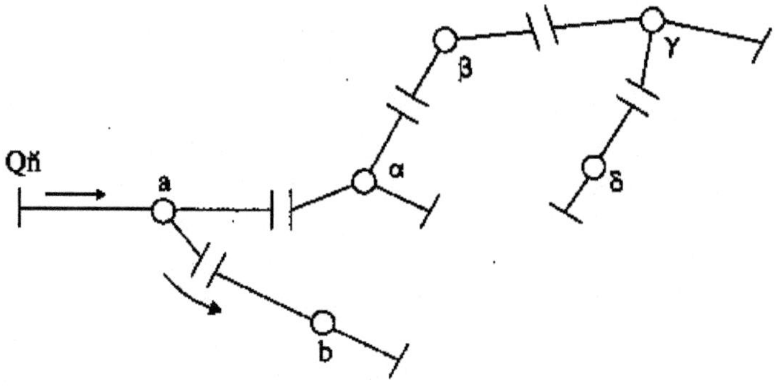

Schema 7.

Mathematicians consider the terms "graph" and "net" to be synonyms. It would have been the same for them if Freud had said "let's picture the id as a graph of invested neurons". Is Lacan's translation correct, if we consider the *"Ich"* as a graph of neurons?

Before going on, I will explain the schema (drawn by Freud himself), which corresponds to the above quotation corresponding to the quotation. On the left "Qñ", the Freudian symbol for quantity; it has an orientation: quantity enters from right to left. Let's explain the letters too: the first one is "a", and there is an arrow going down whose letter is "b". Thus, there are two arrows, one towards "a" and the other one towards "b". If we follow the circuit started in "a", the following letters are: α, β, γ and δ ("alpha", "beta", "gamma" and "delta").

I will propose another series before finishing today:

1. 1895: "Introduction of the Ego" (name given to point 14 in the "Project for a scientific psychology ... ")
2. 1914: "Introduction of the other ego", that is, *On narcissism. An introduction,* where Freud differentiates between libidinal drives of the ego as an object and ego-drives of the other ego; and
3. 1955: "Introduction of the big Other" *(Seminar 2).*

Three "introductions" of three well-differentiated functions: two different egos and the Other. When Lacan has to translate the *"Ich"* of *"Wo Es war, soll Ich werden"*, he chooses "subject" because he understands that this is a Freudian reference to the first ego, the ego as a "network of neurons". "Neurons" which Freud will refer to as "mnemic traces", firstly, and "representations", later. Modern linguistics calls them signifiers. This "ego" is a graph of signifiers, namely, the subject; it has to be well differentiated from the "ego" as the captured object of narcissistic libido.

The first ego, the one from the "Project ... " is a net of representations, that is, a graph. Lacan finds the subject at the same place Freud does: the system of signifiers, which has the structure of a graph.

Notes

1. To follow Lacan's construction of the "graph of desire" see Jacques Lacan, Le Seminaire, Livre 5, "Les formations de l'inconscient", Seuil, Paris, 1998; Jacques Lacan, Le Seminaire, Livre 6, "Le désir et son interprétation" (unpublished); and Jacques Lacan, "The

Subversion of the Subject and the Dialectic of Desire in the Freudian Unconscious", in Écrits, The First Complete Edition in English, Translated by Bruce Fink, Norton, New York, 2006, p. 671.

2. In Spanish 'sujeto humano': literally 'human subject'.

3. *Instanz* in German. Also translated as "agency".

4. A (*Autre*) both the French word and the initial letter in the original.

5. "Mother" and "father" are places in the structure, structural functions that can be fulfilled by any person no matter the biological relationship he or she has or has not with the subject.

6. '*L'objet petit a*' in French. Translated sometimes as 'object small *o*' or '*o* object'. We prefer to keep the original letter as Lacan considered it algebraically.

7. Lacan introduces the "optical model" in Seminar I ("Freud's Papers on Technique", edited by Jacques-Alain Miller, New York, Norton, 1988). He refers to it several times during the course of his work, but especially in his writing "Remarks on Daniel Lagache's Presentation: Psychoanalysis and Personality Structure", in Écrits, The First Complete Edition in English, translated by Bruce Fink, Norton, New York, 2006, p. 543; and in Seminar VIII ("Le Transfert", établi par Jacques-Alain Miller, Paris, Seuil, 1991), Seminar X ("L'Angoisse", établi par Jacques-Alain Miller, Paris, Seuil, 2004) and Seminar XI ("The Four Fundamental Concepts of Psychoanalysis", edited by Jacques-Alain Miller, New York, Norton, 1978).

8. In mathematics, unaffected by a designated operation, as a transformation of coordinates.

9. Direct translation of a commonly used Spanish language expression.

10. Jacques Lacan, "Seminar on 'The Purloined Letter'", in Écrits, The First Complete Edition in English, translated by Bruce Fink, Norton, New York, 2006, p. 6.

11. We must not forget two of the possible meanings of *letter*: "written or printed message sent to somebody" and also "any of the signs in writing or printing that represent a speech sound" (Longman Contemporary English).

12. Jacques Lacan, "The Instance of the Letter in the Unconscious, or Reason Since Freud", in Écrits, The First Complete Edition in English, translated by Bruce Fink, Norton, New York, 2006, p. 412.

13. Unpublished in English. Also known as "The Other Side of Psychoanalysis" and "Psychoanalysis Upside-down".

14. *Sens* in French, sometimes also translated as "meaning". We decided to translate it "sense" not only for its resemblance to the original word but also for its ambiguity.

15. Polysemy: The fact that a word has different meanings.

16. In Spanish *'sujeto hablante'*: literally 'speaking subject'.
17. *"Fantasma"* in Spanish in the original. We decide to keep the French word that Lacan uses: *"fantasme"*, different from *"fantaisie"*. Accordinging to *Le Petit Robert* the former suggests an unconscious idea, whereas the latter seems to be a product of the conscious imagination (perhaps closer to "phantasm" in English). There is also *"fantôme"* in French, equivalent to the English "phantom". This concept is spelt "phantasy" in Freud's Standard Edition.
18. Translated in the SE 'Where id was, there ego shall be' (SE, XXII, 80). Lacan is opposed not only to this translation but to the interpretation of Freud's ideas that it implies.

CHAPTER TWO

Object *a* and mathematical graph and nets theory

Today we will refer specifically to the object *a*. The first thing to be considered when we say "object *a*" is that it fulfils the same function as the value "x" in mathematics: it is an unknown variable.

The letter "*a*" corresponds to an algebraic maneuver, according a name to something that cannot be said. That is why it is hard to tell you what I am going to talk about today; for you to know I must start talking. That is the reason why it is called object *a*, without any attribute or value, just object *a*.

There are several dimensions of the object *a*. I believe it is convenient (I am not saying it is necessary) to distinguish at least three dimensions of the object *a*: spatial, temporal and logical.

Strictly speaking, these are artificial cuts with regards to the notion of the object *a*; they allow us to see more clearly from which perspective we are facing the problem. There is no possibility of working on the spatial dimension of the object *a* without considering the other two dimensions, and vice versa.

To be more explicit, I will say that it is the spatial dimension of the object *a* which is at stake in the graph of desire. The graph of desire, as such, is a device built mainly to work on the spatial dimension

19

of the object *a*. We will start with two already known dimensions: *res cogitans/res extensa*. Although they are Cartesian notions, we will consider them from a different perspective than that of Descartes. The *res cogitans* will be taken as signifying chain and the *res extensa* as body (the notion of body that psychoanalysis operates with).

Hence, we will work on the spatial dimension of the object *a*—as it is presented in the graph of desire—in order to better account for its localization in the signifying chain and the body.

As for the temporal dimension of the object *a*, I chose a quotation from *Seminar 8, Transference*, where Lacan says 'the only true object *a* is the child'. It is not very clear what the child is, but at least it is obvious that this is a temporal dimension of the human subject; child refers to something in the human subject understood from a temporal perspective. The difference between a child and an adult is temporal. We do not know very well what "temporal" means; but we know it is a temporal distinction.

And finally I will say a few words about the logical dimension of the object *a*. Since Freud, a very intimate relationship between the unconscious and a type of logic is proposed. According to Freud, one of the fundamental properties of "his" unconscious is that it cannot inscribe "truth-values" which correspond to their representations. That is, it cannot inscribe which one is true and which one is false, thus, an eminently logical problem. Freud stated that both true and false representations may be inscribed, and that it is not possible to acknowledge the truth about the true ones. He said that the principle of non-contradiction does not operate (although it has been understood that he was referring to the principle of bivalence).[1] It is Lacan who advances towards a better and deeper articulation between psychoanalysis and logic; and he does this by means of his notion of the object *a*.

The notion of object *a* as in its logical dimension requires a certain type of logic to be considered: modal logic. And this is because, from the logical point of view, the object *a* will be the impossible.

In order to work on the structure of the object *a* in its spatial dimension let us recall the definition of the graph which we introduced last week. A "graph" is a tripartite structure "G", which includes "V"—vertex-, "E"—edge- (V and E being finite sets) and the relation which links each E element with each pair of V elements, in the manner specified by φ.

G: (V, E, φ)

It is with this formula in mind that I question the graph of desire in respect of its unusual edges: two have departure points but not arrival points, and the other two have arrival points but no points of departure.

We have already said that regarding graphs, it does not matter how they are drawn; the diagram does not have any function. The graph is not a drawing; shape, distance or size have no function.

We are going to develop this definition of the graph, using a graph which has not been overly studied (although it should be) called the "1-2-3 Net", which appears in Lacan's *Seminar on "The Purloined Letter"*. It is as follows:

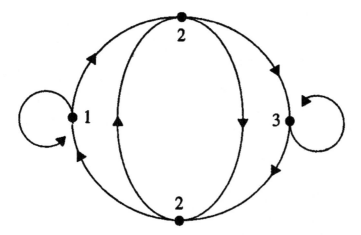

Schema 1.

This is the graph Lacan produces in the *Seminar on "The Purloined Letter"* when he formalizes Edgar Allan Poe's story. This graph represents the relations among the terms 1-2-3 and the way in which these relations are presented. Here, Lacan goes back to the Freudian *fort-da*, in terms of "+ and –". Chance has to do with the plus (+) and the minus (–). But after considering chance we have the inscription of the plus and minus in trios (which Lacan names 1-2-3). What does "1"-"2"-"3" produce? A diachronic series, whose Lacanian name will be "signifying chain".

Then, the "1-2-3 Net" is the graph of a signifying chain.

How many vertices does this net have? Four. Here we find a surprise and another problem: because 1-2-3 leads us to believe that there will be three vertices, but in fact there are four. The "1-2-3 Net" has four vertices (the "2" above is not the same as the "2" below).

We will apply some definitions from graph theory on this 1-2-3 Net, in order to advance further with the graph of desire. We will define: loop, path, chain, connection and orientation or direction.

Once the four vertices are established, I propose to define "loop". It is an edge which begins and ends on the same vertex. This is the case for points "1" and "3" (see schema above).

What is a "walk" in graph theory? It is a sequence of consecutive edges linking one vertex to another, where each edge finishes at the beginning of the next edge.[2] For instance, in the 1-2-3 Net a possible path would be to depart from 1, on the left, to go towards 2, from 2 to continue towards the other 2 below, and from there again to the 2 above, arriving finally at 3.

Let us introduce now the notion of "chain" (it is interesting to note that graph theory uses the same word as de Saussure and Lacan). A chain is a sequence of vertices and edges where all vertices are different. For example, 1, 2, 2, 1 cannot be a chain. Why? Because 1 is repeated and the definition says the vertices have to be different. In a chain one cannot go back to the same term. Therefore, one can take any walk one wants but a chain implies there has to be no repetition of the vertices.

When is a graph connected? (The function of connectivity in graph theory is equivalent to the notion of continuity in topology. We are going to work today on the notions of connectivity and continuity precisely because it is in relation to these notions that

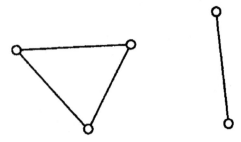

Schema 2.

the concept of object *a* can be defined in its spatial dimension). Both notions of connection and continuity fulfill the function of "invariance" which we have already seen. Hence, a graph has a connected element if in that part a vertex is reachable from any other vertex.

This graph is characterized by having two connected parts not themselves connected. One tends to think they are two graphs because there are two drawings; but actually it is one graph with two unconnected elements.

Regarding the problem of orientation, we find that there are directed edges and undirected edges. With graphs what matters is the structure. A graph can be directed or undirected depending on its edges (whether they are directed or not).

Directed graphs are also called "digraphs" (the bridges of Königsberg graph, for instance, is undirected, given that for crossing the bridges it does not matter which direction the person takes). The 1-2-3 Net, on the contrary, is a directed graph or digraph. Some authors call directed graphs "nets" and undirected graphs "proper graphs".

However, this does not solve the problem of knowing why Lacan called this graph a "net" and the graph of desire a "graph". Because as the graph of desire is a directed graph, he should have called it a net. Otherwise, he should have called both either "graph" or "net".

As we have already said, the notion of connectivity in graph theory is equivalent to the notion of continuity in topology. Continuity is the main property topology operates with (this property is unaffected by stretching or compression). Continuity refers to the consideration of whether there are cuts or glued parts on a certain surface. Two surfaces are topologically equivalent[3] (they have the same structure) if there exists a biunivocal relationship between all of their points without cuts or glued parts. Let us remember that a relationship is "biunivocal" if a term or element of the set is in correspondence with one and only one element of the other set, and vice versa. This is the way in which topologically equivalent surfaces are defined.

I would like to link now the question of continuity to some fundamental elaborations of psychoanalysis in order to show you how, although all this may seem foreign, it is actually "topologically equivalent" to many psychoanalytical problems you have long known.

Let us first examine two quotations from Freud's "Project for a scientific psychology"[4]:

> Whereas in the external world the *processes* exhibit a continuum in two directions, according to quantity and period (quality), the *stimuli* corresponding to them [to the processes] are as regards quantity, firstly *reduced* and secondly *limited* owing to excision, and, as regard quality, are discontinuous (p. 313).

The external processes, to the subject, are continuous. But those processes' effects are, inside, discontinuous. According to Freud, the difference between the inside of the subject and the external world is topological.

Regarding internal processes, so important in their relation to the drive, Freud says in the "Project ..."

> What we know of the *endogenous* stimuli may be expressed in the assumption that they are of an intercellular nature, that they arise continuously and only periodically become psychical stimuli (p. 317).

That is, external processes are continuous, but they are registered discontinuously at a psychical level. And internal stimuli are continuous but psychically registered as discontinuous. What differentiates the subject from the external world and from the biological body is explained by Freud in terms of topological continuity.

Now let us consider a quotation from *The Interpretation of Dreams*[5]:

> But the exigencies of life interfere with this simple function, and it is to them, too, that the apparatus owes the impetus to further development. The exigencies of life confront it [the child] first in the form of the major somatic needs. The excitations produced by internal needs seek discharge in movement, which may be described as an 'internal change' or an 'expression of emotion'. A hungry baby screams or kicks helplessly. But the situation remains unaltered, for the excitation arising from an internal

need is not due to a force producing a *momentary* impact but to one which is in continuous operation. A change can only come about if in some way or other (in the case of the baby, through outside help) an 'experience of satisfaction' can be achieved which puts an end to the internal stimulus (p. 565).

Can you see the problem which arises here? That in the human structure, as conceptualized by Freud, there is a fundamental failure: whereas the stimulus is continuous, the answer found by the subject is discontinuous; and if something other does not come about, this system collapses, there is no escape. Precisely, continuous *versus* discontinuous is the structure of the blind alley (*"cul-de-sac"* in French.). We are facing, again, a topological problem.

We will intensively work on these notions of continuous and discontinuous, formulated by Freud and formalized by Lacan. As we have just now introduced the question, it is clear that this is a problem in Freud's work, and that it is at the heart of the most important issues for psychoanalysis. In order to underline for you the relevance of topology for psychoanalysis, I would like to present another aspect of the same problem. These functions are not only related to the problems of the body and the object *a*. We know the importance Lacan gives to the function of the cut in the session; that is obviously a function of discontinuity. Let us pose the most naïf question, which is frequently the best one: do not non-Lacanians cut the sessions as well? Yes, they do; the problem is to know what the "right cut"[6] is. How is a right cut conceived? This problem is posed by Lacan. Freud missed it.

If an analysis (in its structure) is finite, then psychoanalysis as such implies the right cut. That is, there is the right cut and it is practicable. However, Freud did not see it thus. According to him, the analysis could only finish with an *impasse*[7]: castration anguish[8] for men and penis envy for women.

I think Freud has an absolutely Borgesian[9] way of conceiving the *"cul-de-sac"*: there is no way out because it is infinite. The problem of the terminable (finite) and interminable (infinite) analysis is directly related to one's conception of continuity. This is valid for the session and for the structure of the analysis itself. And this is how Lacan concludes that there must exist a right cut for the session: it will only exist in so far as there is a right cut in the analysis itself, its end.

How is that discontinuity to be conceived in order to know that we are moving in the right direction?

To answer this we must now consider invariants for graphs, the laws of construction for graphs.

The first invariant is that graphs must be constituted by connected parts. Thus, the minimal structure required for a graph would be two vertices and the edge by which they are connected, as a certain φ relation establishes it.

The second invariant is that there must be an even number of vertices of odd degree in every graph. Let us go back for a second: why am I introducing you to these invariants? Our point of departure is that the structure of the psychoanalytic clinic is that of the "case by case". Then, how can something be valid for every case? From the same perspective: what sense does it make for us to be here together? If each of our cases is structurally condemned to have nothing in common with any of our colleagues' cases, how is it possible for the psychoanalytic discourse to organize itself and to progress?

Once again, why are graphs important?

It is crucial to understand that although there are graphs that nobody yet has invented, and consequently there will always be new graphs, the invariants of their structure are already known to us.

Do you remember the tenet that Lacan addresses to psychoanalysts in "The function and field ..."? He proposes that we train ourselves by doing cross-words. In the same sense I would give you the following piece of advice: make graphs. In this way you will be able

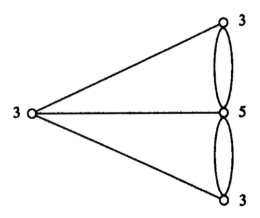

Schema 3.

to verify that these structural properties always work, inevitably: every graph will always be composed of connected parts and it will always have an even number of vertices of odd degree.

What is a vertex degree? It is *the number of edges coming in and going out of it.* Let us analyze this in the graph of the seven bridges of Königsberg.

Last week I wrote numbers for each bridge in order to identify them; but in this case I will renumber the graph:

This time each vertex has a number and is represented by a circle. The number indicates the vertex degree. Thus, we have three vertices whose degree is three and one vertex whose degree is five; so, they are all vertices of odd degree. How many vertices of odd degree are there in this graph? Four. Then, the law has been fulfilled: an even number of vertices of odd degree. Let us enunciate the third invariant: only graphs having all their vertices of even degree can be entirely crossed without repeating trajectories.

You must be aware that these invariants only work if loops are not considered.

So without considering loops, the 1-2-3 Net can be completely crossed following this path: 1-2, 2-3, 3-2, 2-2, 2-2, 2-1. This is how we can say that all of the vertices in this graph are even, because for vertices 1 and 3 the degree is two, and for vertices 2 -up- and 2 -down- the degree is four. Therefore, the law has been fulfilled again.

Strictly speaking, this is only one form of this invariant. Also graphs having only vertices of even degree and graphs having only two vertices of odd degree can be entirely crossed without repeating trajectories. That is why the "school graph" could be included here. It has even vertices except two whose degree is three. In order to cross it one has to start from one of the vertices of odd degree and finish in the other one.

The fourth invariant (this is extremely important) is that any graph can be done in a three-dimensional space without needing cuts. In the case of the "school graph", for instance, the cross of diagonals is what we call a "cut". An alternative is to make one of those "diagonals" pass outside the rectangle in the second diagram of the graph (see schema 6, Chapter One).

Let us do the following exercise: three consecutive houses need to be connected to the gas, electricity and water supply. Can this connection be made by means of a two-dimensional graph or, on the contrary, is a three-dimensional graph required? Let us assign a designatory letter to each house, A, B and C, and a designatory number to the gas, the electricity and the water, 1, 2 and 3 respectively. A three-dimensional graph is needed (note the difficulty in connecting house A to net 3, as shown by schema 4).

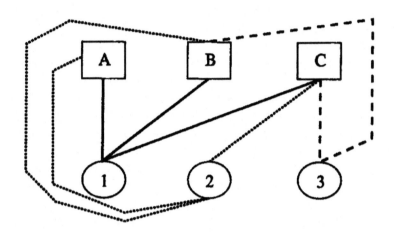

Schema 4.

Is the graph of desire two-dimensional or three-dimensional? I pose these questions so you may apply them to Lacan's graph—which accounts for the structure of the subject of the unconscious.

One more digression. We are going to work on the structure of two Freudian schemata. To the one we saw in our first class (the neural net) we will add the "comb schema" from *The interpretation of dreams* and the "ovum schema" from *The Ego and the Id*. After that we will have considered the three most important Freudian schemata.

The "comb schema" has a different structure than the "neural net". I made an oriented graph of the "comb schema".

Schema 5.

Which, structurally speaking, is equivalent to:

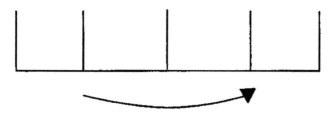

Schema 6.

It is equivalent because the vertical lines have no function in any dimension apart from the horizontal. It can only be crossed from left to right, in the same direction that we write. My interest is to show you that the structure involved in the "comb schema" cannot be the graph structure required in psychoanalysis, precisely because the "comb schema" has the problem of being one-dimensional. In order to work on the structure of the subject of the unconscious, we need a two-dimensional structure. That is why I propose to oppose both Freudian schemata: the network of cathected neurons and the "comb schema". Remember that Freud includes the "comb schema" in the chapter on regression, for it cannot be represented by the one-dimensional schema of the psychical apparatus.

In fact, there is a problem at this point concerning the reading that is made of Lacan's "S_1 and S_2". I think they are usually read as if they were two vectors and one edge graph. Within the 1–2 context, we tend to believe that for the second S to be S_2, another S must have been previously considered as S_1. I believe it is read like the "comb schema", it is read as if it were a graph structured like schema 5, and this is a mistake. This mistake has to be thought of in relation to other theories. Neither the notion of chain in graph theory (I have already given you its definition), or that of linearity of de Saussure's linguistics are enough for conceiving the psychoanalytical notion of signifying chain. In mathematical graph theory the notion of chain implies that each vertex where the edge arrives has to be different. Consequently, it is impossible for repetition to be represented there; the unconscious as "an other scene"[10] is unthinkable in de Saussure's conception. Roman Jakobson criticized Saussure's notion of "linearity" considering it a "prejudice" of the Genevian master (cf. *Fundamentos del lenguaje*, Editorial Ayuso, p. 109).[11]

Let us consider a well-known quotation which is seldom taken into account; it is in "The agency of the letter …", in *Écrits*. Lacan says:

> With the second property of the signifier, that of combining
> according to the laws of a closed order, is affirmed the necessity
> of the topological substratum of which the term I ordinarily use,
> namely, the signifying chain, gives an approximate idea (p. 169).

Lacan's notion of signifying chain requires topological support.
The Lacanian notion of the signifying chain is not equivalent to the
general notion or to mathematical graph theory one; it is his. And so
he defines it:

> [...] rings whose necklace is sealed into the ring of another
> necklace made of rings.[12]

I will add two elements in order to clarify the problem. On the one
hand, the word "ring" is referring here to one of the topological surfaces, the torus. And on the other hand, the expression "is sealed",
ambiguous in Spanish, can mean both "to close" and "to mark".
Lacan says that a torus is marked and closed when it embraces
another torus.

Although a torus can be "imaginarized"[13] as a ring, it is important to note that it could never be represented as a link within a
chain represented as a three-dimensional object. It must not be
considered as linear or one-dimensional either: it is, in topology,
two-dimensional.

What use do we make of the opposition between the "comb
schema" and the neural net? What are we tying to work on? For
given that they do not have the same structure, the "comb schema"
being one-dimensional and the neural net being two-dimensional.
It is only by reviewing this opposition that we will understand why
Lacan reads the Freudian 'Wo Es war, soll Ich werden' the way he does.
Even for non-German speakers, there are two words that deserve
to be recognized: "Es" and "Ich". Lacan proposes to translate them
as "it"[14] and "subject",[15] respectively. He reads then "Where it was,
there the subject shall be",[16] because he considers that Freud is referring there to the Ich of the neural net.

That is why I am insisting on the graph's structure: because Lacan's
proposal is that the subject has the same structure as a graph.

Let us consider again the sequence of text presented in our last
class: "Introduction of the Ego", "Introduction of Narcissism"
and "Introduction of the big Other". It is a fundamental series in

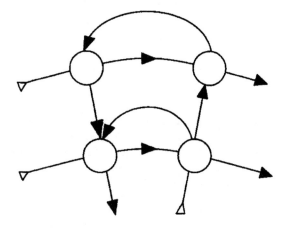

Schema 7.

psychoanalysis: subject, ego and Other are not the same. As you can see, Lacan has been a unique reader of Freud; there are Freudian writings which only Lacan "has read".

Let us go now into Lacan's graph. We are going to consider this graph in order to answer the question we left open in our last class:

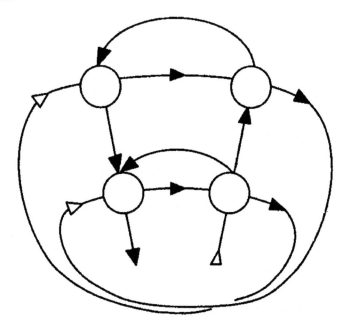

Schema 8.

We will consider the above schema in opposition to the following:

As far as I know, Lacan never published this "closed" graph. However, he clearly indicated that it had to be conceived in this way; he did it in his first class of *The Seminar, Book 9* (unpublished). I think he trusted his readers: he supposed that he could be read exactly as he could read others. If we do not suppose that we can still read, there is no future for psychoanalysis. If the analyst does not suppose that the patient can read, there is no possibility for an analysis. The possibility for analysis to exist is to suppose that subjects are able to read. We can doubt they want to read, but they are capable of doing so. I state that Lacan built his graph having in mind the same idea: my readers can and must read me. Let us try it.

The solution I propose to the "crazy" edges (those that come from and go nowhere) of the graph of desire in Schema 8, is supported by an extremely important Lacanian notion: the "interior eight". It can be obtained by making an eight and folding one circle on top of the other.

Why do I think this is the right solution? Although there are several, I believe the two fundamental solutions are the "interior eight" and the following:

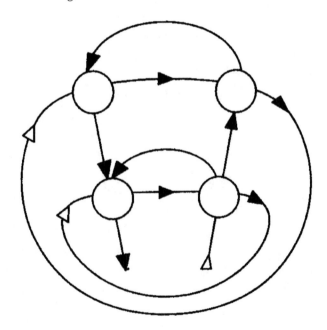

Schema 9.

They are fundamental because they both must be taken into account in order to correctly understand the notion of the unconscious in psychoanalysis.

Topologically speaking, the solution of the "interior eight" is a continuous solution; what is at stake is, precisely, the notion of the divided subject. The notion of the divided subject is taken by Lacan from Freud, more specifically, from a posthumous Freudian text: "Splitting of the ego in the process of defence"[17] (*"Ichspaltung"* in German). Now, which is the split ego? Is it the ego in "Introduction of the ego"? Is it the cathected network of neurons that Lacan reads as subject? And also, which fundamental property of the ego is highlighted in "On narcissism. An introduction"?

I am thinking of another famous Freudian paragraph, the one on the "new psychical act" (surely you all remember it). What is that ego's fundamental property? It is unitary, it is unity *par excellence*. And what is the new psychical act? Again, unity.

There is nothing unitary in biology. At the level of the cells unity does not exist. It is the symbolic order that must introduce it.

Can then *"Ichspaltung"* be referred to the narcissistic ego? No, because the structure of that ego is unity and not division. The ego that for Freud is divided is the neural net's ego, namely, the divided subject.

What is the structure of this division? Between the two parts of what is divided a continuous relation is maintained. Answers in the form of discontinuity do not belong to the psychoanalytical field. Division understood as discontinuous division is previous to psychoanalysis; it is the famous "ego into the ego". In order to account for the difference between these two forms of division, I will ask you to consider the following schemata:

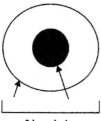

2 boundaries

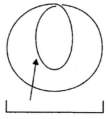

1 boundary

Schema 10.

The notion of the divided subject with which psychoanalysis operates (the subject of the unconscious) implies a continuous division. It is exactly the same logic posited by Freud in "Negation" ("de-negation"): to affirm by means of denying or to deny by means of affirming; that is, a continuous type of solution. This is the subject's division as posited in the "graph of desire". It is the only one that allows us to understand the pulsating unconscious of *Seminar 11*, always opening and closing, for it only has one boundary.

Therefore, we require a continuous solution. I have suggested one, the "interior eight", which connects the four terms with the four vertices. Each of these vertices contains a series of letters: "S(Ⱥ)", "(Ȿ◊D)", "A" and "s(A)". The four terms are: "signifier", "voice", "*jouissance*"[18] and "castration".

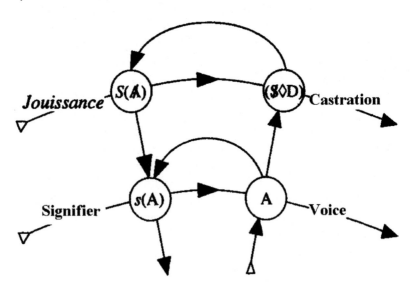

Schema 11.

On the one hand, it seems reasonable for the voice to be linked with the *jouissance*. Since they are on separate levels, their link is impossible. In the discontinuous solution the voice, which is an object of *jouissance*, remains separated from *jouissance* itself. This is contradictory. And on the other hand, it seems reasonable for castration to be in continuity with the signifier. For if there exists castration it is, precisely, due to the signifier.

The problem is how to separate them, or better, how to justify the separation between upper and lower levels. The instrument we will use in order to solve this problem will be the "interior eight". We have said that graphs can be planar or non-planar. This means that any graph may be constructed in a three-dimensional space, and some of them can be formed in a two-dimensional space. According to mathematicians, a planar graph is a graph that can be made on a sphere. Planar and spherical are topologically coincidental; I can cover a sphere with a plane, or transform a sphere into a plane by doing certain cuts. So, a planar graph can be made on a sphere, and a non-planar graph cannot. The graph of desire is non-planar.

However, contradictions appear when we make this statement, we say that the graph of desire is non-planar and we know Lacan states the subject is two-dimensional. This means that we affirm that the graph requires three-dimensions and at the same time we affirm that the subject's structure (the subject of the unconscious) is two-dimensional. We have to choose between the relation planar-spherical and the relation non-planar-two-dimensional.

Let us pose the same problem in a different way: how is it possible for a ring, a torus, to be two-dimensional? Considering that the notion of "spherical subject" is the common notion, the opposition planar-spherical *versus* non-planar-toric is the opposition between the psychoanalytical notion of the subject and the ordinary notion of subject.

The spherical notion of the subject is supported by the idea of the subject as an individual: a *continuum*, something indivisible. This ordinarily considered subject is fundamentally divided with regards to the other. Not self-divided but divided in relation to the other. It has to be a separate unit concerning what is not itself. This is what an individual is: indivisible as such, divided regarding that which surrounds it. This is the philosophical opposition between "internal world" and "external world".

According to this conception, the subject is spherical. The spherical shape predominates as "good form",[19] and this characterizes much of our Western culture.

Let us go to Freud, to *"The Ego and the Id"*[20] (1923). Let us remember that Lacan says that the schema in this text was designed for fools, given that his students were not at his level. He, in order to make himself clear, had to invent this schema. Lacan also says that

Freud already knew, by 1923, that nobody understood him. I believe, however, that the problem is more complicated; that there is a problem in what Freud says here:

> We shall now look upon an individual (*Individuum*) as a psychical id, unknown and unconscious, upon whose surface nests the ego, developed from its nucleus the Pcpt. System. If we make an effort to represent this pictorially, we may add that the ego does not completely envelop the id, but only does so to the extent to which the system *Pcpt*. Forms it [the ego's] surface, more or less as the germinal disc rests upon the ovum (p. 24).

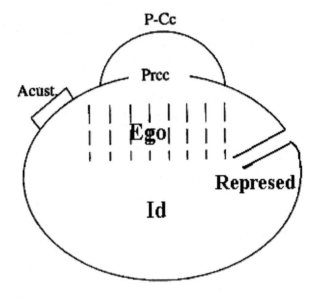

Schema 12.

According to Freud, the structure of his second topography is three-dimensional. And as with anyone, the problem of the closed three-dimensionality is that it ultimately becomes spherical. It becomes an "ovum", as Freud himself calls it.

This is not new. The circular, the spherical has represented the "good form" in Western culture for a long time, as was the case in Ancient Greece. Let us take Aristophanes' intervention in the *Symposium* as an illustration of the ancient roots of this conception:

First of all, you must learn about human nature, and what has happened to it. Long ago our nature was not the same as it is now but quite different. For one thing, there were three human genders, not just the present two, male and female. There was also a third one, a combination of these two; now its name survives although the gender has vanished. Then "androgynous" was a distinct gender as well as a name, combining male and female; now nothing is left but the name, which is used as an insult. For another thing, the shape of each human being was a rounded whole, with back and sides forming a circle. Each one had four hands and the same number of legs, and two identical faces on a circular neck. They had one head for both the faces, which were turned in opposite directions, four ears, two sets of genitals, and everything else was as you would imagine from what I've said so far. They moved around upright as we do now, in either direction, as they wanted. When they set off to run fast, they supported themselves on all their eight limbs, and moved quickly round and round, like tumblers who do cartwheels by keeping their legs straight as they go round and round[21] (pp. 22–23).

Do you see how this is a spherical conception of the original human being?

This conception of the origin of the human race is very interesting for it posits three sexes. We say, following Lacan, that "there is no such thing as sexual relation" because there are two sexes. If there were three, there would be sexual relation. The conceptual problem we are facing is the passage from 1–2 (*Fort-da*) to 1-2-3 (net), from a dual structure to a triadic structure.

The conception about the spherical nature of the human being and the two sexes as a result of its being cut is nothing but the notion of the "other half". Do you remember how that social link, engagement, used to be agreed? By means of a half-medal. While looking for the etymological definition of "symbol", I found that it comes from "*sumballein*". This Greek word means "to throw" and also "to put together". From this word derives "*symbolon*", which means "recognition sign". You will see how, in the etymological definition of symbol I will quote, a great part of Lacanian theory on symbol is included. My dictionary says that *symbolon* was primitively a recognition sign, an object cut into two parts, each of the halves being kept by each of the hosts ("host" names both the person who receives and the person who visits). So, each host kept one half, and then that half was transmitted from parents to children. The reunion of both parts was used for recognising the carriers, and it was the proof of previously established hospitality relationships. That is, if someone comes to me carrying the symbol of an ancient pact, I know who he is, I recognize him. Exactly like the half medal. It is a theory of recognition by means of the symbol. Also among the most common meanings of the word "*symbolon*" we find: commercial treaty, mark, signal, sign or password, emblem, insignia, omen, auspice, agreement and treaty. If you studied all these words, you would understand much of Lacan's teaching.

Surprisingly, there is another word derived from *symbolon*: "*sumbolaion*", which means "symptom".

What I would like to propose to you is that this theory of the subject as spherical, as individual, comes to us via the etymology of the word "symbol", being exactly what produces castration. Do you note the tricky sort of interior eight that is produced? The symbol produces an opposite illusory effect, precisely concerning what it produces as real effect: the function of the symbolic ideal and the interval, which we will study further on during this course.

"Symbol" means: let's put the parts together for building the whole. The problem is that there is an effect of the symbol itself which prevents the parts from being reunited in order to make a complete whole. What is then the relation between the symbol as effect and the etymology of the word "symbol"? They are in continuity, in an interior eight; although they are opposites, they must be placed as having certain continuity.

According to the "*ego-psychology*",[22] we call the conflict-free part of the "ego" the "sphere". If we were to build a graph of this theory, there should be two spheres: one above and one below. It could also be a sphere inside another sphere (if we wanted to be more subtle), but we would remain within the logic of the individual anyway.

Hence, it is important to have the structural opposition sphere-torus in mind, in order to avoid the millenarian confusion between individual (three-dimensional) and subject (two-dimensional). We could metaphorically state that the torus is a holed sphere. However, this introduces a complication, for the hole does not belong to the torus; strictly speaking the torus is a surface without holes.

Let us remember that the subject, the theme of this class, is the object *a* as a cut. We have already posed the problem about the right cut, for instance at the end of the session or even the final cut of the analysis, "the pass"; but the problem remains. The problem of the structure of the surface on which we operate and the structure of the cut made on that surface, the cut able to reveal and transform that structure itself.

There exists a procedure for uniting topology and graph theory, this allows us to establish when there is a hole on a surface and when there is not. Let us consider a sphere and a Jordan closed curve (the topological equivalent of a circle) whose definition is: *a closed curve which does not cross itself and divides a plane into inside and outside.*

The following schema shows what we name "interior" (shaded) and is the result of having drawn up a Jordan closed curve.

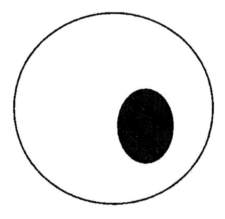

Schema 13.

The theorem of Jordan posits that any Jordan closed curve divides a sphere's surface into two parts. The Equator is an example of Jordan closed curve: a closed line divides the planet into two hemispheres. But, strictly speaking, any closed line (no matter what shape it is) divides the sphere into two surfaces, as seen in Schema 13. The same happens with the torus, but not for any closed curve, that is to say, it does not always happen.

We know now how closed curves allow us to distinguish the torus' and the sphere's structures, for they reveal both surfaces' structural properties. Right cuts are capable of revealing the structure.

Structure always operates, however there are cuts which hide it and cuts which reveal it. Let us think of a cut like this (schema 14) on the torus; we represent the closed curve as a cut using a pair of scissors, the line drawn up by a pencil is equivalent to the cut made by a pair of scissors.

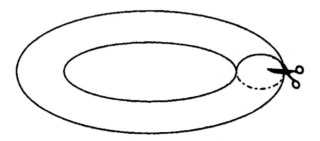

Schema 14.

The torus is not divided in two in this case. The result is a cylinder, but the cut does not divide the torus into two (see schema 15).

Schema 15.

Therefore, there exist Jordan closed lines which do not divide the torus into two. This shows how the toric structure is different from the sphere, where any Jordan closed curve would divide the surface into two.

There is another cut we can make on the torus (schema 16):

Schema 16.

This cut does not divide the torus into two either; it opens the cylinder, but it remains as one piece. We made two cuts, which are twice intersected, and the torus has not been divided into two. If we homologate lines to edges, and arrival and departure points to vertices, closed lines (cuts on surfaces) are made equivalent to graphs. By drawing a graph on the sphere (in this case a loop) and another graph on the torus, we discover that they have different structures. This is knots theory, as used by Lacan. They are graphs built not with "lines" but with "strings" onto the same topological structures.

In order to advance in our conception of the object *a* as a cut, namely, in its spatial dimension, let us consider these four graphs. They are graphs which account for the presence, or not, of a hole on a certain surface.

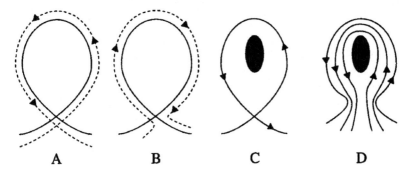

A   B   C   D

Schema 17.

Graph "A" shows a path following an already established direction, where lines cross. "B" is a similar case, except for the fact that lines do not cross. These two paths have in common that both are reducible to a point.

On the contrary, neither "C" nor "D" are reducible to a point. They are not reducible as their "minimal" presentation can not abolish the hole they border.

This means that only the paths which do not have a hole can be reduced to a point; and those which have a hole are not reducible to a point.

Lacan says this in *Seminar 7, The ethics of psychoanalysis*[23]:

> The detour in the psyche isn't always designed to regulate the commerce between whatever is organized in the domain of the pleasure principle and whatever presents itself as the

structure of reality. There are also detours and obstacles which are organized so as to make the domain of the vacuole stand out as such (p. 152).

But there is also something to differentiate "C" from "D": the way in which each one borders the hole. In "C" the existence of a hole in the structure is always revealed. "D", on the contrary, disguises it. In this case the cross point—which we call "cut"—is a false cut. The cut becomes less apparent as we move away from the hole. This is the difference between the right and the false cut. A false cut is, for instance, cutting the session according to the clock, for it eliminates the cut's subjective function. For that function to exist the cut must be an act; and for an act to be such it is a necessary condition that it implies a subject. The cut which results from a subjective act reveals the structure (as in graph "C", where the hole is revealed).

The fact that the graph of desire is not folded-in on itself, defining not a circle but an interior eight, is the proof of the existence of the hole in the graph, the spatial equivalent of the object a.

We do not place the graph of desire's hole in the interior circle because that would be confusing (the imaginary effect that makes believe both circles can become one); we place it in the space in between one and the other circles of the interior eight; by doing so we are able to sustain the impossibility of any encounter whatsoever among the repetitions drawn as circles of the interior eight).

It is definitely established thus, that both the interior eight and the hole are irreducible; this has to do with the spatial dimension of the object a, which gives the graph of desire its fundamental structure.

By analysing the notions of *fantasme*[24] ($\$ \lozenge a$) and drive ($\$ \lozenge D$) we will come back to the elaboration of the notion of the object a in its spatial dimension.

Notes

1. The principle of bivalence: every statement is either true or false. The principle of *non*-contradiction: no statement is both true and false.

2. A *walk* on a graph of length n is a sequence $v_0, e_1, v_1, e_2, ... , v_n$, where v_i are vertices while e_i are edges of the graph such that vertices and edges adjacent in the sequence are *incident*.

3. Another definition could be: "Two surfaces are topologically equivalent (or homeomorphic) if one can be obtained from the other by a topological transformation; that is, a sequence of 'stretching and bending' distortions."

4. Sigmund Freud, SE, Vol. 1, The Hogarth Press and the Institute of Psychoanalysis, London, p. 313.

5. Sigmund Freud, SE, Vol. 5, "The interpretation of dreams", Chapter VII, The Hogarth Press and the Institute of Psychoanalysis, London, p. 565.

6. In Spanish "*el buen corte*". Literally, "the good cut", meaning the "exact, precise cut", but excluding any moral connotations.

7. Which in French means also "*cul-de-sac*".

8. In French *angoisse* and in Spanish *angustia* (Freud uses the term *Angst*). We consider that the traditional '*anxiety*' better translates the French '*anxieté*' and the Spanish '*ansiedad*' (its definition including fear or expectation). These two concepts are radically different and their translation has important connotations for the clinic.

9. Argentine poet, essayist, and short-story writer, whose tales are classics of the 20th-century world literature, Jorge Luis Borges was born in Buenos Aires and he learned English before Spanish. In 1914 the family moved to Europe, and seven years later returned to Buenos Aires. There he started his career as a writer by publishing poems and essays in literary journals. Borges shared the Prix Formentor with Samuel Beckett in 1961. Borges died in Geneva, Switzerland on June 14th, 1986. Among his major works are: Fervor de Buenos Aires, 1923; Inquisiciones, 1925; Historia universal de la infamia, 1935—A Universal History of Infamy; El jardín de los senderos que se bifurcan, 1942; Ficciones, 1944; Nueva refutación del tiempo, 1947; Otras inquisiciones, *1937–1952*, 1952—Other Inquisitions, *1937–1952*; El Hacedor, 1960—The Doer/The Dreamtigers; El otro, el mismo, 1964; El libro de los seres imaginarios, 1967—The Book of Imaginary Beings; Elogio de la sombra, 1969: El informe de Brodie, 1970—Dr. Brodie's Report; El oro de los tigres, 1972—The Gold of Tigres; El libro de arena, 1975—The Book of Sand, and many others.

10. Reference to Freud's expression: "*eine andere Schauplatz*".

11. English version: *Fundamentals of Language*, Walter de Gruyter Inc; Reprint edition. January, 2002.

12. The original French states: "*anneaux dont le collier se scelle dans l'anneau d'autre collier fait d'anneaux*" (*Écrits*, Points Essais, Éditions du Seuil, pp. 498–499). Sheridan's translation leaves a fragment of the definition outside. "… rings of a necklace that is a ring in another

necklace made of rings" (*Écrits: A selection*, p. 169). The pertinence of the author's subsequent clarification on the expression "to be sealed" cannot be fully appreciated if we consider this English version.

13. Emphasizing the function of the Imaginary register (as opposed to "imagined").
14. Although this is the same word in French for Freud's "Id", we prefer not to use the Latinized word (chosen in the SE) for this context, in order to emphasize Lacan's original reading of Freud's categories.
15. In French "*ça*" and "*sujet*" respectively; "*eso*" and "*sujeto*" in Spanish.
16. See Note 12, Chapter One.
17. Book 23. Standard Edition.
18. "*Goce*" in Spanish in the original.
19. Reference to the *Gestalt* theory. Also "good shape".
20. Sigmund Freud, SE, Vol. 19, The Hogarth Press and the Institute of Psychoanalysis, London, p. 24.
21. Plato, *The Symposium*, Trans Christopher Gill, Penguin Classics, London, 1999, pp. 22–23.
22. In English in the original.
23. The Ethics of Psychoanalysis (1959–1960), The Seminar of Jacques Lacan, Ed. By J.-A. Miller, Book VII, Trans. Dennis Porter.
24. See note 9, Chapter One.

CHAPTER THREE

The structure of language: Need, demand and desire

We shall work today on the articulation between linguistics and psychoanalysis. In order to elaborate that articulation I shall profusely quote *"The subversion of the subject and the dialectic of desire in the Freudian unconscious"*. This writing by Lacan will be, from now on, our main reference.

My work today will turn around two categorical statements by Lacan; we will make use of them for progressing in relation to the point we reached last week. The first statement says that "the unconscious is structured like a language" and the second one that "since Freud the unconscious has been a chain of signifiers that somewhere (on another stage, in another scene, he says) is repeated, and insists on interfering in the breaks offered by the effective discourse and the cogitation that it informs".[1]

As the structure of the "graph of desire" is supported by those two phrases, we will advance considerably today in its investigation. From next class on we will introduce clinical articulations. We have been working on the structural foundations, and this will allow the clinical articulations to be more that mere clinical descriptions.

In both quotations Lacan affirms that the signifier is a fundamental notion. In "The subversion of the subject ..." he says that "signifier" is a word that modern linguistics borrowed from ancient rhetoric. Lacan proposes to limit that modern linguistic: he call the inferior level "the dawn of modern linguistics" and he refers it to Ferdinand de Saussure. And he calls the superior level "modern linguistics' culminating point", referencing Roman Jakobson. What we do not know is whether Jakobson's work will continue to be this culminating point, or whether it will have to be changed with the passage of time. You know that when the superior level is changed and for reasons that are intrinsic to the theory of the signifier, the inferior level might have to be changed too. Anyhow, it was like this for Lacan, in Lacan's times.

First question: why is the theory of the signifier (as modern linguistics starting from Saussure posits it) needed in order to account for the structure of the unconscious?

Let us take a quotation from Saussure's *Curso de lingüística general*[2] (a version his students established, given that he never wrote it nor published it):

> "The linguistic sign is then a two-sided psychological entity [...]
> the two elements are intimately united, and each recalls the
> other" (p. 66).

So they are two that make one; they are two intimately joined. If you know Saussure's elaborations, this is the problem represented in his sign through the ellipse and the arrows.

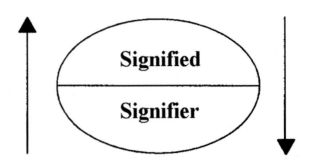

Schema 1.

"Only the associations sanctioned by that language appears to
us to conform reality, and we disregard whatever others might
be imagined" (p. 67).

The unity that both elements of the language [*langue*][3] form is what
constitutes reality, according to Saussure, and reality is based on
these relations; any other would seem to us outside of reality. Do
you realize that the notion of "psychical reality" does not belong
exclusively to Freud? Let us remember that for Saussure, the union
between signifier and signified constitutes a psychical unity. The
quotation continues:

> "I call the combination of a concept and a sound-image a sign,
> but in current usage the term generally designates only a sound-
> image, a word, for example" (p. 67).

The speaker believes it is only one element, but they are always two.

> "One tends to forget that *arbor* is called a sign only because it
> carries the concept 'tree', with the result that the idea of the sen-
> sory part implies the idea of the whole" (p. 67).

The mistake is, precisely, on one side, the sensory one, to imply the
set; the fact that there is another element hidden, and its association
with the first one, is forgotten.

> "Ambiguity would disappear if the three notions involved here
> were designated by three names, each suggesting and opposing
> the others. I propose to retain the word sign [*signe*] to designate
> the whole and to replace concept and sound-image respectively
> by *signified* [*signifié*] and *signifier* [*significant*]; the last two terms
> have the advantage of indicating the opposition that separates
> them from each other and from the whole of which they are
> parts" (p. 67).

The second reference is that signs, says Saussure, are discrete elements, units that are distinguished, separated from other units.
Then, if the unconscious is structured like a language, this will
mean that we must take these Saussurean teachings as our departure point.

The thesis is the following (I will consider a quotation from "The subversion of the subject ..." which seems to confirm it):

> Lets the hunt be in vain for us analysts, [he is referring to the hunt for the subject] we must bring everything back to the function of the cut in discourse, the strongest being that which acts as a bar between the signifier and the signified.[4]

We have to notice that, according to Lacan and concerning the subject of the analytic experience, everything has to be reduced to the function of the cut; and the strongest cut is the bar between signifier and signified.

> There the subject that interests us is surprised.

Let us pay attention to the modulation of terms Lacan uses; he does not say, "there the subject is hunted", he says, "there the subject is surprised". That is, the subject is effectively there, but he himself does not know it—otherwise he would not be surprised.

Let us see know what Lacan considers the culminant point of modern linguistics, Roman Jakobson, who says in "Los conmutadores, las categorías verbales y el verbo ruso", en *Ensayos de lingüística general* (Seix Barral, 1981).[5]

> The message (M) and its subjacent code (C) are vehicles of linguistic communication, but both work in a double way.[6]

Once again they are two, as Saussure said; but now they are two which function in a double way; message and code may be both utilized and referred to. I propose to you, in order to make the exposition more eloquent, to employ it as it is denominated in logics: use and mention.[7] That is to say, one may use the code and use the message, as well as one may mention the code and mention the message.

> Thus, the message can be referred to the code or to another message, as well as the general meaning of a unity of the code will imply a reference to the code or to the message. Therefore, four double types must be distinguished: (1) two types of circularity— the message refers to the code (M/M) and the code refers to the

code (C/C)—; (2) two types of overlapping[8]—the message refers
to the code (M/C), and the code refers to the message (C/M).

"Overlapping" can be translated into Spanish by two synonym words
deriving from a Latin term that designates the floor and implies a
peculiar form of covering a surface totally or partially.
   We will briefly define each of these four types:

> (M/M) A quoted discourse is a discourse inside a discourse, a
> message inside a message, and at the same time, a discourse
> about the discourse, a message about the message.

After that we have:

> (C/C) First names [...] have a particular place in our linguistic
> code: the general meaning of a proper name cannot be defined
> without referring to the code.

That is why proper names are impossible to be translated, precisely
because they indicate a place in the interior of their code/language.[9]

> In the English code Jerry means a person named Jerry. Circular-
> ity is evident: the name means any person to whom that name
> has been given. The appellative "pup" means a young dog;
> bloodhound, a dog for hunting rabbits, whereas Fido means a
> dog whose name is Fido.
>   (M/C) When we say the pup is a nice animal, or the pup
> cries, the word "pup" designates a young dog, whereas in sen-
> tences like "pup" is a noun that means young dog, or simpler,
> "pup" means young dog or "pup" is a one-syllable word, the
> word "pup" [...] is used as its own designation.

In the message "pup" indicates the pup as a term of the code; it
is being mentioned. The word is not being used to designate a
dog; in any case it is being used to designate precisely that same
word.

> Any explanatory interpretation of words or sentences—
> both intra-linguistic (circumlocutions, synonyms) and inter-
> linguistic (translation)—is a message, which refers to the code.

(C/M) Every linguistic code has a particular class of grammar unities which Jespersen named shifters [...][10]

In telephony, the telephonist operates a "switchboard",[11] which receives stimuli (electricity) through a line, and transfers it on to another line. According to Freud's expression, it is a device that allows us the "*Wechsel*", that is, "switch-words".[12]

> [...] the general meaning (significance) of a shifter can not be defined without referring to the message [...] The sign "I" cannot represent its object without "being in an existential relationship" with it: the word "I" designating the speaker is existentially related to his elocution. [...] Each shifter, however, possess its general meaning. Thus, "I" means the addresser (and "you" the addressee) of the message it belongs to. [...] In fact, shifters differentiate themselves from all the other constitutive elements of the linguistic code only for their obligatory reference to the current message.

At this stage, it seems to me that could it be useful to employ the graph theory. I propose to you that we do something that Jakobson does not, namely that we build a graph of what his theory proposes. We have four cases; the first two cases of overlapping and the other two of circularity.

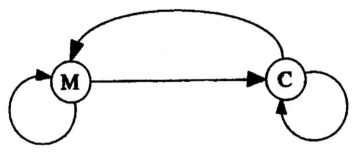

Schema 2.

This graph has four edges and two vertices, and two of the edges are loops.
John has told me that *fries* means *chips*.

This statement proposed by Jakobson includes the four cases: "John has told me that": that is a message inside a message; we are quoting a message. "Fries means chips": a code particle is referred to another code particle; at the same time, there is in the phrase a message referring to a code particle—that means it is also a (M/C) case. And finally, it is a (C/C) case. The *shifter*[13] is in "has told me"; (to me) but, who am I? That who is speaking. That is, those code particles in the message whose only means of establishing their value is the message itself.

This last case is extremely important, as it relates to a problem we will work on today. It is an important problem because it places us before a misinterpretation of Lacan's teaching concerning the function he would have assigned to the "*Je*" as subject of the unconscious.

You have surely noticed how subtle Jacobson's example is: the *shifter* is indicated there by a particle that is neither "I" nor "you".

> This simple elocution includes the four types of double structure: quoted discourse (M/M), autonomous form of discourse (M/C), proper name (C/C) and shifters (C/M), that is, the pronoun of the first person and the perfect tense that indicates an event prior to the transmission of the message. In language and its use, duplicity carries out a basic function.

In the graph I drew it could seem to you that there are only two double cases and two simple cases, but do not forget that the loop implies a relation C/C which is double, and the other loop implies a relation M/M which is double too.

> Particularly, the classification of grammar categories, verbal especially, requires a coherent discrimination of the shifters.

Let us remember that the graph, as long as it implies the basic double structure of language, clearly indicates as well that if the unconscious is structured like a language and that this is the structure of language, the subject's division is not which we criticized last week. If the graph did not have the loops it would appear as an ego inside the ego. But here is when duplicities begin to duplicate themselves.

And then Jakobson continues:

> *"Attempt at classification of verbal categories"*.

(I shall tell you that this is a classification of the verbal categories that is valid for any language).

> In order to classify the verbal categories in two groups, two basic distinctions must be taken into account: (I) the discourse itself, speech (s), and its subject, the narrated matter (n).

Thus, the first duplicity is speech—the fact of saying- and the content of what is said—narrated event.

> (II) The event itself (E) and any and each of the participants (P), whether active or passive.
> Therefore four elements must be distinguished: a narrated event (E^n), a speech event (E^s) [...]

For example: "I went to the cinema yesterday". If I say that I went to the cinema yesterday, for the narrated event it is past tense, whereas for the act of saying it, it is present tense. A temporal discordance is posited.

> [...] a participant of the narrated event (P^n) and a participant of the speech event (P^s).

They may match or not. In the example of the cinema the participant matched, but it may not—as in the example of John. In the case: "It is not that I think it, but John has told me that you are a ..." This position in the enunciation[14] is always complicated, given that the subject of the narration and the subject of the speech[15] [discourse] are not easily distinguishable. In ancient and classic times, emissaries paid with their lives for the bad news they transmitted. This is very clear, for instance, in *Antigone*.

One more quotation:

> Any verb refers to a narrated event [...] Thus, both designators and connectors may characterise the narrated event (statement) and/or its participants, by referring or not to the speech event (enunciation) or its participants. Categories implying

this reference will be called shifters; categories lacking it will
be designated non-shifters.

It is clear through this quotation that a shifter is what allows the
passage from the statement to the enunciation, it works as a key for
shifting from statement to enunciation and vice versa.

Our last quotation from Jakobson:

Any generic verbal category could be defined considering these
basic dichotomies.

Jakobson proposes that any verbal category (generically speaking)
will have this basic dichotomy, and also these forms of relationships
between statement and enunciation.

This is, then, the structure of language. After having seen topology, graph theory, we have finally arrived into linguistics, which is
the last reference for the context of our work on the graph of desire.

So, if this is the structure of language (a fundamental dichotomy
between code and message, between statement and enunciation,
between signifier and signified) and if we sustain—with Lacan—that
the unconscious is structured like a language, what sort of subject
can we conceive for the unconscious? (I am paraphrasing Lacan
with this question).[16]

In "*Subversion of the subject ...*", Lacan answers his question like
this:

We can try, with methodological rigour,[17] to set out from the
strictly linguistic definition of the I [*je*] as signifier, in which
there is nothing but the 'shifter' or indicative, which, in the subject of the statement, designates the subject in the sense that he
is now speaking (p. 330).

That is to say—for us—in the enunciation. Lacan states that if the
unconscious is structured like a language, and we wonder about the
subject of the unconscious, "with methodological rigour" the first
thing we should ask ourselves is whether this subject is the same as
the subject of the structure of language, the "*je*" in French, or not.

Last week somebody asked me after the class was finished, why
hadn't I used the opposition *moi-je* for talking about the subject's

division, given that that was precisely the way Lacan worked on it. I answered him that, although I had planned working on it today, I had not done it basically because it is a mistake: the subject's division is not the opposition *moi-je*. If it was, then psychoanalysis would remain absolutely attached to linguistics.

Lacan distinguishes "*je*", the shifter, from the subject of the unconscious, by saying:

> That is to say, it designates the subject of the enunciation, but it does not signify it (p. 330).

The shifter[18] designates the subject of the enunciation but it does not signify it; and there lies the problem: that although the "*je*" particle designates the subject of the enunciation, it does not tell us what it is. Put it in a more intuitive way: to localize ourselves in a particle of what we say, for example in the place of the "*je*", does not answer the question *what am I?*

> This is apparent from the fact that every signifier of the subject of the enunciation may be lacking in the statement, not to mention the fact that there are those that differ from the I [*je*], [...] (p. 330).

It is clear that the subject speaking in the unconscious cannot be localized in the *je*; there are an infinite number of phrases where the *je* is not even there. That is, for instance, the case in "John has told me ..." *Moi-je* is not an opposition which would allow us to oppose I (*moi*)—subject of the unconscious ($). Those who do not have French as mother tongue tend to consider the opposition *moi*-subject of the unconscious using the French distinction *moi-je*, but this is incorrect. By designating it with the letter S barred it is clearly indicated that it is incorrect to choose the "*je*" as the subject of the unconscious.

Lacan goes further, proposing what in the French code would be the particle indicating the mark of the subject of the unconscious.

> I think for example, that I recognized the subject of the enunciation in the signifier '*ne*', which grammarians call the expletive, a term that already prefigures the incredible opinion of those, and they are to be found among the best, who regard its form as being a matter of mere chance (p. 330).

In French negation has a double structure, for instance, *"ne pas"*, *"ne guere"*, *"ne rien"*. Contrary to what a Spanish speaker would believe, the negative particle is not the *"ne"* so close to the *"no"*, but the second one: *pas, guere, rien*. There exists a whole series of expressions that, containing this *"ne"* are, however, affirmative; they are the ones we are interested in. In order to say correctly some affirmative phrases in French, it is needed to introduce the *"ne"* in them. An example of this is: *"Il craint que je ne sois trop jeune"*, it means: "He fears I am too young". There we have the expletive *ne* working. It is a grammatical category whose definition is to be a grammatical function which is necessary to the phrase but is semantically unnecessary. It does not deny nor change the meaning [sense]; it does not turn an affirmative into a negative nor a negative into an affirmative.

Hence, if there is a particle in the French code for designating the subject of the unconscious, Lacan says it is for example the expletive *ne*.

The problem is that not having the function of that particle in Spanish, we cannot use the same example.

Let us now make a key distinction. By means of the *ne* we are localizing the subject of the unconscious in the code, detecting the mark of the subject of the unconscious in language. But language is not the same as discourse [speech]; and in the clinic, the subject we are interested in is the subject of discourse, the particular subject. Clinically speaking, then, this signal of the subject of the unconscious is not the one we look for in the analysis. What is at stake in an analysis is a subject localized within a particular discourse. Let us say it using Jacobson's words: in the analytic experience, the subject of the unconscious is localized in the message, not in the code.

But Lacan believes that a trace, a mark of the subject of the unconscious, can be localized in the structure of language. For Spanish this is a complex question, although we have those phrases including double negations where it is never clear if it is yes or no. Those are the marks in our code, in the Spanish language, in the knowledge of a language [langue], of the subject of the unconscious, double negations.

One more quotation by Lacan:

> Namely, the right way to reply to the question, 'Who is speaking?', when it is the subject of the unconscious that is at issue. For this reply cannot come from that subject if he does not

know what he is saying, or even if he is speaking, as the entire experience of analysis has taught us (p. 331).

More interesting than the fact that the subject says something other than what he says, is the fact that, sometimes, what the subject says and his truth does not seem for him to be a said.[19] This is Freud's discovery. For example a symptom, a pain: it is presented there where something is said, precisely where one does not believe it is being said. It is not some other "ego", some kind of "I tell you that I love you but there is something in me that hates you". It is the fact that my own message is produced in what I do not even register as being a message.

Who speaks? Then, this is not something which can be asked of the subject, because sometimes, even when he speaks, he does not know he is speaking.

> It follows that the place of the 'inter-said' [*inter-dit*], which is the 'intra-said' [*intra-dit*] of a between-two-subjects, is the very place in which the transparency of the classical subject is divided and passes through the effects of 'fading' that specify the Freudian subject by its occultation by an ever pure signifier: that these effects lead us to the frontiers at which slips of the tongue and witticisms, in their collusion, become confused, even where elision is so much more allusive in tracking down presence to its lair, that one is surprised that the *Dasein* hunt hasn't done better out of it (p. 331).

I would like you not to forget the importance Lacan gives to this "between", this "inter": "the inter-said is the intra-said of a between-two-subjects".[20]

Thus, it is necessary to accept that the subject does not know he is speaking; not only that he says something other than what he wants to say. That is to say that, by means of someone else, the existence of a message which the subject does not know exists, can be established. A problem not considered by the linguist, which Lacan introduces, begins to appear: that the duplicity of "between-two-subjects" has to be taken into account. Neither of one nor of the other, the problem is between them. It can no longer be affirmed that the emitter emits the message which the receptor receives. Whose is the message?

If it does not belong to one nor to the other, it remains in the middle, in the 'between', in the inter. It has to be remembered that it remains hidden, "*fading*" (vanishing, eclipsing), given that it could only be seen if it was on one side or the other. "That specify the Freudian subject by its occultation by an ever pure signifier" says Lacan; meaning that the clearer it becomes, the purer the signifier which determines it is, the more obscure becomes the determination itself, because the subject will fall between that signifier and another signifier.

> [...] that these effects lead us to the frontiers at which slips of the tongue and witticisms, in their collusion, become confused, even where elision is so much more allusive in tracking down presence to its lair (p. 331).

The elision, an absent term, is the most allusive form of presence. If we capture what Lacan is saying to us, we will have already an answer for the Freudian example in *Beyond the pleasure principle*. Freud was wrong; the *Fort-da* does not contradict the pleasure principle, but the child reproduced, precisely, this case: the presence of the mother being indicated by means of the elision. It is an effect of the structure, and not beyond the pleasure principle. Freud did not have this theory of language. Freud asks himself: how is it possible that through the term "absence" (*fort*) and "throw the object", somebody can recover his absent mother? If to throw the object produces displeasure, then it means that it is against the pleasure principle. We should notice today that it is not, it is pleasant; but it is paradoxical: the best way of having the presence in the symbolic level is through elision, absence.

> Lest the hunt be in vain for us analysts, we must bring every-thing back to the function of the cut in discourse, the strongest being that which acts as a bar between the signifier and the sig-nified. There the subject that interests us is surprised, since by binding himself in signification he is placed under the sign of the pre-conscious [...] This cut in the signifying chain alone verifies the structure of the subject as discontinuity in the real (p. 331).

If the subject has a real localization, this will be discontinuity. Any-thing of the real that might be homologated to the cut will constitute an offer for the localization of the subject, for instance, the holes in the body. If something makes a discontinuity in the real, there the subject will localize itself. Which would be the fundamental discontinuity that, as real, would become the subject's localization? That is the cut in the signifying chain, the fundamental form that this "inter", "between", acquires.

I propose that we name it the "subject of the interval". In order to account for the structure of the subject as subject of the interval we will work on another opposition, which consists of a triad: need-demand-desire. For conceiving the subject—if it is localized in the interval—the conceptual device one has to manage is the triadic opposition *need-demand-desire.*

If the localization of the subject is third (neither here nor there but in the middle), then a device that rescues us from the language's duplicities is required. That device will be the aforementioned triad.

Let us take Lacan's writing *"The signification of the phallus"* (1989). Let us remember we have already said that of both formulae concerning the structural relationship language-unconscious, Lacan considered the signifier to be the fundamental notion. I will begin with the paragraph where Lacan announces he will examine the effects of the presence of the signifier. He says:

> In the first instance, they proceed from a deviation of man's need from the fact that he speaks, in the sense that in so far as his needs are subjected to demand, they return to him alienated. This is not the effect of his real dependence [...] but rather the turning into signifying form as such,[21] from the fact that it is from the locus of the Other that its message is emitted (p. 316).

What Lacan proposes here is that as an effect of the subject being a speaking being, there is a deviation of man's needs.

Let us relate the notion of demand to the notion of need. It is as a consequence of demand that a deviation from need is produced; that is, need is alienated. To produce an inversion is a structural effect of every demand. For us, the concept of demand implies that one receives his own message from the Other—and not that the emitter codifies and emits the message which the receiver receives and decodes.

In rigor, there are two inversions: one, the subject receives its own message from the Other (that is to say, the emitter is the receiver and also the true receiver is the emitter); and another (which the graph of desire allows us to study) the subject receives from the Other its own message back in an inverted form. We are only working today on one of the two inversions. This is well worth distinguishing, so that in our next class (chapter four) we may work on the opposition neurosis-psychosis.

Precisely what Lacan says is that if need is determined by demand, the consequence is that need will in the end come to the subject from the Other, it alienates itself. Need no longer belongs to the subject, it belongs to the Other, which obviously denaturalizes it in an absolute way. He also says that this is not the effect of a real dependence, but of the presence, in the human world, of the signifying function. That is, this dialectic is not caused by any prematuration of birth.[22]

> That which is thus alienated[23] in needs constitute an *Urverdrän-gung* (primal repression), an inability,[24] it is supposed, to be artic-ulated in demand, but it re-appears in something it gives rise to that presents itself[25] in man as desire (*das Begehren*) (p. 317).

We will see further on how Lacan localizes in several different places the Freudian notion of primal repression; this is one of those places, but it is not the only one.

Primal repression is the psychoanalytical way of talking about a loss without return; in this case it is a pure loss that becomes coher-ent with the offspring of desire. If it were "repression proper" the return of the lack within need, would return as another need. Here it does not return but it has a 'sprout': desire.

Lacan proposes to us to substitute, in psychoanalysis, the notion of frustration with the notion of demand: because if we reduce demand to frustration we will loose characteristics that structure demand itself. On the contrary, he invites us to think of frustration as being an effect of the demand.

> Demand in itself bears on something other than the satisfactions it calls for. It is demand of a presence or of an absence—which is what is manifested in the primordial relation to the mother,

pregnant with that Other to be situated *within*[26] the needs that it can satisfy[27] (p. 317).

The mother's function is not to be pregnant with the child, that is a female. A mother is that who is pregnant of the Other for a certain child. The child perceives that the language is all "in" the mother. That is why that language is called "mother tongue", for it is supposed to be "of the mother". What the child demands of the Other, concerning his needs, is not satisfaction but the presence of that Other which must situate itself within [*au deçà*] the needs it can fulfil.

Let us consider the following schema:

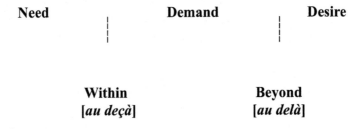

Need | **Demand** | **Desire**

Within | **Beyond**
[*au deçà*] | [*au delà*]

Schema 3.

Let us situate in one border the "within" [*au deçà*] of the need-demand relation and in the other border the "beyond" [*au delà*] of the demand-desire relation. In the demand's sector I would like to add the word "power", because Lacan clearly says that this demand the child addresses to the mother (as Other) is a request for presence and not for the satisfaction of needs. And this is because the mother incarnates the locus from where needs can be fulfilled, although not through or by means of the need's object.

The Other has the privilege of satisfying needs; that is, he has the power of depriving needs of the only thing that can satisfy them, namely, the presence and not the object.

In primal repression, then, Lacan localizes the function of privation; he says that whoever occupies that place of demand—the place of the Other—will have the privilege of being able to deprive need of the only thing that satisfies it. What satisfy man's needs then, if the function of demand is already present? The presence of that who incarnates the place of power, namely, the Other (A).

Let us include a very well-known quotation from *"Subversion of the subject ..."* in order to clarify our arguments:

> The first words spoken [*le dit premier*] stands as a decree, a law, an aphorism, an oracle; they confer their obscure authority[28] upon the real other (p. 338).

The mother, real other, has that obscure authority only due to the fact that she enunciated the 'first said'. Why the sole enunciation of the 'first said' gives the mother (insofar as she embodies the place of the Other of language) the possibility of incarnating the place of power? This is the problem of the so-called mother tongue.

What is the mother tongue?[29] It is a language [*langue*] learned before letters; a language learned exclusively through words. And it is evident that for the child faced to the 'first saying' the symbolic order is inside that other who speaks. Is there any possible limitation for that power of the Other in possession of language? From this perspective, there is not. What is at stake is its omnipotence.

An example: mothers present here surely remember their children's furious reactions when, between the second and third year, they did not understand what their children where saying or telling them. They do not give chances: if they are not understood the furious or anguished reaction immediately emerges. And what is that anger. It is not the fact of not being understood, but the recognition that the language [*langue*] is not of the mother. That is, that the mother does not understand the mother tongue. That is why they despair. The incomprehension of the mother undermines her omnipotence: the omnipotence whose attack anguishes him the most, the other's not his. For the child it is not the undermining of his own omnipotence what anguishes him, rather the Other's.

However, cases of 'hospitalism' when, although somebody with the language exists (i.e., the nurse), the child lets himself die, prove that someone occupying the position of the Other is not enough. This dual logic need-demand is insufficient. Therefore, our journey is still partial; I am opening the path for introducing the desire of the Other. Then, what power does the Other have? It can deprive the need of the only thing which may satisfy it, namely, the presence of the Other itself.

> This privilege of the Other thus outlines the radical form of the gift [*don*] of that which the Other does not have, namely its love.
>
>   In this way demand annuls (*aufhebt*) the particularity of everything that can be granted by transmuting it into a proof of love (p. 317).

Lacan sustains that the demand annuls—and he proposes the German word "*aufhebt*". This word belongs to the Hegelian dialectics and is also the word Freud uses when talking about the abolishment of repression. It is here, at this stage, says Lacan, that the *aufhebt* of the Hegelian dialectic takes place. It means "preservation with change" and "change with preservation". Therefore, it is through demand that this function of abolishment of what belongs to the level of need, is produced (what Lacan calls particularity) as long as it is substituted by the proof of love. But he also says that the particularity, in addition to being cancelled is preserved.

Which is that particularity at the level of the species? It is the specific object that satisfies the need for the species in question. For the newborn, cow's milk does not satisfy his need, that is why a new born fed like that dies.

What Lacan states is that because of the presence of demand, this particularity is abolished. And in its place the subject begins to demand a proof of love. And that proof of love will be the presence of the Other.

> It is necessary[30] [logically], then, that the particularity thus abolished should reappear *beyond* demand (p. 317).

Let us notice the kind of use Lacan makes of the term need: what reappears is a logical necessity. Lacan asks himself: which is that logical necessity? It is that what the signifier produced as a loss at the level of the species' particularity reappears as the subject's particularity. The field of desire is a recovery, beyond demand, of what the demand—the articulated signifier—produces as loss in the field of need. It is because the signifier causes something to be lost in the world of the human species, in the famous "natural given being", that this 'sprout' that is desire is produced.

Lacan emphasizes that the particularity lost at the level of the species is recovered as particularity at the level of the subject: that is desire.

> It does, in fact, reappear there, but preserving the structure contained in the unconditional element of the demand for love (p. 317).

The unconditional element of the proof of love is, precisely, the trace of the demand's effect on the need's particularity. Given that there is no need, structurally, that is by itself a condition for the proof of love. Not even the "need for life" is a condition, a limit for love. It is for this reason that every demand is a demand for love, regardless of what is requested. Thus, the particularity of the need will reappear with the property of absolute condition of desire.

> *Renversement*[31] that is not simple a negation of the negation [he already separates himself from Hegel here], the power of pure loss emerges from the residue of an obliteration. For the unconditional element of demand, desire substitutes the 'absolute' condition (p. 317).

As an effect of the signifier and its functioning as demand, a radical loss (abolishment, says Lacan) is produced at the level of the need.

What is it that in need is abolished? Lacan characterizes it as the particular object. For the human species that is maternal milk. And in its place, the subject demands the mother's presence, but the particularity's necessity, now logical,[32] reappears, though preserving the traces of the demand. And which are those traces? Precisely, the mark left by demand. And what is the most characteristic of demand? Its unconditional character. No hunger, then, will be a limit to love. And, at the same time, the subject's position with relation to this Other is unconditional. Demand is unconditional regarding need and the Subject is unconditional regarding the Other.

But desire, as an 'offspring' of the lost object of need does not receive conditions from demand. If demand is unconditional regarding need, desire will be an absolute condition regarding demand, due to the traces that the unconditional element of demand leaves in the sprout of the abolished object of need.

The figure of the Other outlined here is omnipotent; the Other of demand is omnipotent precisely due to the structure of demand itself. It is an Other which is completely unconditioned with regards to the need.

Let us advance a little bit more. We will consider the following quotation:

> For the unconditional element of demand, desire substitutes the 'absolute' condition: this condition unties the knot that element in the proof of love that is resistant to the satisfaction of a need. Thus desire is neither the appetite for satisfaction, nor the demand for love, but the difference that results from the subtraction of the first from the second, the phenomenon of their splitting (*Spaltung*) (p. 318).

Desire as such, implies the residue that remains from the structural difference between need and demand. Need minus demand leaves a remainder.[33] Obviously, we are stating that there is something in the need that cannot pass into the demand; and that remainder is what we call desire.

There is a great advantage in conceiving desire as a remainder: to see ourselves led to the theory of the object *a* as a remainder. What is it that in need does not pass into desire? The particularity. For us, human beings, it does not matter the particular required in order to satisfy the need, we substitute it by proofs of love. But this "does not matter", that is what is lost, will imply a remainder that we will call desire. Which are then the properties we assign to desire based on this relation? They are particularity and absolute condition. The particularity abolished at the level of "everybody" of the species, is recovered, precisely, in the difference of each one (what in the subject is particular). Let us notice that they are different particularities: both are particularities but they are not the same; there is a fundamental transformation.

The definition for "unconditional" in French (Lacan thinks in French that is why I search for the references in that language) is: absolute and imperative. Thus, it can be said that the super-ego is an effect of the structure. It is the power of the Other of the demand that, by means of a "reverse", passes afterwards onto the subject's side of the equation and opposes via the super-ego.

And what is a condition? Let us define it in relation with the cause. How to differentiate one from the other? Cause is often considered as a positive term, whereas condition would be a negative one, but the issue is more complex. Let us see:

- Necessary condition: A being a necessary condition for B means that there cannot be B if there is no A first, and that there can be A without B.
- Sufficient condition: Every time there is A there will be B. It is a different case. Within the sufficient conditions there are absolute conditions and relative conditions.
- Relative sufficient condition (when the first term implies the second, once the other conditions have been presupposed): For A to exist there has to have been always B before, as well as the other required conditions.
- Absolute sufficient condition (it is when a first term implies the second one by itself): If B exists, there must have been A before.

Therefore, to affirm that the subject's particular position is an absolute condition means that it is a non-relative sufficient condition; that is, it is not relative to the demand. Why did Lacan not use the same word, namely, "unconditional", both for demand and desire? Because whereas unconditional leads to omnipotence, absolute condition does not.

For a subject's position, insofar as he is a desiring subject, the remainder between need and demand will be a particular residue. This is his particular way of recovering the abolished particularity at the level of need. And at the same time, all that happens to him as a desiring subject—at the level of the cause- will have the form of the absolute condition regarding the demand.

Let us, before finishing, consider the relation need-demand-desire as a Möbius strip structure, equivalent to the interior eight that I proposed as the fundamental structure of the graph.

What I am trying to show you is that the graph of desire is desire, precisely because it is founded on the opposition need-demand-desire. To say "structure of the subject of the interval" is the same as saying "subject of desire".

We will posit, through the graph's sections, the described relationships: mythical subject of the need, going through the demand, through the Other (A) of demand, its beyond, desire.

I write the demand as signifying chain. The intersecting point will be the Other of demand; and last, beyond demand, remains that element of need that will not be included in demand, the field of desire.

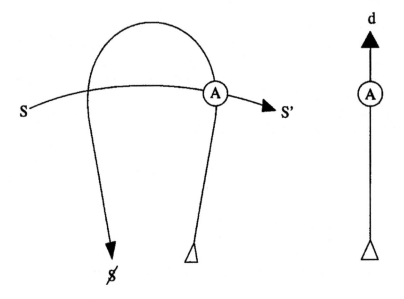

Schema 4.

If Lacan states that "desire is articulated, but it is not articulable", he does it precisely based on these relations among need-demand-desire. The remainder between need and demand implies already the articulation of a chain of the Other, for instance, the 'first said'; but it will not be articulable because it is precisely that of the need which does not pass into the demand. And that of the need which does not enter into demand is the particular object. That is to say, that the articulated but non articulable residue will be the object, the object *a* cause of desire, abolished from need due to the 'going through' of the demand but always being a 'beyond the demand'. It is precisely desire, as a beyond demand, which will allow us to work, next week, on the opposition between neurosis-psychosis.

I propose that we write down the principal articulations concerning the triad need-demand-desire that we worked through today, using the following schema:

Schema 5.

Given the relation abolishment-offspring on each side of the demand, it is obvious that the relationship has a Möbius strip structure, where the notion of *"renversement"* takes its due place. We will consider demand as the torsion itself and we will localize the 'within' and the 'beyond' accordingly.

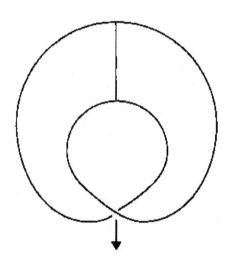

Within   *renversement*   **Beyond**
    [*au deçà*]   [*au delà*]

Schema 6.

In the following classes we will attempt to substitute, within this triad, the word "need" (for being mythical) with the word *"jouissance"*,[34] of which the psychoanalytical clinic attests to it being anything but mythical.

Notes

1. Jacques Lacan. *Écrits: A selection.* p. 320.
2. English version: *"Course in General Linguistics"*, trans. W. Baskin, Ed. Ch. Bally and A. Sechehaye, Mc Graw-Hill Paperbacks, 1966.
3. F. De Saussure isolates *langue* and *parole* in the vast field of *langage*. English does not have three words for translating the original French. Language [*langage*] would be, according to the author, the *matière* of linguistics, whereas *la langue* would be its object (clearly delimited from then on). In this context, *langue* is defined by Saussure as a "formal system of signs" whereas *parole* refers to the effective and concrete use that speakers make of that system (its "enacting"). Because of this Saussurean definition, *'parole'* is translated into English as 'speech' and not as 'word'.
4. Jacques Lacan. *Écrits: A selection.* p. 331.
5. English version "Shifters, Verbal Categories, and the Russian Verb" in *Selected Writings: Major Works 1976–1980 Completion Vol.*, Ed. Mouton de Gruyter, 1988.
6. My translation from now on.
7. Gilmore Logics.
8. In brackets in English in the original.
9. *"Lengua"* in Spanish in the original. Equivalent to the French *"langue"*.
10. In brackets in English in the original.
11. The Spanish translation for "shifter" is *"conmutador"*, also "switch-board".
12. According to Strachey's translation. In Spanish *"cambio de vía"*, literally "changing way".
13. In English in the original.
14. The French *énontiation/énoncé* will be from now on translated as enunciation/statement.
15. In Spanish *'discurso'*, equivalent to the French *'discourse'*. In linguistics and other fields linked to semiotics it is usually translated by 'speech' rather than 'discourse'.
16. Jacques Lacan. *Écrits: A selection* (p. 330).
17. In the original version *"On peut ici tenter, dans un souci de méthode, de partir de ..."* Lacan, J. *Écrits* Ed. Du Seuil, 1999, p. 280. I would rather

translate "*dans un souci de méthode*" as "because of a methodological concern". Lacan's statement seems to be rather: "if we were only worried about methodology, we would depart from the linguistic definition of the subject". The following paragraph shows that that is not the subject which interests psychoanalysis.

18. In English in the original.
19. Lacan distinguishes between *dire* and *dit*, which will be translated onwards as "saying" and "said" respectively.
20. Contrary to the English words, both in Spanish and French these particles share similarities: 'inter-intra-entre (between)'.
21. In the original version "*de la mise en forme signifiante comme telle*". Lacan, J. *Écrits* Ed. Du Seuil, 1999, p. 168.
22. Lacan separates himself here from his own initial perspective (cf. "The family complexes in the formation of the individual" for instance).
23. The author refers to the mistranslation of this verb in the Spanish version of the *Écrits* (the English version does not pose that problem).
24. In French: "*ne pouvoir, par hypothèse, s articuler dans la demande*": it seems that what is at stake in this use of the verb "*pouvoir*" here is less 'inability' or 'impotence' than 'impossibility'. Ibid. p. 168.
25. In the original "*qui apparaît dans un rejeton*". Probably the word was directly omitted due to the difficulty with translation. Literally: "it appears in a sprout" (also offspring). Desire would be thus defined as that part of the need that cannot be articulated in demand but emerges as a sprout. Ibid., p 168.
26. In French "*au deçà*" as opposite to "*au delà*" (beyond). Ibid. p. 169.
27. The verb Lacan uses is "*combler*" (to fill in, or to fulfil) and not "*satisfaire*".
28. There is a difficulty here due to translation: the authority is conferred on the real other by this "first said" [*dit premier*].
29. In Spanish "*lengua*" means both '*langue*' (language) and 'tongue'.
30. The author's clarification refers to the fact that French and English have two words (need/*besoin* and necessity/*necessité*) whereas Spanish only has "*necesidad*" for expressing both terms (biological need and logical necessity).
31. In French in the original. Translated "by a reversal" in *Écrits: A selection* (p. 317).
32. See note 28 above.
33. In the original "*resto*", in the sense of "residue" or "left over".
34. "*Goce*" in Spanish in the original.

CHAPTER FOUR

Graph one

Today's subject is graph number one.
In order to exhaustively work on the graph we are going to articulate it with the following quotation from *"Subversion of the subject ..."*, with which we ended last class:

> "[...] It is precisely because desire is articulated that it is not articulable" (p. 335).

The fact that desire is not articulable may be clear to us because we already worked on the idea of desire being that effect of the demand that demand itself cannot recapture. Necessarily, desire will always imply a field that is beyond any demand. This justifies the fact that in the analytic practice with neurotics it is not possible for desire not to be there. Lacan is particularly subtle when he states that, regarding desire's rejection, a neurotic subject can only go as far as "to desire not to desire". We call desire then, the structural effect of demand over need, which is not recoverable through demand, but which has to be distinguished from any "I desire *x* object".

We must keep in mind that in lacanian algebra, "demand" is written with a capital D, and "desire" with a small *d*. If you pay attention

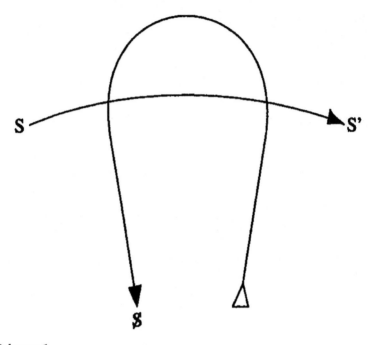

Schema 1.

to the logic according to which Lacan distributes small and capital letters (at least at the beginning of his teaching), you will find a surprise. When referring to the Symbolic, Lacan uses upper-case letters, and he uses lower-case letters when referring to the Imaginary (cf. for instance schema Lambda in *Seminar* 2).

Does Lacan mean, by writing desire with a *d*, that it is imaginary? It is not this, which is at stake. The problem is that it is not possible to account for a three-element system (Imaginary-Real-Symbolic), one by one, by means of a two-element system (capital letters—small letters). Anyhow, it is very interesting that, despite this fact, Lacan chose a D for demand and a *d* for desire. What happens is that desire as such, in spite of being an effect of the Symbolic, cannot be completely reabsorbed into the Symbolic itself. In other words, this *d* of desire has to be read as follows: it will not be reintroduced in the demand (the Symbolic).

And what does it mean that desire is articulated? This problem directly relates to the structure of the analytic practice. If Lacan had only affirmed that desire is not articulable, we should automatically conclude then that, being desire the ineffable, it is the same for everybody. Desire would then be the ineffable, that which nobody can say. But desire is not that. Desire is articulated for each particular subject. This implies the recovery, through the particular difference, of the function of the signifier in relation to the demand.

It seems to me that it is convenient here to posit the following: desire is articulated in the discourse of the Other (this appears in Seminar 9, "Identification", where Lacan works on this question by means of the structure of the two embraced *tori*[1]). Desire being articulated in the discourse of the Other clearly indicates that each subject's desire is determined by the demand of the Other. A more intuitive version of this problem is the phrase: "This is what you say to me, but what is it that you want?" where "what is it that you want?" is still determined by "what you say". Be aware that I say "determined" and not "caused".

Concerning the Other, every subject is faced with a disjunction between what is said to him and the margin, which does not fit into what the Other says (the question about his desire). But without any doubt, the particular question (namely, the articulated one) that each of us has regarding the desire of the Other depends on the determination received from the demand of the Other.

I am not saying that there is not a profound relation between the desire of the subject and the desire of the Other (that would be a relation of causation), but I want to say that there exists an intimate relation between the desire of the subject and the demand of the Other (a relation of determination).

Let us analyze this quotation from *"Subversion of the subject ..."* which precedes graph 1 in that text:

> For far from ceding to a logicizing reduction where it is a question of desire, I find in its irreducibility to demand the very source of that which also prevents it from being reduced to need. To put it elliptically: it is precisely because desire is articulated that it is not articulable, I mean in the discourse best suited to it, an ethical, not a psychological discourse (p. 335).

It is precisely because desire is articulated that it is not articulable (and be aware of the fact that Lacan is saying all of this elliptically). Elliptic speech is one of the figures in the art of rhetoric, the art of *well-saying*. It is a saying searching for emphasis and based in a certain not saying. The subject, then, in the direction of the cure, approaches the path of its desire, for example, via ellipsis (which is one of the ways in which the articulated but not articulable problem can be solved).

Graph 1 will allow us to present the point where desire is situated regarding a subject defined within its signifying articulation. Notice that in graph 1 (which Lacan himself defines as topological) desire is not included. Now, why does Lacan say that that graph will allow us to localize desire?

Strictly speaking, neither graph 1 nor graph 2 nor 3 exist as such; they are parts of the deductive argument accounting for the complete graph. Clinically speaking, then, graphs 1, 2 and 3 do not exist. They are nothing but devices of transmission. We could say it even more radically: they are didactic devices that Lacan invented in order to discursively account for the structure of the graph of desire.

We have already said that the virtue of a graph is to say everything it says synchronically; and that if one wanted to account for everything the graph says in the synchrony, it would take hours and hours (that is diachrony). But in order to anchor crucial elements of what is being said, we introduce partial cuts into the complete graph, and those are graphs 1, 2 and 3. In the same way as we also say that we never find Oedipus 1, Oedipus 2 or Oedipus 3. What we find is just Oedipus. If the paternal metaphor operates then there is Oedipus it is a complete metaphor. So, this graph is the beginning of an argument that will allow us to access to the complete graph. Only then will Lacan be able to localize desire, the subject as desire.

Lacan calls graph 1 the "elementary cell".

> This is what might be said to be its elementary cell. [...] In it is articulated what I have called the 'anchoring point' [*point de caption*],[2] by which the signifier stops the otherwise endless movement [*glissement*][3] of the signification (p. 335).

Graph 1 allows us to posit the function of the quilting point or 'stopping point'.

I do not know if you know the structure of what upholsterers call *'point de capiton'*, 'upholstery buttons'. It is a kind of knot that is also called a point. This is highly indicative of the function that the full stop[4] has in the phrase. For instance, stopping the sliding (otherwise indefinite[5]) of the signification, given that signification is character-ized by leading always to another signification. What Lacan says, thus, is that signification leads to another signification. He does not say that the signifier leads to another signifier; the signifier does not always lead to another signifier, only sometimes (in holophrases, for example, it does not). What does always happen is that significa-tion leads to another signification. And what stops that sliding is precisely the function of the point ('full stop'). But this point, the point at the end of the phrase, the full stop, is not enough in order to account for that notion, it is necessary to appeal to the structure of the quilting point, which is a point but has the structure of a very particular knot.

What is an 'upholstery button'? It is the point that allows a cush-ion, one with big dimensions, not to loose its shape. In order to pre-vent it from loosing the good shape, buttons are put in both sides, sewed one to the other. The upholstery button [point de capiton] links the knots that link the buttons in each side, forming a continuous bow. It is not that one is tied to another one in the other side, but they are taken in pairs, and without closing the bow that links them, one goes on to the next two, and so on until every pair is included. And it is made like this in case the lower buttons require more string (due to the stuffing concentration, which tends to thicken it). The excess string above yields and thus the form is kept. It is a system used for knotting several levels, and this refers us to the structure of the graph of desire. It is a knotted structure implying at least the continuous relation: two to two. Its relationship with the structure of language, as we considered it last class, is evident.

In the context of Lacan's teaching then, whenever the function of the point is involved, what is at stake is the fact that it has the struc-ture of a point de capiton. I am saying this because the end of the ses-sion is usually understood, very naively, as a full stop (final point). Which analyst does not know, and even, which analysand does not know that the vast majority of most of the sessions are not in reality true full stops? Only some of them produce the effect of things not being the same any more, only some of them are true cuts.

Lacan has always assigned to the Other the function of punctuat-ing the discourse, that is, it is not the subject emitting his message but the Other receiving it who punctuates the discourse. Lacan calls this the "listener's discretional power".[6] Because of this, we say that one receives one's own message from the Other. Not because it is not me who speaks the words, but because it is the Other who punctuates them. (And examples abound that show it depends on how a phrase is punctuated for its signification[7] to be one or another). However, as we have said previously, a punctuation made by the other will not necessarily be "an interpretation".

In the elementary cell of the graph, Lacan proposes that we work on the notions of diachrony and synchrony. Diachrony:

> The diachronic function of this anchoring[8] point is to be found in the sentence, even if the sentence completes its signification only with its last term, each term being anticipated in the construction of the others, and, inversely, sealing their meaning by its retroactive effect (p. 336).

There is a problem here concerning the translation of the *Écrits* into Spanish.[9] In the original it does not say "the sentence ´completes´ its signification". The term used by Lacan is *"boucle"*, and although it is said in the dictionary that the verb *"boucler"*[10] means, "to close", we should not forget that it is to close with the shape of a curl.[11] For example, one could never say "to close a door" using this verb. And regarding the term *"boucle"*, the dictionary says: "objects with the shape of a ring, and by analogy, everything that curls in the shape of a ring". What Lacan proposes here is, thus, that signification, within the elementary cell closes as a ring does.

The other thing that Lacan proposes to us is that the temporality, which is at stake, is that of anticipation and retroaction. It is retroaction that closes as a circle would. The structure is that of a curl. However, it has to be noticed that retroaction (which we situated in the function of the quilting point, ending the sliding of the signification) is not the only temporality in play; there is also the time of anticipation.

In the first place, we have to be able to distinguish this anticipation from the one posited, for instance, by the logic of the optical model: the imaginary anticipation. Imaginary anticipation refers to totality, to the unity one is able to see in the other's body, but that is not yet, as such, a real unity in one's own body (and this is why the other's image is seductive, captivating). This is an anticipation that will never be able to be rectified (not even in an analysis oriented towards the relocation of the ego, given that the ego remains forever structured with this temporal failure, precisely because it is constituted trough identification).

In this case, to the contrary, what is at stake is that in the same way as the last element, understood as a quilting point, has the virtue of stopping signification, the first element has the power of affecting those coming after it. You can begin to connect this already to the S_1, the master signifier: once the signifier one is chosen, then it is not possible for 'anything' to follow.

For this relation anticipation-retroaction shows that one can never account categorically for the present, Lacan proposes a "sealed" interaction. And do not forget that although "to seal" implies to close (desire is finite, it is fundamentally closed), it also means to leave a mark, a seal, a trace. It does not only "close" but also remains as a "mark". The mark left by the Demand of the Other on the desire of the subject. This desire will remain, thus, connected to these marks.

Let us go now to the synchronic dimension:

> But the synchronic structure is more hidden, and it is this structure that takes us to the source.[12] It is metaphor in so far as the first attribution is constituted in it—the attribution that promulgates 'the dog goes miaow, the cat goes woof-woof', by which the child, by disconnecting the animal[13] from its cry, suddenly raises the sign to the function of the signifier, and reality to the sophistics of signification, and by contempt for verisimilitude, opens up the diversity of objectifications of the same thing that have to be verified (p. 336).

The synchronic structure is, doubtless, more obscure. It is that of the time without time, and Lacan states that it takes us to the origin: even more, that it is the metaphor of the origin, the first metaphor, the first attribution. Let us remember that the attributive judgment logically precedes the existential judgment.

Here is Lacan's example, which I believe has a similar strength to Freud's *fort-da*. It is the following: the dog goes miaow the cat goes woof-woof. Between the dog and the "woof-woof" there is a relationship that may be that of the thing and its cry. The cry may be thus considered as the sign of the thing. There are signs within the animal world; the question is to be able to determine what does it mean for a child to say 'the dog goes miaow the cat goes woof-woof'. Lacan affirms that by separating the thing from the sign, putting the former in relation with the sign of another thing, the first thing produced is the destitution of the sign as such; it becomes a signifier. Automatically and because of this metaphorical substitution, when we are faced with someone who is able to say "the dog goes miaow", then he no longer knows what he says when he speaks, given that it is neither signs nor things which are at stake.

Thus, the sign becomes signifier, but the question is what happens with the thing. When we situate ourselves at the level where the sign has become a signifier, an effect is produced over the thing: let us say that the reality of things becomes the sophistic of signification.

And what is sophistics? It is nothing else than the use of sophisms; and "sophism" means argument, reasoning in terms of true or false statements.

So once one no longer has signs of the thing, the problem that emerges is that truth acquires the sophism's structure, it becomes an argument. Truth acquires the structure of fiction. Dora for example, was a victim, but she was also an accomplice; that is, Dora's truth has the structure of a sophism, it is a truth hiding a falsity. Or if we would like to think of it the other way around, it is the same thing: it is a falsity that hides a truth. Something similar occurs in Freud's Rat Man case concerning Freud's interpretation referring to the patient's father as an obstacle to his marriage choice. For it was his mother who had actually contrived to the "convenient marriage", when the father had already been dead for a while. It was "true" that the father was the obstacle, but it was at the same time inexact.

Within traditional logics, a sophism is a reasoning according to the rules of logic that leads to a false conclusion. And colloquially, in a vulgar use, sophism means "captious" (this shows us how lie captures).

It is interesting that Lacan writes, "cry" (and not "said" for example); the same happens with the child and his own cry. When the child's cry is no longer a sign for the mother, it is because she takes it as a signifier. We do not understand children's cries precisely because they have become signifiers to us.

The cry, having become a signifier, is a call; and a cry is not the same as a call. And that which was a thing has become a child. Everything has been denaturalized, has been devitalized.

In order to better think about this problem, which I believe is fundamental, let us consider the following quotation by Lacan; it is in *"The metaphor of the subject"*, written between 1960 and 1961, *Écrits 2, 1987*.[14]:

> The radical metaphor is given in the tantrum of rage reported by Freud of the child, still unarmed with coarseness, which was his Rat Man before he became an obsessional neurotic, who whenever opposed by his father, challenges him: "Du Lampe, du Handtuch, du Teller usw." (You lamp, you napkin, you plate, etc.).
>
> In what we also hear [understand], the dimension of insult in which metaphor is originated, is not lost. Insult more serious than one imagines it when reduced to the invective of war. Because it is from that that the injustice rendered for free to every subject of an attribute by which any other subject is provoked to start it. "The cat goes woof-woof, the dog goes miaow." Here is how the child spells the powers of speech and inaugurates thinking (p. 757).

Lacan states that it is through this inversion that thinking (*la pensée*), thinking proper, symbolic thinking is originated. Lacan mentions also an insult, absolutely unjust damage that leads us to an ethical issue: it is an unjust damage perpetrated on every subject. The child will be damaged simply by being told that he is this or that, or that he wants this or that object. That is to say, he is damaged so long as any attribute is applied to him. He will be damaged at the level of the natural, as a thing. We must consider that any signifier chosen as an attribute implies the substitution concerning all the others; this is the metaphor which is involved here.

So, both diachrony and synchrony already participate in the elementary cell. Diachrony implies anticipation and retroaction, and synchrony implies attribution (which implies, as such, both the existence of the subject at the level of the Symbolic and its damage).

Let us consider another quotation from *"Subversion of the subject …"*:

> I will spare you the various stages by giving you at one go the function of the two points of intersection in this simplified graph. The first, connoted O[A], is the locus of the treasure of

the signifier, which does not mean the treasure of the code, for it is not that the univocal correspondence of a sign with something is preserved in it, but that the signifier is constituted only from a synchronic and enumerable collection of elements in which each is sustained only by the principle of its opposition to each of the others. The second, connoted s(O) [s(A)], is what may be called the punctuation in which the signification is constituted as a finished product (p. 336).

The following schema corresponds to this quotation:

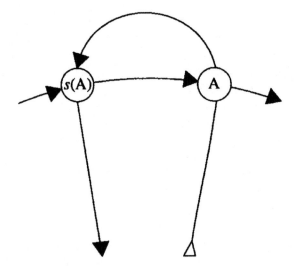

Schema 2.

We call A the crossing point on the right. Lacan proposes to define it as the "treasure of the signifier" and he warns us that the treasure has to be distinguished from the code. He defines the code as the univocal relationship between a sign and a thing. The treasure of the signifier, on the contrary, is formed by signifiers which need, for constituting themselves, the opposition regarding all the other signifiers. It is important not to forget that Lacan states that this synchronic reunion is "enumerable"; meaning: for each case in the clinical practice we must be able to find the number of signifiers put into play.

If a signifier is over-determined by three others, for instance, it is necessary that the function of all four signifiers is established; three of them are not enough; we would be not even close: none of the found signifiers acquires the right meaning unless all the others are present. And it is not "all" in the sense of completeness that is at stake, but "all" in the sense of "all the involved ones". This is what happens in the case of the Rat Man: despite the fact that several articulations around "rats" had already been uttered (heiraten, Spielratte, ratten-Raten, etc.) nothing is solved until Ibsen's Little Eyolf's Lady of the Rats and Gisela's sterility (castration of the idealized Lady) are reached.

Lacan calls this Other, A, which is not a code (not only because it is not a complete set, but mainly because there is no relationship between signs and things); Lacan calls it "treasure of the signifier". The word "treasure" is extremely interesting. Doubtless it leads us, on the one hand, to the problem of value; things will have a value or not according to what happens in the A for each subject; but it always leads us to the notion of treasure itself: place where valuables are kept, and even the safe, that is, a direct reference to the place. Finally, it suggests the idea that the treasure is what it is, no matter how much it contains. That is to say that the treasure is not, in spite of lacking nothing, an "all", whereas the code is. Every code is complete, and there is no empty place in it (given that if there was, it could not be used as a code any more). The code is complete and it is an "all". For instance, if we consider the treasure of the U.S as a metaphor for the world's largest concentration of gold, it is not however all the gold in the world. If it was, gold would immediately loose any exchange value, which is the actual value of gold.

On the other side of the graph we have another crossing point, that we call the signified of the Other—s(A). There is no doubt that this has to be in opposition to Jakobson's notion of message. Here Lacan develops how the subject's message is, by structure, a message of the Other. Here you have one of the inversions: the message no longer belongs to the subject, it belongs to the Other. And Lacan places there the function of punctuation, but within the logics of the anticipation and retroaction. Let us notice that Lacan places the function of the full stop (final point) on the left, subverting the legality of our writing. If we represented it by means of a schema it would look something like this:

$$\text{"S}_1\text{ S}_2\text{."} \qquad \text{contrary to:} \qquad \text{". S}_1\text{ S}_2\text{"}$$

where it can clearly be seen how it is not the same when we consider the point as a cut, than when we consider it as a punctuation mark.

Thus, we refer back to what I anticipated: that Lacan conceives the function of punctuation as a function of the Other (it is from there that psychoanalysts operate). If psychoanalysts can produce any effect, it is precisely by placing ourselves, artificially, in that place where from we exert a power. This is why Lacan had to write "The direction of the treatment and the principles of its power": psychoanalysts occupy a place of power (at least that of the listener's discretional power).

The quotation continues:

> Observe the dyssymetry of the one, which is a locus (a place rather than a space) [...] (p. 336).

A is a symbolic locus, strictly symbolic. What Lacan means by "place" is that A is also a signifying place, the place of the signifiers is a signifying-signifier itself, it is not an actual place. As it is not an actual place, it has no measurements, dimensions. It is a place, then, but it has neither measures nor sizes. It is a place in the sense of topology.

> [...] to the other, which is a moment (a rhythm[15] rather than a duration) (p. 336).

When the message that comes from the Other is produced, it is produced because of punctuation. And punctuation (that has a temporal dimension) will be as such a symbolically structured time too; a time of cut, scansion, and not of duration.

The question is: what structure does this time have? The answer is: a time of scansion. The problem is not "for how long?" or "since when?" but how this "too soon/early or too late" is produced for somebody. Psychoanalytically speaking, the question is why the scansion is anticipated, delayed or does not come at all, and that is not a measurable temporal dimension. Time corresponds here to a reality that has lost its actual connotation and has now a symbolic connotation; it is a symbolic time itself. We have thus condensed here the entire logic for the variable-length sessions. The same happens with space.

Therefore, space becomes localization and time becomes scansion.

After the quotation on the synchronic function, Lacan continues with the following paragraph:

> Does this possibility require the topology of a four-cornered game? That is the sort of question that looks innocent enough, but which may give some trouble, if the subsequent construction must be dependent on it [the subsequent construction of the graph of desire] (p. 336).

Are the two crossing points enough in order to account for the structure? Is the dual organization enough or is a quadripartite structure, a topology of four required? This is the type of question which may seem naïve, but which is useful for the subsequent construction of the complete graph and the direction of the cure.

We justify the pertinence of considering the "quilting point" as a bow joining two to two precisely in this indication by Lacan to a topological relation of four places. The structure of language as a quadripartite one is thus recovered for the structure of the unconscious. We conclude that the unconscious as such cannot operate within a dual structure as the one presented in graph 1. We will take this perspective in order to work on the opposition between neurosis and psychosis in our next meeting.

We have not comment yet—I did it on purpose—on the fact that Lacan calls this graph 1 "the graph's elementary cell". I have the impression that there is a trend to read this as the "graph's fundamental unity"; but Lacan names graph 1 a "cell" for a different reason.

The word "cell" has at least two meanings: The first one is the one it has in biology: what has a membrane that isolates the cytoplasm from its nucleus, an inside and outside. The other one is the one it has in the field of memory: repetitive element. I think the second meaning is the most relevant one. The first one is particularly inadequate for accounting for the subject's (S) relationship with the Other (A), given that the subject receiving his own message from the Other eliminates the possibility of establishing the opposition inside outside between them. I propose to you that we add the notion of repetition, as a fundamental character, to the circuit of the graph.

The subjection[16] of the subject to the signifier, which occurs in the circuit that goes from $s(A)$[17] to A and back from A to $s(A)$ is really a circle, even though the assertion that is established in it—for lack of being able to end on anything other than its own scansion, in other words, for lack of an act in which it would find its certainty—refers only to its own anticipation in the composition of the signifier, in itself insignificant (p. 337).

Lacan says that if the cell was closed and limited to the dual circuit, then it would be in itself insignificant, worth nothing, even though the circuit is made of signifiers. And if one tried to constitute an act in which the subject finds a certitude through this circuit, he will fail, because this circuit is insignificant. And it is so, precisely, because the thing is lost and the circuit itself has no way out (from A to $s(A)$ and vice versa). I propose to name this circuit with a Lacanian designation: "infernal circuit of the demand". He is considering it within several articulations. Firstly, it indicates the horror, the hell (inferno) produced by this functioning. Secondly, it leads us to the Inferno as conceived by Dante in *The Divine Comedy*: structured as a circle. They are concentric circles that Dante crosses from the exterior/outside to the interior/inside, for example in the Third Canto he says:

> And when his hand he had stretch'd forth to mine, with pleasant looks, whence I was cheer'd, into that secret place he led me on. Here sighs, with lamentations and loud moans, resounded through the air pierced by no star, that e'en I wept at entering. Various tongues, horrible languages, outcries of woe, accents of anger, voices deep and hoarse, with hands together smote that swell'd the sounds, made up a tumult, that forever whirls round through that air with solid darkness stain'd, like to the sand that in the whirlwind flies.[18]

Notice that Dante is indicating to us that those who are in Hell are trapped into an infernal circle of the demand. Those who are being punished complaint, lament and moan; those are forms of the demand, which lead them nowhere, their punishment is eternal. That is what is circular. Demand, as such, is a circularity, which has no way out.

Lacan says that the only way out is an act which would allow the possibility of certitude. But the logic of such an act is beyond demand, the "beyond" we already know as desire. What can break the infernal circle of demand then is an act corresponding to desire. Having arrived at the dialectic of desire, we must first establish an extremely important clinical distinction. Let us depart from this quotation:

> Code messages or message codes will be distinguished in pure forms in the subject of psychosis, the subject who is satisfied with[19] that previous Other (p. 337).

That is, for the psychotic subject demand operates. Therefore we can sustain that there is a subject in psychosis, and also that there is an Other in psychosis. And this Other, doubtless, has the structure of language, that is: the division between code and message does operate and, consequently, there is circularity and overlapping.[20]

The subject of language means the consideration of the human being as being strictly different from any natural given, and it implies, as in graph 1, not the encounter with *the* signifier, but with at least two of them. In terms of graph 1, at least two crossing points that have to be considered as signifying/signifier themselves. Therefore,

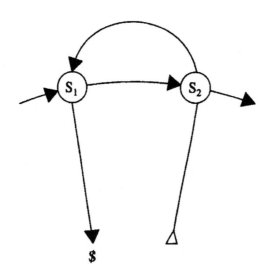

Schema 3.

the subject of language, crossed by language, the $, is the product of the encounter with at least two articulated signifiers. In graph I:

The subject of language is posited as an effect of the encounter with the function of the demand, that is, with the Other (A), with at least two articulated signifiers. Thus we can say that it is not *the* signifier which kills the thing but the articulation among signifiers. It is this which introduces "the lack of being into the object relation". Regarding this, both the neurotic and the psychotic are subjects of language. What produces the distinction in this opposition is whether the function of the 'beyond demand' (that we will soon define as "between the lines") operates or not.

The problem within the field of psychosis is precisely that the psychotic subject remains trapped in the circuit of the demand. There is no 'beyond' demand for him, and let us remember that that beyond demand is desire.

The last quotation I selected in order to think of these problems is from *"Subversion of the subject ..."*:

> But we must insist that *jouissance* is forbidden to him whom speaks as such, although it can only be said between the lines for whoever is subject of the Law, since the Law is grounded in this very prohibition[21] (p. 352).

"Interdict" within this context, does not essentially mean "prohibition" but it posits the "between".[22] Thus, for the human subject (given the structure of "interdict") *jouissance* can only be voiced between the lines. And be aware that this "between the lines" is not founded by the Law, but on the contrary, it is the Law that is founded in the 'between the lines'. This subverts the way we used to posit the structure of the function of the father in neurosis and psychosis. The question of a clinic orientated 'beyond the father' emerges.

The problem of the infernal circle of the demand is that, in so far as it is circular, it does not account for the "in-between". Therefore, the act which would allow the subject to egress from this infernal circularity (in which the psychotic subject is, structurally speaking, trapped) must point beyond demand. That is, it must point towards desire. In sum, a four-cornered topological interplay is necessary.

Notes

1. Plural for the topological surface called 'torus'.
2. In French '*point de caption*'. Literally: 'upholstery button'; also translated as 'quilting point' (we will keep this term).
3. "Sliding".
4. "Point" in Spanish and French.
5. '*Indéfini*', translated as 'indefinite', is the term Lacan uses in the original.
6. In the original French "*pouvoir discrétionnaire de l auditeur*" (J. Lacan. "Variantes de la cure-type" in *Écrits II*, Ed. du Séuil, Paris. 1999, p. 330).
7. Spanish "*significación*" and French "*signification*". Also translated as "understanding" or as a synonym for "meaning". We will use the English "signification" from now on exclusively when translating this term.
8. See note 1 above.
9. Since the same (or even worse) problem emerges from Sheridan's English version (his translation: "*completes*"), we transcribe the author's comment on the term "*boucler*" almost unmodified.
10. Literally: to curl.
11. "*Bucle*" in Spanish.
12. In French "*origine*": literally: origin.
13. Here Lacan writes "*en déconnectant la chose de son cri*", that is "by disconnecting the *thing* from its cry".
14. *Écrits II*, Ed. du Séuil, Paris, 1999, p. 361. My translation.
15. Lacan says "*scansion*", that has a reference to the cut (for instance, when talking about "analyzing metric elements of the verses in a poem"). Both the noun "scansion" and the verb "to scan" exist in English, so we will onwards translate the French using them.
16. In the original "*soumission*"; it shares meaning with the English "submission" in terms of "accepting an authority".
17. Translation modified according to notes 2 and 4, Chapter One.
18. Dante Alighieri. *The Divine Comedy*. The Harvard Classics. 1909–14.
19. In French "*... celui qui se suffit de cet Autre préalable*". Literally: "for whom that previous Other is enough". The reflexive form of the verb in French when referred to people has the connotation of 'find by one's own means how to satisfy one's needs' (cf. Petit Robert Dictionary).
20. In English in the original.
21. The author substitutes in the Spanish translation "interdicción" for "prohibición", closer to Lacan's term (*interdiction* in French). In English it can be translated as "interdict", thus maintaining its Latin root (*inter-dire*).
22. *Inter*: between. *Dict*: said / saying.

CHAPTER FIVE

Questions and answers:
The impossible—neurosis
and psychosis

I shall begin with some questions or issues posed by you.
   The first question I was asked by one of you was about the type of relation existing between "absolute condition" and "unconditional", for both terms are linked to desire and demand respectively.

   The terms "absolute condition" and "unconditional" account for the relation between the terms "need-demand-desire" themselves. The problem with this triad is that for one of its terms, need, the subject is mythic. That is why, as we advance and in order to be more precise from a psychoanalytic perspective, we will substitute the triad need-demand-desire with jouissance-demand-desire. We could say that we are now in a mid-point in our way towards that substitution.

   We have to be able, with the triad "need-demand-desire", to make an equivalent maneuver to that which exists in Freudian topography. This implies that each of its elements acquires the status of a *topos*, a non-metric place—that is, a place defined by its position in relation to the others, and not by its autonomous placement in relation to any measure scale whatsoever. Thus, demand is for instance, between need and desire; demand breaks the continuity need-desire and introduces the structural discontinuity in that trio. And if demand produces such an effect due to being "between", what has to be considered then are the relations between need and demand on one hand (unconditional) and the relation between demand and desire, on the other (absolute condition).

The relationship between need and demand is unconditional because (according to our conception of the subject) need does not impose any limitation on demand, and this is a fundamental psychoanalytic postulate. However, the problem we face here is that this triad has been set up incorrectly, given that—strictly speaking—the only need which remains for the speaking being is the logical one[1]: "it is necessary that". And any other vital need is considered as being mythical.

It is our position in psychoanalysis that no need exists for the speaking being—not even the fundamental need of not dying. A transformation which we call "presence-absence" is produced. The presence of the Other, as love object, becomes determinant, more important than any need. Even more, in the realm of the speaking being there is no vital need (although any need of this kind is vital by definition) able to constitute a limit for love. Only logical needs can do that.

So, the first logical effect of demand in the field of need is to be unconditional. For within any human subject, his position being determined by demand, we find the effect of the unconditional, because the demand always introduces the unconditional condition with regards to vital needs.

But there is also another effect of demand, not on the need, but on the demand itself: it is the effect on the demand produced by the presence of demand itself. Given that demand is constituted by signifying elements (signifiers) and not by signs, a new effect is produced: a beyond demand, something that of the demand is a beyond demand itself.

This "beyond" has to be understood in the Freudian sense. When Freud writes "beyond the pleasure principle" he denounces his mistake: to have believed, as it was believed in the history of thought, that the determinant element for the subject was the pleasure principle, that every human subject acts according to the "supreme good". Freud discovers something that it is not determined by the pleasure principle, but it is its determinant. "Beyond", in a Freudian sense means, "determinant".

We say that beyond need is demand. But there exists a really paradoxical effect of demand, which becomes its own beyond, desire. We said that, regarding demand, the need does not constitute any condition. We can now say that desire, regarding demand, is an absolute condition.

We have already said that the expression "absolute condition", given its philosophical connotations, implies the notion of cause. The cause of the subject's true act is always beyond demand; that is, there is a determinant for love not determined by love; there is something determining love and what love itself cannot determine: that is desire.

It is not enough to have three in order to have a trio; that those three constitute a trio has to be demonstrated. In our case ("need-demand-desire") we have not demonstrated it yet. We have only talked about the duo need-demand, on one hand, and of the duo desire-demand, on the other. Then, why must they be considered as a triad? They are a trio because what is produced as the specific loss from need is recovered, in a certain sense, at the level of desire. There is a certain communication between need and desire. The problem is that it is conservation with transformation, there is an inversion in the relationship, from the particularity of the species to the particularity of the subject's desire. There is an offspring of the particular object of the species, in so far as it is unavoidably lost due to demand: the object a cause of desire, "cause-object", particular for each subject. This relation between "need-demand-desire" is a Möbious strip.

Another question that has been posed is why, if Lacan is progressing towards abandoning representation, there are always models or schemata working as representations of his notions?

Those who deal with the pure signifier are scientists (for instance: mathematicians), not psychoanalysts. The psychoanalyst is always facing the fact that the signifier produces effects of meaning (signified) within the subject. People addressing us as analysts suffer precisely from that, from those effects.

The problem Lacan faced was the relationship signifier-signified, and his response was that the signifier determines the signified, something that is absolutely obscure for every neurotic subject.

The progress of Lacan's teaching consists in choosing representations that better respond to the structure of representation of the speaking being; that is, to find those representations able to better account for the material we have to face and operate with in the analytical practice. And that is different from radically abandoning all representation.

According to Lacan, a certain level of intuition has to be maintained, given that intuition never disappears in our subject. What needs to be highlighted is that intuition must be represented as we find it operating in the subject: determined and not determinant.

We advance by abandoning those representations that are not useful which orientates us towards the types of representation that are useful. Our path is ruled by the following logic: the representations we move towards are those which better include—in their internal logic—the fact that saying [dire] determines intuitive representation. It seems to me that this is the problem; and even at the most abstract levels, borromean knots, for example, we will always need a blackboard in order to communicate them.

Physicists, mathematicians and logicians posit that physics, mathematics or logics have a metalinguistic level (namely, which is beyond saying). Lacan tries always to remind them that at a certain stage they will have to communicate it to others (even only to other mathematicians, physicists or logicians) and in that moment they will not be able to escape from the fact that no human communication can be produced at a metalinguistic level.

And now to the last question posed by one of you, a double question. Firstly, can enunciation and the unconscious be overlapped? We can answer, partially, yes, at least according to the way Lacan presents it in the "graph of desire"—although after Seminar 12, during the last part of his teaching, Lacan seems to invert this—.

What should be noticed is that the localization of the subject of the enunciation is always paradoxical with regards to the subject of the statement. The subject of the unconscious is the one between the subject of the statement and the subject of the enunciation. Although strictly speaking we should say that it is closer to the subject of the enunciation, because statements refer to contents and enunciation, to acts. These issues will be further developed in following classes.

And secondly you asked about the "graph of desire" and the diverse structure of the two signifying chains. It is a complex question.

Remember, however, that we said that in the case of the "graph of desire" there cannot be edges departing from one side and arriving nowhere, as there cannot be edges arriving somewhere departing from nowhere. Let us recall that we set up the union of those edges in the graph according to the structure of the interior eight. Thus we postulated the two chains in continuity.

Lacan states that in order to localize the subject, as we find it within the analytic experience, it must be sought in the interval, in the 'between'—and that the logic of the interior eight must be added to that condition. We seek then for an interval subject, but also for a subject in a certain repetition. And that repetition is produced, precisely, as the interior eight. Notice that if one of these two dimensions is missing, the 'between' (the failure in the encounter) and repetition (its searching), we will not have the structure of the neurotic subject we work with.

To sum up, we require the 'between', the clinic of the question, the doubt, but we also require, unavoidably, repetition, a question related to that which returns. Let's say it this way: structurally speaking there is no symptom without repetition.

But we can still turn the screw once again and view the question from another angle. Psychoanalysis demands the presence of repetition for the subject's constitution; but, at the same time, psychoanalysis knows well that repetition as such is some sort of paradox, because in every repetition there is something that fails with respect to the repeated.

We reach thus the question for the localization of the object a. The object a will be localized in the 'between' the first time—the original—and the second time—its repetition. It will then be that which is lost between the first time and its repetition. And put like this, it is clear that it is a symbolic effect. In other words, repetition needs a symbolic structure—account, numeration—able to establish it as such. Only for the subject for whom it is always "the first time" there will not be an object a, and precisely because for him this effect of loss, characteristic of repetition, does not exist.

Let us now address the topic of this class. Our themes will be: the quadrature of the circle, the notion of impossibility and the opposition between neurosis-psychosis.

Let us begin with a quotation from "*Subversion of the subject ...*" that we have already worked on.

> This is what might be said to be its elementary cell. [...] In it is articulated what I have called the 'anchoring point' [*point de caption*], by which the signifier stops the otherwise endless movement [*glissement*] of the signification (p. 335).

We conceive this quilting point as being a knot.

Then Lacan asks himself:

> Does this possibility require the topology of a four-cornered game? That is the sort of question that looks innocent enough, but which may give some trouble, if the subsequent construction must be dependent on it (p. 336).

What possibility is he referring to? It seems to me that he is referring precisely to the quilting point's basic function: to stop the indefinite movement of signification. Are then graph 1 and its two crossing points enough in order to act as a true brake, as a point for halting signification, or do we need a graph bringing into play four points?

> To be possible, the squaring of this circle only requires the completion of the signifying battery set up in O [A], henceforth symbolizing the locus of the Other [...] Yet such a squaring is impossible (p. 337).

Lacan works on this problem, the opposition between a dual structure and a quadripartite structure, by means of the mathematical notion of quadrature of the circle. He states that the quadrature (4) of the circle (2) is impossible. In order to work on them we will first read some quotations from *Mathematics and the Imagination*,[2] a book by Kasner and Newman.

> When it is said that the circle cannot be squared, all that is meant is that this *cannot be done with ruler and compass alone*, although with the aid of the integraph or higher curves the operation does become possible. [...] The difficulty in squaring the circle, as stated at the outset, lies in the nature of the number π (pp. 69–72).

What is called quadrature of the circle is the possibility of calculating the surface of a circle from a square that has the same surface, following the knowledge of ancient mathematicians on how to calculate the surface of straight-sided figures. The problem they found was how to calculate the circle's area, being the circle a curved-sided figure or a figure with no straight sides. So they posited the possibility of calculating the circle's area by means of the calculation of the surface, known to them, of a square of equal area. This is called the quadrature of the circle. But, is it possible? Is it possible to construct, with ruler and compass alone, a square of the same area as a given circle? The whole question is what we understand by 'to can' or 'to cannot', by possibility and impossibility. That is to say, the question about the structural limitation within which possibilities are measured is not to be forgotten.

The solution that ancient mathematicians did not have is related to the π number; and the quadrature of the circle lies precisely in the nature of that π number. Let us go on with our reading of Kasner and Newman:

> This remarkable number, as Lindemann proved, cannot be the root of an algebraic equation with integer coefficients [...] when the Greek philosophers found that the square root of 2(√2) is not a rational number, they celebrated the discovery by sacrificing 100 oxen. The much more profound discovery that π is a transcendental number deserves a greater sacrifice. Again mathematics triumphed over common sense. π, a finite number—the ratio of the circumference of a circle to its diameter [...] (pp. 72–80).

Notice that the problem we are dealing with goes beyond common sense. It is a true monster, a finite number produced as an infinite sum of numbers. That is exactly what contradicts common sense: that the sum of an infinite number of terms results in a finite number of terms. The simplest surface of all geometrical figures, the circle, is precisely the one that presents more problems to intuition. We continue with our mathematicians:

> The √2 when written as a decimal is just as complicated as π, for it never repeats, it never ends, and there is no known law giving the succession of its digits; yet this complicated decimal is easily obtained with exactitude by a ruler and compass construction. It is the diagonal of a square whose side is equal to 1 (p. 110).

This is a fundamental problem for us, for it brings along the question of the incommensurable, exhaustively worked through by Lacan when trying to account for the logic of the relation/proportion between the sexes. For Greek mathematicians, the incommensurable appeared in the lack of common measure within the relations between the square's diagonal and its sides.

Let us now refer to the use Lacan makes of these mathematical notions, through an already partially quoted citation:

> To be possible, the squaring [quadrature] of this circle only requires the completion of the signifying battery set up in O [A], henceforth symbolizing the locus of the Other. It then becomes apparent that this Other is simply the pure subject of modern games theory, and as such perfectly accessible to the calculation of conjecture, even though the real subject, in order to govern his own calculation, must leave out of account any so-called aberration, in the common, that is, the psychological, acceptation of the term, and concern himself only with the inscription of an exhaustive combinatory[3] [...] Yet such a squaring is impossible, but only by virtue of the fact that the subject is constituted only by subtracting himself from it and by decompleting it essentially in order, at one at the same time, to have to depend on it and to make it function as a lack (p. 337).

The squaring of the circle, is it then possible? Is it possible to localize the subject beyond demand within a structure like the graph's elementary cell? Yes, if A was complete; but A is, fundamentally, incomplete (it is treasure and not code). We are stating, together with Lacan, that it is impossible to localize the subject of desire within a dual structure as graph 1 is, and that a four-cornered topological game is essential.

We find an excellent definition of the impossible in *Mathematics and the Imagination*:

> Statements about impossibility in mathematics are of a wholly different character. A problem in mathematics which may not be solved for centuries to come is not always impossible. "Impossible" in mathematics means *theoretically* impossible, and has nothing to do with the present state of our knowledge.

"Impossible" in mathematics does *not* characterize the process of making a silk purse out of a sow's ear, or a sow's ear out of a silk purse; it *does* characterize an attempt to prove that 7 times 6 is 43 (in spite of the fact that people not good at arithmetic often achieve the impossible). By the rules or arithmetic 7 times 6 is 42, just as by the rules of chess, a pawn must make at least 5 moves before it can be queened [...] To determine whether we have the right to say that squaring the circle, trisecting the angle, or duplicating the cube is *impossible*, we must find logical proofs, involving purely mathematical reasoning. Once such proofs have been adduced, to continue the search for a solution is to hunt for a three-legged biped (pp. 68–69).

All these examples of impossibility in mathematics are logical contradictions within discursive chains. A "three-leg biped" has nothing to do with reality, it is a logical impossible produced by the signifying chain, it has nothing to do with nature and its limits.

What is at stake for Lacan is: a) the impossibility of the Other (A) to be complete, for both for neurosis and psychosis; and b) the impossibility of comparing a dual and quadripartite structure. From these statements we conclude that a neurotic cannot be turned psychotic or vice versa. We have localized the subject of psychosis in the graph 1, and we have said that the analytic experience with neurotic subjects requires the complete graph. Notice, thus, that the transformation of the two into four, of the circle into square, of the graph 1 into the complete graph, is impossible (which is completely different from thinking that it is very difficult). Impossible here means logically impossible.

Let us see the following example by Kasner and Newman (2001), which is really eloquent:

The French philosopher, Auguste Comte, demonstrated that it would always be impossible for the human mind to discover the chemical constitution of the stars. Yet, not long after this statement was made the spectroscope was applied to the light of the stars, and we now know more about their chemical constitution, including those of the distant nebulae, than we know about the contents of our medicine chest. As just one illustration, helium was discovered in the sun before it was found in the earth (p. 67).

This was not impossible. The problem was wrongly posed; it was just a "we do not know how to do it yet".

For psychoanalysis then, the transformation of the graph 1 into the complete graph, of a neurotic into a psychotic would be possible only if the signifying battery was complete. But it happens that it is not: at least one signifier is lacking. We must distinguish between two qualifications of the Other (A) which are often confused: a) the Other as battery and b) the Other as treasure. Any battery, of cannons, casseroles or signifiers, no matter how many elements it contains, is complete. It lacks nothing. On the contrary, the treasure, no matter how valuable and rich it is, can never be 'all', 'whole'. If treasure meant to have all the gold in the world, it would be worthless, as gold would lose its exchange value. Lacan sustains, for each speaking subject, the function of the Other's treasure incompleteness, as well as he affirms that no signifier lacks to any speaking subject, in order to say what he wants to say. In that sense any signifying battery will be always complete. Let us go to a quotation from the writing "On a question preliminary to any possible treatment of psychosis", where the lack is specified at the level of the treasure of signifiers:

> The L of the questioning of the subject in his existence has a combinatory structure that must not be confused with its spatial aspect [he is referring to the schema L]. As such, it is the signifier itself that must be articulated in the Other, specially in its position as fourth term in the topology.
>
> As support for this structure, we find in it the three signifiers in which the Other may be identified in the Oedipus complex. They are sufficient to symbolize the significations of sexed reproduction, under the signifiers of relation, 'love' [the mother] and 'procreation' [the father].
>
> The fourth term is given by the subject in his reality, foreclosed as such in the system, and entering into the play of the signifiers only in the mode of death, but becoming the true subject to the extent that this play of the signifiers will make it signify (pp. 216–217).

Fundamentally what is at issue regarding the subject is that A is incomplete. The treasure of the Other is incomplete because the term that designates and signifies the subject is foreclosed. Therefore, the opposition neurosis-psychosis is not the opposition repression-foreclosure. The hinge of this opposition depends on the place where foreclosure operates, for psychosis it is the foreclosure of the signifier of the Name-of-the-Father, for neurosis it is the foreclosure of the signifier of the subject.

Because within psychosis the foreclosure operates on the signifier of the Name-of-the-Father, which is the signifier of the law in the Other, because of its foreclosure the structure of the Other will be lacking the inscription of the law, and thus, the lack of one signifier will not be legalized for the psychotic subject. The signifier of the Name-of-the Father will be the quilting point, that is, the knot fastening in a stable way the quaternary topology, the four crossing points in the graph of desire, thus establishing the interval, that locus 'between' for the localization of the subject of desire.

There exists in *"Subversion of the subject ..."*, as we studied it last week, a strong association between the interdiction (saying between-the-lines) and the Law, for the subject of the law, a version of neurosis:

> [...] that *jouissance* is forbidden to him who speaks as such, although it can only be said between the lines for whoever is subject of the Law, since the Law is grounded in this very prohibition (p. 352).

The interdiction, as the means by which *jouissance* is said by the subject of the law, has to be opposed to that which the clinic of psychosis presents to us in its place, namely, the infinitization. The infinitization, the lack of the function of limit, is what the infernal circle of demand—infernal for being infinitely repeated—represented in graph 1 shows. The subject of psychosis, the one who is satisfied with that previous Other, is localized.

These Lacanian elaborations can be distinguished from the Freudian ones, as long as for the latter the Oedipus complex implies a triadic structure, whereas for Lacan, the paternal metaphor is essentially bringing into play a quaternary structure for the subject.

Let us retake the "eternal" question: is there a subject in psychosis? We can say that, rigorously speaking, there is more subject in psychosis than in neurosis, for neurosis is precisely the foreclosure of the signifier of the subject, as we shall see in following classes. It is in my own counting, where I do not count myself in, where I find the lack of the Other (A). Remember the quotation from "*Subversion of the subject ...*" that we worked on last class:

> Code messages or message codes will be distinguished in pure forms in the subject of psychosis, the subject who is satisfied with[4] that previous Other (p. 337).

which accounts for a "pure speaking subject" in psychosis.

According to Lacan, the fundamental clinical index of the psychotic structure is certitude, which is the certitude of self-reference and not of anything else. In the case of neurosis, the fundamental position of the subject in relation to demand is self-exclusion. Neurosis is characterized by the failure in the position of the subject in the signifier which designates it. Psychosis, on the contrary, is the solid and intimate relationship of the subject with the signifier that designates him and that is precisely the psychotic failure, at least from the perspective of the problems we are dealing with for the moment.

The clinical question is, within the field of neurosis, how the subject modulates its response to the inexistence of the signifier that represents him. The hysteric will sustain that lack and the obsessional will deny it. They are two completely opposite answers to the same inexistence of the signifier which represents the subject (S) in the Other (A).

The structural opposition neurosis-psychosis is characterized by the fact that the transformation of one into another is impossible. The difference lies in which term has been excluded.

The constant, then, is that A is never complete. There is no possibility for a term not to be lacking, as long as there is a symbolic order. The foreclosure in psychosis affects the signifier of the Law. A term is lacking but also, that lack is not legalized. The neurotic lack, on the contrary, is legalized because the signifier of the Law, the Name-of-the-Father, operates.

The existence of the impossible does not reduce the subject to impotence; on the contrary, only the impossible opens up and defines, for the subject, its possibilities.

My proposal, to sum up, would be that one of the most important dimensions of the impossible within the psychoanalytic clinic is the transformation neurosis-psychosis, psychosis-neurosis (its impossibility).

Notes

1. See note 28, Chapter Three.
2. References are from the following English version: E. Kasner and J. Newman, *Mathematics and the Imagination*, Dover Publications, Inc. and Schuster, Mineola, New York, 2001 [1940].
3. "… de la seule inscription d'une combinatoire dont l'exhaustion est possible". *Écrits* II, p. 287.
4. See note 16, Chapter Four.

CHAPTER SIX

Ideal (*I*)—ego (*m*)—ideal (*i*): Graph 2

Today we shall work on the articulation between the ego Ideal and the Ideal ego considering how Lacan elaborated these notions in relation to the notion of the Other. In order to do that we shall analyze some paragraphs from "*Subversion of the subject* ..." in which Lacan presents the logic of graph 2.

> Observe, in parentheses, that this Other, which is distinguished as the locus of Speech,[1] imposes itself no less at witness to the Truth (p. 337).

The Other, then, is not only the locus of Speech; it is also witness to the Truth.

At this stage in our pathway, it would be convenient for us to apply the notion of 'signifier', as we have developed it, to the signifiers of psychoanalysis. And although they require a conceptual structure, that is, a precise system of articulation, which we are allowed to elaborate within transmission, we should not forget that because these concepts are sustained by signifiers, they structurally imply ambiguity. I say this because a new way of understanding the Other results, precisely, from Lacan changing the context of this notion. We are considering the Other as a signifier—which it is—and therefore, it will only derive its signification from the other signifiers from which it differentiates itself in each case. And those other signifiers, within diachrony and synchrony, are the context of the notion that it is at issue. The Other will be locus of Speech or the witness to the Truth, or something else, according to the context that is chosen to define its meaning.

When reading Lacan, one has the feeling that he changes, almost all the time, the meaning of the terms he uses, and thus one does not fully understand what he is stating. The thing is that Lacan gives his notions the status of signifiers, and he uses them as such. In order to read him and understand him it is necessary to resolve and to discriminate, within which system of metaphors and metonymies he is localizing the signifier in question.

We must in this case move on to the problem of truth, falsity, lies, deceit, etc.

> Without the dimension that it constitutes, the deception[2] practiced by Speech would be indistinguishable from the very different pretence to be found in physical combat or sexual display (pp. 337–338).

We have here an opposition between registers, which is absolutely necessary in order to present the opposition: Ego ideal–Ideal ego; that is, the opposition Truth-Pretence.

What Lacan proposes to us is that, given that the Other, A, is both the locus of Speech and the witness to the Truth, then Speech and Truth are doubtless articulated. And if Speech and Truth are articulated, this articulation has to be clearly distinguished from the function of deception [tromperie].

> Pretence of this kind is deployed in imaginary capture, and is integrated into the play of approach and rejection that constituted the original dance, in which these two vital situations find their rhythm, and in accordance with which the partners ordered their movements—what I will dare to call their 'dancity' [dancité]. Indeed, animals, too, show that they are capable of such behaviour when they are being hunted; they manage to put their pursuers off the scent by making a false start. This can

go so far as to suggest on the part of the game animal the nobil-
ity of honoring the element of display to be found in the hunt.
But an animal does not pretend to pretend. He does not make
tracks whose deception lies in the fact that they will be taken as
false, while being in fact true ones [...] (p. 338).

Precisely, the key of human Truth is that it can pretend to be false.
What animals cannot do is to pretend that they pretend, that is, to
have genuine (true) tracks considered as if they were false.

What device allows us to do this, to make believe that true tracks
are false? Which is the most usual mechanism employed to make
someone distrust the authenticity (truth) of tracks? For example,
make them too obvious. To say that one is going to Krakovia, to make
the other believe that one is going to Lemberg, when in reality ...
Deception, deceit is then produced in the human world by means of
exaggerating the verosimile of the true.

[...] ones, that is, that indicate his true trail. Nor does an animal
cover up its tracks, which would be tantamount to making itself
the subject of the signifier (p. 338).

Lacan says that animals pretend when they are being hunted (that
is, when the other is a predator). But they can never pretend to pretend, which implies the calculation of a subject in relation to another
subject able to calculate. And then he adds something subtle: that to
erase its own tracks and to produce false tracks, would transform
the animal into a subject of the signifier. It is Robinson Crusoe erasing Friday's tracks. A subject who is completely alone on an island
finds a human footprint on the beach, the footprint of he who he
will call "Friday". But the amazing thing is that what Robinson Crusoe does first, after discovering the Other's tracks, is to erase them.
Notice that it is a completely futile maneuver: if those footprints
connote the presence of a possible danger, of what benefit would it
be to erase them? This maneuver of erasing the tracks of the Other
involves, metaphorically, what we call the bar over the subject, for
the subject does not deny the existence of the Other but, in the most
obvious way, he wants to know nothing about it.

All this has been articulated in a confused way even by
professional philosophers. But it is clear that Speech begins

> only with the passage from 'pretence' to the order of the signi-
> fier [...] (p. 338).

The translation into Spanish does not say "pretence",[3] but "fiction"; the problem is, precisely, that Lacan reserves the notion of fiction to present the structure of Truth as ultimately symbolic. You will also notice that in the same writing, in the forthcoming paragraph, the word "fiction" appears, but this time in the right place.

> [...] and that the signifier requires another locus—the locus
> of the Other, the Other witness, the witness Other than any of
> the partners—from the Speech that it supports to be capable of
> lying, that is to say, of presenting itself as Truth (p. 338).

You can see that if the structure of Truth responds somehow to the structure of the signifier, it is precisely that in order to lie, it presents itself as true. And any speech [word] presenting itself as true, even if it is false, must say about itself that it is not lying.

> Thus it is from somewhere other than the Reality that it con-
> cerns that Truth derives its guarantee (p. 338).

Truth derives its guarantee from a locus Other than Reality (the Other locus). Here Lacan questions the notion of truth as adjustment (*adae-quatio rei et intellectus*), adjustment between what one says and what is said. Such is the scholastic notion of the truth: a statement is true if it coincides with that portion of reality that it is talking about. And Lacan refutes this notion. Although Truth refers to Reality, it does not derive its guarantee from it but from the function of Speech.

> Just as it is from Speech that Truth receives the mark that estab-
> lishes it in a fictional structure (p. 338).

Thus, if Truth derives from Speech its guarantee, that guarantee will be that of the signifier; and we must remember that the structure of the signifier is, at least, ambiguous. Therefore, the Truth can only lead to the lie, and the lie to the Truth (the dual structure, in that context, of *fort-da* in graph 1).

We have already discussed when quoting De Saussure, that Reality is constituted from the structure of Speech. But I shall consider the quotation once again, to show you that this notion of Reality with which psychoanalysis works, is not exclusive to it.

In his *Course in General Linguistics* De Saussure says:

> The linguistic sign is then a two-sided psychological entity [...] the two elements—concept and sound-image—are intimately united, and each recalls the other [...] Only the associations sanctioned by that language appears to us to conform Reality [...] (pp. 66–67).

There is a different idea of adjustment here. De Saussure is saying that the only thing, which appears to us to conform to Reality, is the concordance with what our language proposes to us as related by concept and sound-image, between signifier and signified. Thus, for De Saussure, Reality is also a function dependant on the articulation of language.

Lacan warns us that if Truth concerns Reality, it does so insofar as the former introduces its structure of fiction into the latter. Any word presenting itself as true only tries to say that it is not lying. The only way in which the Truth can be posited as true is by articulating itself to the lie. This is the only guarantee for Truth and it is, as we have already said, a paradoxical guarantee.

Let us proceed now to the I(A) in graph 2:

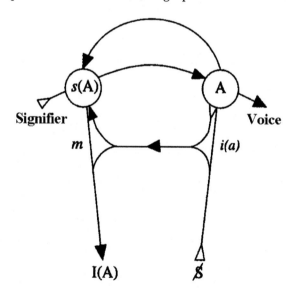

Schema 1.

articulating it to the following quotation from "*Subversion of the subject ...*":

> The first words said [*le dit premier*]⁴ stands as a decree, a law, an aphorism, an oracle; they confer their obscure authority upon the real other. Take just one signifier as an emblem of this omnipotence, that is to say of his wholly potential power [*ce pouvoir tout en puissance*], this birth of possibility, and you have the unbroken line [*trait unaire*]⁵ which, by filling in the invisible mark that the subject derives from the signifier, alienates this subject in the primary identification that forms the ego ideal.

This is a theoretical zone where we have to move with extreme precision, given that we must oppose the Freudian notion of ego ideal to the Lacanian one, for they are not identical. The formula I(A) itself raises the issue of it's reading: Does it have to be read as "Ego Ideal" or as "Other's Ideal"?

The formula I(A) implies that we take a signifier from the other which, isolated and representing the One (I) provides the Other (A) with omnipotence—the omnipotence we think the one embodying the place of Other is invested with. If I(A) is a signifier of the Other, the symbolic ideal could be read as "One of (A)". I am saying that "I" may be taken not as the first letter of the word "ideal" but as the 1 in roman numerals, the "I" as One of the Other, I [1] of (A).

Emitter and receiver are always involved in the logic of any said [*dit*], even the first one. That it to say it always implies two: the subject and the Other. At the same time, by structure, there is no signifier that stops representing the subject for another signifier. The Other embodies the locus of Speech and from that place it receives its power, and there is a displacement which is precisely passing the power of speech on to that who occupies that place by means of isolating a signifier that transforms it into the One of the signifier.

Where word [speech] exists, the problem is related to power; whereas if there exists no word, among the animals for instance, problems have to do with strength. Throughout Lacan's teaching this function—the function of One regarding power—is to be elaborated around the notion of "master signifier", with which S_1 will be characterized. Why does Lacan call that obscure? Because it is the power inscribed with a single signifier, and anything in the order of an isolated signifier, will always be absolutely obscure, given that it does not differentiate itself from any other which, acting as S_2, could clarify it. The problem is that in order to clarify this power of the One it would be necessary to add another signifier, and then it would not be "the One" any more. This means that, as soon as the power of the One is no longer obscure, it is then no longer omnipotent, for it requires the Other, other signifier. Thus, it is clear that the function of omnipotence inscribed through the One must necessarily be obscure in order to be omnipotent.

Let us remember that the graph we are dealing with is number 2 and not number 4, which is the complete one. We are actually working on a part or an aspect of the complete graph. Observe in the complete graph the crossing point up on the left, S(Ⱥ), and the final point down left, (I(A)). The departure point is S(A), the inscription of the lack in the Other, and we arrive at I(A), which says that the Other is not barred (left side pathway of the complete graph).

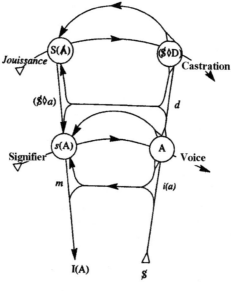

Complete Graph

Schema 2.

Within the graph of desire's relational system, one of the Other, I(A), acts as the inscription of the omnipotence, regarding the signifier of the lack in the Other, S($\cancel{A}$).

However, if I is a signifier that Lacan proposes that we adopt as an emblem,[6] why is not the matheme S(A) instead? If Lacan had been "reasonable" he would have written S($\cancel{A}$) in the upper level and S(A) in the lower one. The problem is that, when it is one and only one that is at issue, it is not yet a signifier; it is, I will say, an 'insignia'. In order to become a signifier, signifier one, it should have been S_1; however, S_1 already supposes S_2 and does not allow the omnipotence of the One to be inscribed.

This is the therapeutic key for people to be able to live a calmer relationship with the ego ideal, to make it become S_1 of a certain S_2 or vice versa.

By writing I(A), One of the Other, Lacan produces a double alteration of the Freudian notions (as they appear, for example, in chapter three of "On narcissism: an introduction"). Freud says that the ego ideal is composed by "cultural and ethical representations", the fundamental cause of repression. Lacan says that the problem is not there, that that is "civilization and its discontents". The problem arises when representation becomes "One". On the other hand, Lacan also states that it is not the ego's omnipotence that is inscribed but the Other's. For the post-Freudians, on the contrary, the emphasis is placed on the subject's narcissism, perhaps facilitated by the name Freud gave to the function: "ego ... ideal". However, it can be read in "On narcissism" that, although ideals are the heirs of primary narcissism, this is, as well, the target of the parents' narcissism. Freud wrote *"His Majesty the Baby"*; his followers read: *"I, the Majesty"*.

Let me remind you of the correction I introduced for the verb "to alienate".[7] By working on the notion of "ego ideal" as "Other's ideal" we are allowed to introduce the notion of alienation (which will have a strong conceptual status in Seminar 11 within the pair alienation/separation).

Why does the notion of alienation have such an important conceptual status in Lacan's teaching? Because the subject identifies itself, precisely with the one of the Other, and that gives you a very paradoxical identity, it results in an alienating identity, because it is the Other's (*"Alio"* in Latin means "other").

Notice that even primary identification—thus understood—is founded on the logic of alienation. Primary identification says 'no' to the possibility of identity within oneself. This is the structural effect of the signifier.

This can be rather clearly seen already in Freud. In Chapter Three of "On Narcissism: An introduction", Freud indicates that cultural and ethical representations are introjected, whereas the ideal ego is projected onto the objects. Language belongs to the Other and, consequently, it has to be introjected. If the subject identifies himself with that, he will never escape from alienation. Lacan called this stage in the subjective constitution 'moment 1, and he called separation 'moment 2'.

However, this notion of moments is a relative thing. Lacan warns us that the Other's Ideal—I(A)—takes the place of the invisible mark left by the signifier on the subject. If you compare graph 1 and graph 2, you will see the substitution of $ as the arrival point in graph 1 and as the departure point in all the other graphs (schema 3).

Where in graph 1 can it be seen that the subject went through the signifying logic that condemns him to alienation? Why do we write down $ in graph 1? Because we already find there, at the two crossing points, the logic of "at least two signifiers". When facing the two signifiers, the subject receives the mark of the signifier. And what is that specific mark? It is the *"fading"*.[8] If in "the cat goes woof-woof" the animal is disconnected from its cry, the subject also looses its animal being through that same maneuver and there we have the place marked by a lack. To that place marked by a lack, which is the place of the subject, the ego ideal comes to rescue it. And that is why it occupies the place, in graph 2, that the subject did in graph 1.

How does the ideal rescue the subject, located between the two, with the lack that is there? If we added another one, a third one—S_3—, it would be of no benefit, we would be only multiplying the between-two. If we moved S_1 (as it happens in *The Purloined Letter*, where it can be clearly seen how due to the successive cuts the function S_1 is displaced onto the different signifiers of the chain) it would be of no benefit either. How then? By pretending that it is one, by denying the fact that they are at least two: that is what I(A) says.

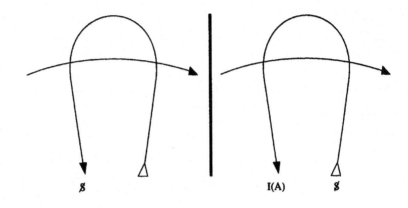

Graph 1   All other graphs

Schema 3.

The subject is barred at the middle as a consequence of facing the logic of the 2, and he is rescued by the 1: what does this one say about the Other? What does I(A) say about A? It says that it is one, and that is why it is not written as barred, because that is the only form of omnipotence capable of rescuing the subject (the only thing that guarantees that one is one, that he is one). What is at issue, then, is the logic of the one. That is the ideal's fundamental function. We are referring here to the one of the totality, which is different from the one of the account, the "one plus one", a very different function of the one.

Both Freud and Lacan propose that the analytic cure must go beyond ideals. The problem is how to know that we are indeed going beyond the ideals in a certain treatment; it is very easy to misunderstand the mere substitution of a representation for another in the place of the ideal, as if it was an effective abandonment of the ideal as the place for the subject's fixation. What defines the ideal as such is the dialectics within which it works; and that dialectics is that of the one.

I would like to present you now with a different dimension of the problem of the One. Instead of thinking, as we usually do, that the subject remains exclusively captured between the one and the

one ('a signifier is what represents a subject for another signifier')
Lacan proposes that we consider that the subject, strictly speaking,
remains captured also between zero ($) and one I(A); this is what
graph 2 teaches us. We are used to thinking that the subject is always
between one signifier and another signifier, but we must also think
of it as being between $ and I(A), between 0 and 1. This is inscribed
in graph 2 (although thoroughly developed in *Seminar 12, Crucial
Problems of Psychoanalysis*). This is how it can be seen in the graph:

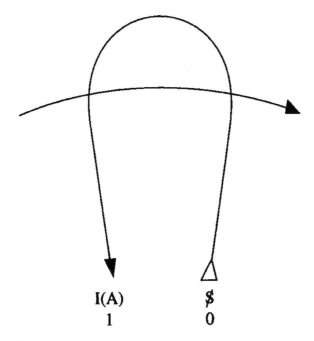

I(A) $
1   0

Schema 4.

As we have already said, there is an inversion in the position of $
from graph 1 to graph 2: it has moved from the departure point to
the arrival point. This passage is described in *"Subversion of the subject ..."* as follows:

> This is a retroversion effect by which the subject becomes at
> each stage what he was before and announces himself—he will
> have been—only in the future perfect tense (p. 339).

This inversion in the graph of desire has a temporal structure, and Lacan assigns it the temporal metaphor of the 'future anterior'. In French, future anterior expresses anteriority in relation with a future to come. It is a completely paradoxical tense: it supposes a past anterior regarding a future; but the problem is that it is only past in relation to *that* future; therefore, it is a past that is also future for that who enunciates it as past in relation to a future, but as future in relation to the present time of enunciation.

We do not have this tense in Spanish (or English), but we do have the future perfect tense. Future perfect is a verb tense that denotes a forthcoming action anterior to another one which is also forthcoming.[9]

We might ask ourselves then how is it possible for place one to exist before place zero does. Lacan says this actually has a temporal structure, but a paradoxical one: in French, that of a future anterior. When inscribing itself, the future anterior inscribes an anterior moment, that of the *'fading'*. Strictly speaking, there is no subject prior to the primary identification, given that prior to the primary identification it could not be distinguished from any other subject. And for psychoanalysis there is no subject without particularity. At the zero stage, we are all the same.

What would a subject prior to the primary identification be? The subject embraces the Ego Ideal primary identification, which gives it a certain consistency in the signifier, and at that moment, the fact that it has to 'have emerged' from nothing is founded. We are henceforth dealing with a totally paradoxical temporality, a temporality that requires the articulation of the notions of retroaction and anticipation.

The word that Lacan uses is "retroversion", a real find in language, for implies a 'retro'—going back—with the structure of a version. And what is a version? The way in which an event or a series of events are interpreted or presented. And also: the manipulation of a foetus in the uterus to bring it into a desirable position for delivery. And one of its strongest meanings: inverted position of the uterus.

Doubtless Lacan states that the birth of the subject is by means of a version: the first said.[10] A subject emerges due to a version that produces, by retroaction, the "anterior" time, that of the *fading*.

What would be a possible therapeutic intervention to operate on this version? To multiply it. That is to say, the exactly opposite maneuver to the one that Freud carried out, for instance, in his analysis of the Wolf Man, where he permanently tried to go towards the One. Freud pushed that case, let us say, towards the neurotizing direction *par excellence*. He advanced with the conjecture that in the origin there was one. Lacan proposes, on the contrary, retroversion: to invert the versions, a maneuver sustained by the fact that every signifying version implies necessarily a plurality of interpretations. And the subject will have to choose (through his act) which is the most truthful interpretation (desire and its interpretation) for that moment.

> At this point the ambiguity of a failure to recognize that is essential to knowing myself [*un méconnaître essentiel au me connaître*[11]] is introduced (p. 339).

"Misrecognize myself" because it is the Other's; that is alienation. Each step the subject takes towards knowing himself via the Other's ideal has no other effect but to render him more Other, to misrecognize himself even more.

> For, in this 'rear view' [*rétrovisée*], all that the subject can be certain of is the anticipated image coming to meet him that he catches of himself in his mirror.

So, how may the subject escape and get to know himself, when being left in this place zero, after his encounter with at least two signifiers? Lacan proposes that the subject's own and anticipated self image of the mirror stage, becomes available then for the subject. The key here is that the subject takes this image as if it were his own.

> I shall not return here to the function of my 'mirror stage', that first strategic point that I developed in opposition to the favour accorded in psychoanalytic theory to the supposedly *autonomous ego* (p. 339).

If the mirror stage somehow rectifies the psychoanalytic theory, it is fundamentally by saying that the ego is not autonomous, for it works as an identificatory resource against the "between" the $(0) and the I(A) (1).

But the subject finds in that altered image of its body that it is also the other's. This is what we have in order to respond, at the imaginary level, to the problem of the Other's ideal. And what is the alteration of that image? The inversion produced by the mirrors. We must not forget here the *alter*, the other: the image belongs to the other precisely because it is anticipated. Thus, imaginary alienation is what we can oppose to symbolic alienation.

> In any case, what the subject finds in this altered image of his body is the paradigm of all the forms of resemblance that will bring over on to the world of objects a tinge of hostility, by projecting on them the manifestation of the narcissistic image, which, from the pleasure[12] derived from meeting himself in the mirror, becomes when confronting his fellow man an outlet for his most intimate aggressivity (p. 339).

Notice that in graph 2 Lacan names the vertex departing from $, at its first crossing point, not m but $i(a)$; it is the image of the other that is at issue. Thus, the subject ($) faces up to two ideals of the Other: I(A) and $i(a)$: the insignia of the omnipotence of the Other, one of the Other, the first one; and the image of the other, the second one.

If the subject tries to escape from the first alienation—that of the signifier—he finds as a resource the altered image of the other.

It is clear at this point what we can see in graph 2: that the subject remains trapped between two "othernesses".[13]

> It is this image that becomes fixed, the ideal ego, from the point at which the subject stops as ego ideal (pp. 339–340).

The fixation of the image is a function that depends on the subject being halted by the ideal. If $ as such is the effect of interval produced between signifiers, to add another signifier would immediately produce the sliding effect: thus, instead of being between S_1 and S_2, the subject will be between S_2 and S_3, and so on. How does the subject stop this infinite metonymy? It identifies itself with one of the signifiers, abandoning the fact that they are two. It tries to escape from the interval and it adheres to one.

How is it, asks Lacan, that there is, for us, an image? There is "an" image because we stop at a signifier; otherwise there would not be any imaginary problems. If the subject did not stop at a signifier there would not be any problem, because we would be passing from one image to another, and there would be no problems with imaginary identifications, given that the one of the image depends on the one of the signifier. Subjects, in analysis for instance, are fixed on an image because they are halted at a signifier.

We should articulate this halting with the problem that Lacan poses in Seminar 11, where the alienation to a signifier produces the subjective effect of the monolith, which Lacan calls "petrifaction". A subject glued to a signifier is a monolith. We remain petrified under the one of the signifier and thus we can become captured by an image.

What does retrovision lead us to? It leads us to the baby, in his mother's arms, looking in the mirror at his mother's gaze, instead of looking at himself. What captures the child in the mirror is the mother's fascinated gaze. But Lacan says that this is not enough. What fundamentally produces the possibility of being captured by an image is the petrifaction under a signifier.

Therefore, the problem is not the imaginary identification as such, but the fixation on an image; and the subject remains fixed to an image as a consequence of the symbolic ideal's functioning.

> In the capture to which it is subjected by its imaginary nature, the ego masks its duplicity, that is to say, the consciousness in which it assures itself of an incontestable existence […] is in no way immanent in it, but, on the contrary, is transcendent, since it is supported by the unary trait[14] of the ego ideal (p. 340).

The subject adheres itself to an image because this image hides this duplicity from him: the "I am that one", "I am that", "I am me". This implies the attempt at becoming one within oneself, to hide the fact that it is the Other who lacks the element of identity. To hide the duplicity by means of the ego allows saying that the ego is not immanent but transcendent.

There exists a whole theory about the ego as immanent, but what interests us here is the fact that this is the theory every neurotic subject has regarding its own ego. And that is why Lacan warns us about the fact that the ego is transcendent and not immanent, for it is supported by the unary trait.

> As a result, the transcendental ego itself is relativized […] (p. 340).

I would like us to consider a few questions concerning these notions: transcendence, immanence and transcendentality. "Immanent": it derives from Latin and means "to reside in", *in-manens*. It is used in philosophy as immanent cause, which is the one that resides in the subject that is at issue. It is the case in which the cause is localized within the subject itself. It is contained within the nature of a being.

What does Lacan mean by saying that, for each of us, the ego is immanent? He means that we believe it is included, contained in our own being nature. Whereas, on the other hand, transcendent is what is elevated upon a certain given level. In philosophy, it refers to those terms that have such a universal meaning that they surpass every category.

What Lacan is saying is that the ego is not caused by itself, that it has not a logic that closes upon its own being. To the contrary, the ego is determined by something that is beyond its limits, that transcends its limits. This transcendence is the ideal ego, the anticipated image of the other. And, on the other hand and more fundamentally, this transcendence is also the signifier of the Other's ideal, the ego ideal.

In scholastic philosophy, transcendentality was the essential, and according to Kant, it was that which constitutes or expresses an *a priori* condition. The notion of *a priori* is in reality part of the phrase that says: *a priori* any experience.[15]

According to Lacan, the ego is neither essential nor *a priori*; it is a primordial effect of the function of the signifier and the mirror stage. And both functions indicate that the ego is determined by other elements: (A) on the one hand, and (a), on the other. Thus, the double virtue of the ego's function is to hide from us that it is not immanent and that it is doubly determined.

I shall continue with another quotation:

> As a result, the transcendental ego itself is relativized, implicated as it is in the *méconnaissance* in which the ego's identifications take root" (p. 340).

Because the ego hides from us the double causality by which it is determined, Lacan will say that any so-called ego identification will always have, as such, a function of misrecognition.[16] What does this misrecognition refer to? To the otherness, to anything that is otherness as source of the ego itself. What is the dialectic of this ego? To project itself into the environment; to try to find the sameness; because the ego fundamentally attempts at sustaining itself as immanent to itself, by saying 'no' to the otherness, both at the symbolic and imaginary levels. And, in order to always find the sameness, it projects.

We know well that ego projection implies rivalry and dispute over dominion. This clearly indicates in what sense the ego is not autonomous: dominion will be a function that is derived from potency (omnipotence) with which the function of the Other (A) is invested. Lacan describes it in graph 2 (schema 5, see grey line).

"Projection" also implies another important articulation. *i(a)*, the image that attempts at rescuing the subject from the *fading* produced by the 'at least two' of the signifier, introduces into our considerations the problem of images as produced on a projective surface, in the sense of the screen where a virtual image is projected. We will reconsider this subject when analyzing the function of (\$◊a), the *fantasme*[17] and its relations to the ego and reality.

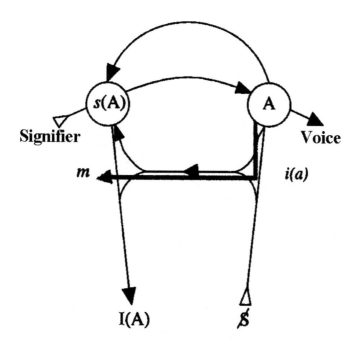

Schema 5.

> This imaginary process, which begins with the specular image
> and goes on to the constitution of the ego by way of subjectifica-
> tion by the signifier […] (p. 340).

Animals do not identify with their own specular image, they are not
even interested in it, because that is not the image of the one able
to rescue them from the duplicity introduced by the signifier; they
have not fallen, and will never do so, into the duplicity generated by
the signifier.

> […] is signified in our graph by the vector $i(a)$-m,[18] which is one
> way […].

The same happens in the Lambda schema: why do vectors go from
the other towards the ego if we are permanently saying that the
ego's functioning dynamic is that of projection? Precisely because in
the graph duplicity is written with a one way vector, but—and here
is the gain—:

> […] doubly articulated.

Duplicity has been recovered.

The graph's pathway is: from $ to $i(a)$, from $i(a)$ to m and from m
to I(A) … and there the circuit is broken and we cannot go on; fixation is produced, stagnancy, petrifaction.

You might remember why we did not close the circle with the
union between $ and I(A)—through the structure of the interior
eight—. Precisely because those are halting points. I(A) is halting.
And the short-circuit is saying so: that the point where the subject
identifies with the signifier of the omnipotence of the Other leaves it
[the subject] petrified, stagnant. There the dynamic of the subject is
stopped; the movement is cut.

Nevertheless, and even when this circuit finishes at I(A), the subject interposes the imaginary dialectics to it: the image of the other
and the ego.

> […] once in a short circuit over $-I(A),[19] and again in a return
> direction over $s(A)$-A. This shows that the ego is only completed
> by being articulated not as the I of discourse but as a metonymy
> of its signification […] (p. 340).

Let us see both ways in the graph:

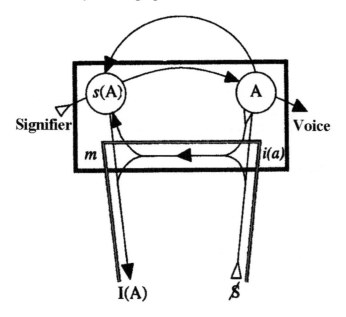

_____ : **Imaginary (metonymic) circuit**
_____ : **Short circuit (petrifaction) at I(A)**

Schema 6.

This is the true circuit. Signification, when stabilized trough the paternal metaphor, is characterized by the fact that it always leads to another signification. A circuit is constituted here, states Lacan, that goes from $s(A)$ towards A, then goes down to $i(a)$, from there to the *moi*[20] (m), and finally it goes up returning (in the shape of a circle) to the signification of the Other—$s(A)$.

This identificatory dialectic leads, then, either to the typical petrifaction of the ideal of the Other—that is the short circuit—or—the subject trapped within the dialectic of the signifier—to the ceaseless metonymy of the signification, the circuit, the circle. Thus, either the subject remains captured within the dialectics of the identification with the one, or it becomes the victim of an infinite movement (sliding) of the signification.

You have probably seen, in your own daily clinic, many subjects trying to find the signification of their ego, when they are in reality trapped in a metonymy that takes them from an "I am/must be this" to an "I am/must be that", and they spent their entire lives believing that they are about to find themselves, and failing each time at the attempt. They are usually subjects who leave a lot behind on the way. Sometimes they loose it all while wanting to gain a being for their ego. This pathway resembles that of desire in the failure of the encounter, but it has to be distinguished from it insofar as it has to be articulated (as we will see further on) with the interval, to the *inter* of that 'beyond the demand' and, specifically, beyond the petrifaction or the closed circuit of the metonymy of the ego's signification.

The 'beyond the ideals' posited by Lacan is, in psychoanalysis, an ethical postulate (not a moral one) because it is strictly speaking the only pathway that offers a way out for the subject. This 'beyond the ideals' is not a moral condition of psychoanalysis, rather it is an essential element in the direction of the treatment (cure) of the barred subject.

Ideals as such, in our theory of the subject, only make possible two ways, both are blind alleys. These two ways never allow, in fact, the dialectic of the subject to take place. This is why the direction of the treatment implies, regarding both ways out in *impasse*, the pass. There are no options for the subject, the pass is only one: to say no to the identificatory way, both imaginary and symbolic.

It is therefore, these theoretical postulates (and not any moral positions) which push psychoanalysts to go beyond the ideals. We must go beyond the ideals because the ideal always implies either a deadly halting point or a heartrending infinitized metonymy.

Notes

1. Lacan uses the term '*Parole*' ('*Palabra*' in Spanish'), literally 'Word', evoking De Saussure's triadic distinction. See note 3, Chapter Three.
2. In French Lacan says: '*tromperie*' (the fact of inducing somebody on purpose into error or mistake. Syn.: imposture, deceit); versus '*feinte*' (simulation, pretence, '*faire semblant de*'). Dictionnaire Micro Robert de Langue Française.
3. Once again the French word is '*feinte*'. See note 2 above.

4. See note 26, Chapter Three.

5. We choose to translate Freud's *einziger Zug* as "unary trait".

6. Lacan uses the word *'insigne'* [insignia] and not *'emblème'*, also available in the French language. The former is homophone of 'one/a sign' (*'un signe'*), evoking I and 1 (i.e., S_1).

7. See note 22, Chapter Three.

8. In English in the original, from now onwards.

9. In English: "Will have been" or also "shall have been".

10. See notes 19 and 27, Chapter Three.

11. The two expressions are homophonous: *'méconnaître'*—which we prefer to translate as *misrecognition*—and *'me connaître'*—to know myself—. The English has only the verb 'to know' to translate the French *'savoir'* and *'connaître'*, whose essential distinction Lacan highlighted many times. This quotation points out that, for the human subject, the pathway towards so-called *self-knowledge* will be marked always by a structural effect of misrecognition.

12. Lacan does not use the word 'pleasure' in this paragraph or in any other of his references to the subjective experience that is at stake in the mirror stage. He always talks about the *'effet jubilatoire'* or the *'jubilation'*, which the English words 'jubilant effect' or 'jubilation' (defined in relation to 'joy' and not to pleasure) translate better.

13. In Spanish *'alteridad'*. There is no English word that maintains the root 'alter'. "Otherness" is the way Lacan himself translates the French *'altérité'*. Cf. i.e., *Communication at the International Symposium*, John Hopkins Humanities Center, Baltimore (USA), 1966.

14. Translation modified. See note 5 above.

15. Meaning not, as it is commonly used, *before* the experience, but *independently* from any experience.

16. See note 12 above.

17. See note 9, Chapter One.

18. Translation modified according to notes 2 and 4, Chapter One. It is read: "the vector going from the specular image towards the ego [*moi*]".

19. Probable by mistake, but significantly, the English version says $\mathcal{S}{\rightarrow}1(O)$.

20. In French in the original.

CHAPTER SEVEN

Graph 3: The question

In this chapter we shall see how to get out, in the neuroses, of the infernal circle of demand, meaning by it the repetition effect of demand as such.

To begin our consideration of this problem we will make use of graph 3 of the graph of desire.

Perhaps it is better to pose the problem, regarding the direction of the cure,[1] as follows: how does one access the new?

This is, in my view, one of the kernels of the psychoanalytical question. According to Freud, the absolutely new is not possible for the human being; and because structurally this possibility does not exist, it does not exist by means of psychoanalysis either. The ideal end at which an analysis may arrive, according to Freud, is the limit of castration anguish[2] for men and penis envy for women.

What I am trying to introduce here, is the idea that graph 3 gives us a first elaboration which allows us to conceive the possibility of the absolutely new for the human being (obviously, within the field of neuroses). And also from this graph we will deduce how to operate in the direction of the cure in order to achieve this.

Let us begin with Freud's approach to the function of the ideal (very close to Lacan's position) in "On narcissism: an introduction".

Departing from the infernal circle of demand in graph 1, we saw the pathway (both in the graph and in life) implied by the imaginary solution (in graph 2) to the problem of the $\cancel{S}$ in the Other. There we differentiated two alternatives: the petrifaction under the one of the Other's ideal and the metonymy of the ego's signification. There is nothing of the order of the new in any of them, even when in certain cases and for certain subjects it might seem different. This is especially so with metonymy, insofar as it seems to introduce the new when, in reality, it is pure repetition. Every time another signifying element appears as if it were 'the new', the subject is unaware that there is no way out through this pathway: aiming to find the signification for his ego will repeatedly and unlimitedly lead him from signification to signification.

Freud's quotation:

> For the ego the formation of an ideal would be the conditioning factor of repression [...] We are naturally led to examine the relation between this forming of an ideal and sublimation. Sublimation is a process that concerns the object-libido and consists in the instinct's directing itself towards an aim other than, and remote from, that of sexual satisfaction; in this process the accent falls upon the deflection from sexuality. Idealization is a process that concerns the *object*; by it that object, without any alteration in its nature, is aggrandized and exalted in the subject's mind. Idealization is possible in the sphere of ego-libido as well as in that of object-libido. For example, the sexual overvaluation of an object is an idealization of it. In so far as sublimation describes something that has to do with the instinct and idealization something to do with the object, the two concepts are to be distinguished from each other (p. 94).

Freud states that idealization and sublimation are different things and must be distinguished. But, strictly speaking, why do we need to distinguish them if they are in fact different? Because at the level of language, the ideal and the sublime belong to very close semantic fields. However, idealization is, according to Freud, the determining factor in repression, whereas sublimation is a process concerning the libido and it consists of the drive pursuing a distant aim other than sexual satisfaction. Regarding sublimation, then, the function refers to the "other aim"; and in respect of idealization, it is a process involving the object "without any alteration in its nature". Notice that the opposition between the sublime and the ideal implies the dialectic between otherness and sameness, the new and the repeated.

Let us continue with Freud's quotation:

> The formation of an ego ideal is often confused with the sublimation of instinct, to the detriment of our understanding of the facts. A man who has exchanges his narcissism for homage to a high ego ideal has not necessarily on that account succeeded in sublimating his libidinal instincts. It is true that the ego ideal demands such sublimation, but it cannot enforce it; sublimation remains a special process which may be prompted by the ideal but the execution of which is entirely independent of any such prompting (1915, p. 95).

We might leave this classroom—as good analysands—with a new ideal: to sublimate; but Freud clearly says to us that the ideal can only incite sublimation but cannot determine it.

> It is precisely in neurotics that we find the highest differences of potential between the development of their ego ideal and the amount of sublimation of their primitive libidinal instincts; and in general it is far harder to convince an idealist of the inexpedient location of his libido than a plain man whose pretensions have remained more moderate. Further, the formation of an ego ideal and sublimation are quite differently related to the causation of neurosis. As we have learnt, the formation of an ideal heightens the demands of the ego and is the most powerful factor favouring repression; sublimation is a way out, a way by which those demands can be met without involving repression (1915, p. 95).

Rather than focusing on the question of "a way other than the sexual one", I would emphasise the fact that sublimation is the way to find otherness, to find the new way: whereas idealization is the most powerful factor favouring repression in neurosis.

We have to keep in mind, from now on, this opposition between idealization and sublimation in order to be able to develop, departing from Freud's work, the possibility of conceiving the new. And by saying 'the new' we refer, on the one hand, to the new for each of us within our analytic experience as analysands and, on the other hand, to the absolutely new that psychoanalysis can contribute.

There is in Freud—although he does not say it explicitly— something absolutely new that psychoanalysis contributes, that is the function of the analyst. Before Freud there had never been a bond between two subjects like the analytic one. But the problem is (continuing with Freud) that he did not conceptualize the radically new for the analysand; according to him, psychoanalysis ended for each subject at a certain *impasse*, at a blind alley.

When Lacan conceives the absolutely new that psychoanalysis contributes for the analysand, he does it through his notion of the end of analysis which consists of a pass.[3] Precisely, the position of he who undergoes the pass at the end of the analysis would be the result of having found the absolutely new. According to Lacan, that person is an "analyst". Not in the sense of being in fact a practicing analyst, but because of a change in his position as an analysand. Lacan states that "the analyst" does not exist; but he who makes the step we are describing as a step into the new, will be an analysand that has became an analyst. Thus, surprisingly, we discover that once again Lacan derives the most radical meaning from the Freudian work: by calling the analysand after going through the pass "analyst", he finds the new invented by Freud, namely, the analyst as a subjective position.

We will work on this step, towards the absolutely new, by means of the notion of 'beyond the demand of the Other'. Our question is thus, how to conceive this beyond the demand of the Other?

It was clear in our last class, and also with the aforementioned quotations from Freud, that the imaginary solutions of the ideal ego and the ego Ideal were not, strictly speaking, solutions which go beyond the Other.

Let us go back to "*Subversion of the subject ...*":

> I will now explain by what bias this opacity produces, as it were, the substance of desire.
>
> Desire begins to take shape in the margin in which demand becomes separated from need: this margin being that which is

opened by demand, the appeal of which can be unconditional only in regard to the Other, under the form of the possible defect, which need may introduce into it, of having no universal satisfaction (what is called 'anguish').[4] A margin which, linear as it may be, reveals its vertigo, even if it is not trampled by the elephantine feet of the Other's whim. Nevertheless, it is this whim that introduces the phantom[5] of the omnipotence, not of the subject but of the Other on which his demand is installed (it is time this idiotic cliché was, once and for all, put back in its place), and with this phantom the need for it to be checked by the Law (p. 344).

We will see that Lacan uses, in the following paragraph, the word *fantasme*. As it was Lacan himself who introduced this notion to psychoanalysis, we have to pay attention to the reason why he might have used a different word in this case, which at the same time is very close, and has the same etymology. I think the most convenient thing to do, is to leave in brackets the word in French as Lacan wrote it.

But the problems do not end here. The word "need" appears three times in this paragraph. The translator's omission is brutal, for in the first two cases it says *"besoin"* and in the third one it says *"necessité"*. The difference is that while the first one is a biological need, the second one is a logical one. Lacan is the psychoanalyst who focuses the most on the difference between these terms. In the first two cases, then, he refers to the need that we worked on within the triad "need-demand-desire".

Lacan begins by posing the question of desire. It could be thought, he says, that the substance of desire was opacity, since desire is presented as being a margin in relation to every demand. Every demand produces a margin that opens a field up—which he names the 'beyond the demand'—that is called desire. And this field implies a certain recovery of the lost object of need (*"besoin"*), as biological need—loss in the human world, caused by the signifying demand.

We have also seen the notion of the particularity of the need, and how it reappeared on the side of desire. Lacan adds that the unconditional character of demand in relation to the biological need is transformed into the absolute condition of desire. This margin regarding every demand (desire) imposes a condition on the Other's Omnipotence; and if it imposes a condition on the Other's omnipotence, then we can conclude that the Other is no longer Omnipotent. Precisely because the Other is not Omnipotent, Lacan says that this margin implies—for the subject—the experience of an abyss that produces vertigo, namely, the clinic of anguish.

Thus, he warns us that the old imbecile fantasy—"imbecile" means "with no support"—of the Omnipotence of the subject has to be attacked. The problem is not the Omnipotence of the subject, but the Omnipotence of the Other. And it is time, says Lacan, to revisit that cliché: the Omnipotence of the subject must be relocated.

There are two imbecile phantasies [*fantasmes*⁶]; one is that of the Omnipotence of the subject (*fantôme*), and the other one is the idea that that *fantôme* has to be restricted by the Law, through the "it is not possible", or the more pseudo-analytical "everything is not possible".

This is very interesting, given that you are used to think that the restriction of the Law, the paternal function, concerns the essence of desire; that is relocated there. It is precisely by this bias that we will introduce the opposition between the pass and the *impasse* at the end of the analysis (namely, the opposition between Lacan and Freud). The question is how to theorise the function of the Law, the paternal function.

Lacan continues:

> But I will stop there and return to the status of the desire that presents itself as autonomous in relation to this mediation of the Law [...] (p. 344).

He is saying here that desire is autonomous in relation to the paternal metaphor, which in Lacanian psychoanalysis is the way of theorizing the introduction of the Law.

> [...] for the simple reason that it originates in desire [...] (p. 345).

It is because of desire that the Law originates. We usually think it is the other way around: that there is desire in so far as the Law originates it. We all have a very neurotic version of this: the father is a certain Other who causes desire. And, being an Other who causes the lack in another Other, the maternal Other, we therefore arrive at the "Other of the Other". The father would be the Other of the mother, the latter representing the primordial Other.

> [...] by virtue of the fact that by a strange symmetry it reverses the unconditional nature of the demand for love, in which the subject remains in subjection to the Other, and raises it to the power of absolute condition (in which 'absolute' also implies 'detachment') (pp. 344–345).

This quotation is essential: Why? Lacan states that the subject remains in a relation of subjection to the Other. In French, like in Spanish, the notion of subject itself implies the idea of subjection. And what is the subjection specific to the subject? The subjection to the Other. And where can it be seen that this subjection is a subjection to the Other? Precisely in the unconditional nature of demand; there is a subjection to the Other in the unconditional nature of the Other's demand, because according to the subject the Other's demand is unconditional. That is why Lacan says that the absolute condition of desire is a condition which does not remain subsumed in the unconditional nature of the demand of the Other; it has a power. And what is that power? "To disjoint"[7] the subject from the unconditional nature of the demand of the Other.

Freud stated that the Law introduces the lack by means of the father. This lack could be metaphorized by saying "at least not one woman". Concerning the set of all women, the father says: at least not one woman, the mother. This is the way in which Freud theorizes the function of the lack.

In Lacan there is a peculiar inversion of this Freudian statement: it is because there is a lack in the structure, precisely, that the paternal operation can be inscribed. This is something extremely new as a conception of prohibition [interdiction] at a social level.

What is the importance of this discussion? We—neurotic subjects— have the same theory of desire as Freud: that the subject desires that which is marked by the Law: that which is forbidden. But Lacan's proposal is to think that desire as the desire for what is forbidden is a way of veiling the true structure of desire. That each of us desires what has been forbidden to him derives from a typical neurotic eagerness: to veil, to hide the fact that there is a lack in the structure.

It is enough to think of those subjects who are fixed to the position of desiring what is forbidden. What are they called? Rebels without a cause. That position implies the putting on the horizon of everything which is denied to them in order to annul the function of the lack (of that which nobody has ever forbidden) as cause.

This detachment from subjection we are referring to is a de-subjection of, not a mutable element, but of the structure of neurosis itself. From these theorizations, then, we conclude that there is, for the subject, a possible position beyond neurosis.

Let us "see" some of these questions in graph 3, our reference during this class (schema 1).

Notice how desire (*d*) is inscribed beyond the Other (A), going out thus from the two circuits with no way out of the imaginary as we described in the past class. This beyond the Other implies beyond any demand because it is not localized on any line, but between the lines. Thus we also see that the question *Che vuoi?* is between the lines, whereas the *fantasme* ($ \$ \lozenge a$) is located as the top that closes the opening of the "between the lines".

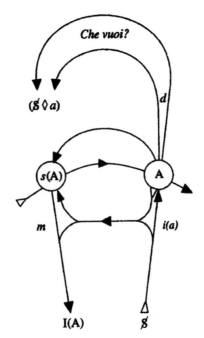

Schema 1.

Graph 3 is the one which (having the shape of a question mark) indicates the function of the question as such, and not the content of any question. It simultaneously presents: a) the desire as beyond any demand; b) the *Che vuoi?*, the way in which desire is distinguished from the ineffable, and c) the *fantasme* as support of desire. Desire, its question and its support, are presented in graph 3 in their interrelation.

In the past class we saw how both the bias of the signifier of the ideal I(A) and that of the metonymy of the signification implied a blind alley (*impasse*) for the subject; now we shall see how the object implies a way out. This is valid both regarding the consideration of the subject in general, and the direction of the analytic cure.

We shall continue with some quotations from *"Subversion of the subject …"*:

> For the gain obtained over anguish with regard to need [*besoin*],[8] this detachment [of the subject] is successful in its first, humblest form, that in which it was detected by a certain psychoanalyst [Winnicott] in the course of his pediatric practice, and which is called 'the transitional object', in other words, the bit of 'nappie' or the beloved bit of material[9] that the child never allows to leave his lips or hand.[10]
>
> This is no more than an emblem, I say; the representative of representation in the absolute condition is at home[11] in the unconscious, where it causes desire according to the structure of the phantasy [*fantasme*] that I now extract from it[12] (p. 345).

Lacan says that we have the humblest example of the detachment from the Other in the transitional object. Notice that when naming them, Lacan does not say "nappie", he says "the bit of nappie" or "the shard". What is characteristic of a transitional object? The fixedness (it has to be this and not any other) which inscribes the absolute condition. They are objects that inscribe a peculiar form of dialectic of the absolute condition. Then, if there is a subject to whom the problem of the detachment from the Other is posited by means of using an object (as the transitional object works for some babies) that object will inscribe the absolute condition for that subject: the object becomes condition. The point is that this detachment is not the true detachment. Lacan says that the object works as an emblem. It is an object, not a signifier, but preserves the signifying property since it is an emblem, and also, since it is partial. There is already a cut.

By making it work as an emblem, the subject's manoeuvre is to deny the lack in the Omnipotence of the Other, because the object itself becomes its emblem.

The actual problem—says Lacan—is the representative of the representation, which is in the unconscious and is the cause of desire. That representative of the representation (which Lacan will call object *a*) has to be well distinguished from the emblem object. Lacan highlights both the differences and the similarities; thus, he states that the theory of the object *a* is founded on Winnicott's theory of the transitional object.

There are two ways of inscribing the function of the object *a* as emblem (both within the logic of the detachment from the signifier): that of the transitional object as it has been here described, namely the detachment which produces an inversion and becomes the emblem of the Omnipotence of the Other. If you want to think of this problem in terms of Lacan's later ideas, this is the theory of the agalma [ἄγαλμα] in *Seminar 8, Transference*. It is in fact a detachment, but an interesting inversion is produced here: that the object implying detachment may also have the opposite function: to be the emblem of the Omnipotence of the Other.

The other way for the inscription of the detachment is the fetish object. What is the fetish object—according to Freud—emblematic of? Of one's stopping at the point where the lack, the failure, the absence in the mother's body is unveiled. The fetish is another form of functioning of the object *a* as an emblem of the Omnipotence of the Other: it says 'yes' in so far as it indicates the way for the unveiling, but also says 'no' to the lack of the Other, in so far as it stops and fixates itself to an object that works as a veil or screen.

Our problem now is that of representation. What is the problem of representation? That there is no representation which directly indicates the thing. The signifier—as such—is not able to lead us to the thing. Therefore, to affirm that an emblem is indeed able to give us the thing is to attempt to transform the signifier's functioning.

Let us consider again the quotation we departed from today, where Lacan talks about the opacity of desire.

"For it is clear that the state of nescience in which man remains in relation to his desire is not so much a nescience of what he demands, which may after all be circumscribed, as a nescience as to where he desires.

This is what I mean by my formula that the unconscious is *'discours de l'Autre'* (discourse of the Other), in which the *de* is to be understood in the sense of the Latin *de* (objective determination) [...]

But we must also add that man's desire is the *désir de l'Autre* (the desire of the Other) in which the *de* provides what grammarians call the 'subjective determination',[13] namely that it is *qua* Other that he desires (which is what provides the true compass of human passion)" (p. 345).

If we are tying to posit that the true detachment of the subject regarding the Other is via desire, how do we make this compatible with the obvious fact that the desire is the desire of the Other and not one's own? The problem we believed we had solved returns.

Lacan relates two formulae which have almost the same structure: "the unconscious is the discourse of the Other" ["the unconscious is the Other's discourse"] and "man's desire is the desire of the Other" ["man's desire is the Other's desire"]. They are generally regarded as though they were the same or at least equivalent; and this is due to the strongly ambiguous nature of the genitive "of".[14]

In order to understand this I will present some quotations from a very good grammar book: *"Esbozo para una nueva gramática de la lengua castellana"* ["Outline for a new grammar of the Castilian language"] by the 'Real Academia Española'.[15]

In Spanish the preposition *"de"* ("of") produces an ambiguity, and as the same occurs in French, this has led us to misunderstand, to confuse these two Lacanian formulae, taking them as if they were identical.[16]

"El burro del herrero."
"Los animales de los forasteros."
"El parque del Retiro."

However, there are certain uses of the *"de"* which are not ambiguous at all. For instance (from the same book):

"The fear of death."

This is not ambiguous; it is not death who fears, is the human being who fears death (in so far as he is a mortal animal and he knows it). This is an example of objective genitive.

Lacan states that the "*de*" [of] in the phrase "the unconscious is the discourse of the Other" has to be understood in the sense of the Latin "*de*": objective determination.

Lacan himself tells us that he is not using this formula in an ambiguous sense—although the "*de*" is ambiguous: that is why he explicitly tells us how to use it. According to Lacan then, "the unconscious is the discourse of the Other" has the same grammatical structure as the phrase "the fear of death".

And then he adds that in the formula "the man's desire is the desire of the Other" the determination must be the one referred to as subjective by grammarians.

Taking into account the differences between the languages, and the impossibility of translating many of the examples, we can still say that the objective determination implies that the last particle ("of the Other") is a direct object that clarifies the meaning of the transitive verb, denoting at the same time the object (person, animal, thing) to which the action refers. Therefore, it is objective because it is a necessary complement for the phrase to acquire meaning. The ambiguity is usually avoided by adding another complement (e.g., "the discourse of the Other on ...").

That the formula "the unconscious is the discourse of the Other" has to be understood as necessarily objective, means that we have to suppose the following structure for it: "the unconscious is the discourse of the Other". My proposal is to consider it as equivalent to "the unconscious is the discourse in relation to the Other". And the Latin example that Lacan gives in that same paragraph seems to confirm my hypothesis:

"[...] *de Alio in oratione.*"

Which is translated: "in relation to the Other in the sentence". What is the sentence about? About the Other. What does the unconscious speak of? Of the Other.

What we usually understand is that it is the Other who speaks when the unconscious is speaking; but here Lacan clarifies it and says that the unconscious means to speak about the Other.

This is further confirmed when he tells us that we must understand the "of the Other" in the phrase "man's desire is the desire of the Other" as a subjective determination: it is in so far as he is Other that the subject desires. No one is ego within desire.

It is because these phrases must not be considered as ambiguous, that Lacan says that nescience should not be confused with misrecognition. That is, it is not a defensive manoeuvre, in the sense of not wanting to know. It is simply of the order of what cannot be known.

We are dealing with the notion of the opacity of desire: a margin beyond any demand. And if it is a margin beyond any demand, no demand will ever cover it. Desire is, therefore, what escapes the demand; this concretely implies the impossibility of building a theory of desire.

But if it is true that it is an opacity which is at issue, an impossibility of knowing, a nescience, a margin beyond what may be said, it is a greater nescience than the one implied in 'the unconscious is the discourse of the Other'. Finally, something regarding the unconscious could be sifted out: what is said about the Other at the level of demand. The key point is the nescience of desire. Why? Because it is as Other that the subject desires, it is from the place of the Other that it desires.

We must distinguish the structure in 'the unconscious is the discourse of the Other' from the structure in 'man's desire is the desire of the Other'. The former means to speak about the Other, the latter implies to be Other in order to desire. This speaking about the Other (our demand to and of the Other) can be finally captured. We ourselves, as analysands, can determine what our demand for analysis is, what do we demand of the Other (no matter how unconscious it is)? What will always remain as opacity is our desire. Precisely, due to the fact that it is never our desire, it is never ours. Thus, the structure that is in play is not "I desire" but "it is desired".[17]

It is time now to rethink what the function of the transitional object as an emblem may be. The fiction "I desire that" is produced there. Think about it, for it is emphasised not only in the clinic of the transitional object but also in the entire dialectic of the future obsessional child. Within the anal mode—says Lacan—the obsessional transforms the cause of desire (always alienated, according to us) into the absolute condition of a certain object. This accent on the object, as a whim, implies veiling the cause of desire. Many neurotic subjects confuse that with a decided desire. And what is the fiction produced there? Not that that is the object, but that it is me, the subject, who desires it. The fundamental point of the fiction regarding the object (when this object becomes an emblem of the detachment from the Other's demand) is the "I desire it".

Finally, the last quotation of today's class:

> That is why the question *of* the Other, which comes back to the subject from the place from which he expects an oracular reply in some such form as '*Che vuoi?*', 'What do you want?', is the one that best leads him to the path of his own desire—providing he sets out, with the help of the skills of a partner known as a psychoanalyst, to reformulate it, even without knowing it, as "What does he want of me? (p. 345)

We are now at the point where, for structural reasons, the maximum nescience is placed for every neurotic subject in what it desires: fundamentally, from where it desires and not what it desires. One could find what one desires, but what one will never find is from where is that desired, since the man's desire is the desire of the Other.

In order to progress along this structurally obscure path of desire, Lacan states that the necessary map course is a psychoanalysis: to find a psychoanalyst travelling companion. Why? Because the question that the subject addresses to the Other: "what does it (the Other) desire?" will return to it (the subject) in an inverted form due to the structure of demand (the structure of every demand is that the subject receives from the Other its own demand in an inverted form). The subject demands of the Other its own desire (it is obliged to pose this question to the Other for the structure of desire implies the misrecognition); and how does this question come back from the Other? ("what do I want?"). It returns as another question: "what do you want?" Lacan says that this question received from the Other as an answer, leads the subject to the act of its own desire.

This circuit continues with a third inversion. The subject inverts the question of the Other (which was in a second instance an answer to the subject's question) and asks the Other: "what do you—Other—want of me?" This is a structural inversion; given that my desire is the desire of the Other, if my question concerns my desire, it will be as Other that I desire. And I will only be able to solve this by establishing the function of the Other's object of desire. There the subject offers itself and is captured as the object of the Other's desire.

This circuit of questions, between the Other (A) and the subject (S), consists of the function of the question, between one and the other, as a pure question, rather than as content corresponding to each personal history.

We find pure examples of this function of the question, beyond content, in the "why?" questions addressed to the Other by children. They are preserved by them as questions that are functioning purely by rejecting again and again every answer that is proposed to them.

Through the articulation of question and desire, we are positing that there is no desire that is independent from the demand of the Other. The relation between the demand of the Other (Other's demand) and my desire is posited in Lacan's formula, in so far as he proposes desire as articulated, articulated to the signifiers of the demand of the Other. But it is, at the same time, not articulable, since desire indicates, precisely, that margin beyond all the particular demands of the Other. This is expressed in graph 3, where the question mark is placed above the Other (A).

This can be clearly observed when simplifying graph 3:

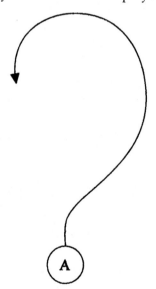

Schema 2.

In Lacan's later teaching the essential articulation between desire and demand will be conceptually built through a topological surface: the torus.

The manoeuvre proposed by Lacan in the analytical practice is not to meet the demand (not to respond to the demand), which aims at making the dialectic of the object emerge, in this case due to the frustration that not meeting the demand implies. By means of this manoeuvre the analyst leads the analysis (as an experience of speech) through the object of frustration, to the horizon of the beyond demand.

What is the function of the psychoanalyst, after the object effect that frustration implies is produced? To hold the position of 'desiring'. This is why the function "desire of the analyst" is required in the analysis. This also firmly demonstrates the logical impossibility of self-analysis. Because desire has the structure of the desire of the Other's determination, and because the Other (who will embody the place necessary for the subject to work through the question of its desire) will be in that place as desiring, the subject is left in the position of the desired object of that desiring Other.

Do you understand what the fiction of the desire of the analyst is? That the analyst bears to be placed as desiring by the subject in relation to it as an object. The analysand will be considered as object and not only as desiring subject. "Desired object" and "desiring subject" are the two poles of the true position, that of the "desiring object".

At this point we need to introduce the structure of the *fantasme*,[18] given that the structural mode of the question is what we call *fantasme*.

This is how the notion of *fantasme* is introduced in Lacan's teaching: as a support for desire. It is the only way in which the subject may work through something of the obscurity, the greatest of all, produced in the neurotic's life. This is why we theorize the clinical practise with neurotics as the 'clinic of the question'. And maybe now many of you will be able to understand why the function of the *fantasme* has such prevalence in Lacan's teaching: because to state that neurosis is the clinic of the question is to say that the analytical practice with neurotics is the clinic of desire; and such a clinic can only be supported, borne, carried out, by means of the question (that is, the question in so far as structured by the *fantasme*).

We will study the relations between desire, *fantasme* and symptom in depth during the following classes.

Notes

1. See note 22, Chapter Six.
2. On anguish/anxiety, see note 4, Chapter Two.
3. In French '*passe*' and '*pase*' in Spanish.
4. Translation modified. See note 4, Chapter Two.
5. Twice in this paragraph Lacan uses the word '*fantôme*'. See note 9, Chapter One.
6. See note 12, Chapter One.
7. The author uses a neologism in Spanish: "*desjuntar*".
8. Translation modified. See note 4 above.
9. « *Tesson* »: is a fragment or part (bit) of something that has been broken (especially glass). In English: shard.
10. Lacan sentence states: "*le tesson chéri que ne quittent plus la lèvre, ni la main* ». The agents of the action (to abandon) are the lip and the hand (the 'child' is never mentioned).
11. Literally: 'in its place'.
12. All the words in brackets in this paragraph have been added.
13. Objective and subjective determination are said, in these cases, in the same way both in French and Spanish (i.e., "*le désir de l'Autre*" translates both "the desire of the Other", "the Other's desire" and "the desire for the Other"). This resource of language has been widely exploited by Lacan, and it will be analyzed in depth in the following passages. Whenever it is the case of this double reading we will add in brackets the alternative.
14. This is valid, strictly speaking, for the preposition '*de*' in French and Spanish and not for English, as we have seen above.
15. 'Real Spanish Academy' official regulatory body of the Spanish language (Spain).
16. Some of the examples the author cites in Spanish to illustrate this cannot be translated sensibly into English. We transcript them, however, for those who can benefit from them.
17. In Spanish the impersonal is used: "*se desea*" (equivalent to the French "*on desire*"). The closest English expression is the passive voice.
18. See note 9, Chapter One.

CHAPTER EIGHT

Desire and *fantasme*: A pathway (I)— the symptom

While preparing this class the first thing I concluded was: to give a class on the *fantasme*[1] makes no sense. It is completely incoherent to say that one is going to give a class on the *fantasme*. But after that I realized that is also impossible to give a class on the desire, for similar impossibilities appear. If one wants to give a class on desire and *fantasme* then, it would be necessary to articulate them; that is, to talk about the articulation between desire and *fantasme*. So we will approach the theme: desire and *fantasme*, emphasizing the "and". I propose to add to that title an indication that will organize our work: the idea of a pathway or (as Freud would put it): a way. So we will begin this class, number 8, by entitling it: Desire and *fantasme*: a pathway.

I believe what I just said is clearly articulated by Lacan in his graph, for what characterizes graph 3 is the simultaneous, articulated entrance of desire (*d*), the question *Che vuoi?* and the *fantasme* ($\$\lozenge a$).

The idea is thus that the question of desire and fantasme cannot be worked on or worked through except via a certain route, a certain diachrony. Actually, the entire graph supposes the idea of a pathway; this is expressed by the fact that it is an oriented graph. Its edges have an orientation, a direction. Thus, the graph of desire inscribes the logic of the discourse "ways", and that of the "defiles" of the signifier. In turn, I shall also posit "a pathway" in order to approach in this class, the pathway from *fantasme* to desire.

The central landmarks of this pathway on the pathway will be:

a) "On a question preliminary to any possible treatment of psychosis" (1957);
b) "The direction of the treatment ..." (1958);
c) "Remark on Daniel Lagache's report ..." [*Remarque sur le rapport de Daniel Lagache*] (1958);
d) "Subversion of the subject and the dialectic of desire" (1960);
e) Two quotations from *Seminar 8. Transference* (1960/61);
f) Some quotations from *Seminar 10. Anxiety*, 1962/63); and,
g) "Kant with Sade" (1963), which is dedicated entirely to this problem.

It is, obviously, a Lacanian pathway. My impression is that the notion of *fantasme* has, in Lacan's work, a greater importance than the notion of unconscious phantasy in Freud's.

Lacan supports the conception of the clinic of neurosis in the function of *fantasme* more than Freud supported his in the function of unconscious phantasy. This links Lacan to other post-Freudians like, for instance, Melanie Klein, as if this primacy of the function of phantasy in the clinic was a delayed effect of Freud's work, on the second and third generation of psychoanalysts.

I want to read you a quotation from Freud's case study of the Rat Man in order to show that what I have just said needs to be relativized when it comes to Freud's clinical practice.

Out of the five Freudian case studies, only four of them were patients of Freud and, among them, the Rat Man has the particularity of being having been "cured".

Some people believe that the Rat Man's symptom was the phantasy of his father and his beloved lady having rats introduced into their anuses; but this was by no means the symptom. This is just a metaphor taken by Freud, from one of the patient's own metaphors, in order to indicate one of the structural questions of the case. This patient's symptom (proper) was his "delay in life".

As Freud discovered and transmitted it, every symptom has a meaning [sense], at least a tendency towards something. So this delay had for this subject a benefit: it allowed him not to make a decision, and that decision he postponed was a particularly difficult one for him: he had to choose between two women. The subject decided to begin an analysis in order to attack this problem of his delay in life. But at the same time (this must be kept in mind), in order to do an analysis he had to leave his life pending. Because Freud lived in a distant place, the Rat Man had to move to be analyzed by him. Nobody solves his or her life in "another place". A long footnote is included in Freud's text regarding these questions. There Freud discusses the problem of phantasy, connected to infantile events of an erotic nature. Freud says:

> It was impossible to unravel this tissue of phantasy thread by thread. The therapeutic success of the treatment was precisely what stood in the way of this (p. 207).

It is truly amazing: given that the symptom was the delay in life, the Rat Man had to interrupt the analysis in order to be able to go and live his life where he had to; if not (notice how paradoxical this is) the continuation of the analysis—which would mean the progress of the subject- would have become the reverse of the goal sought by the analysis itself, namely, the delay.

According to Freud then, one thing is the therapeutic result regarding the symptoms and a different thing is to unravel, thread by thread, the tissue of phantasy. Freud uses the metaphor of a tissue, so we understand that it is a net he is referring to. But it seems to me that we can also refer to a tissue as a weave, in the sense of a plot.

Freud distinguishes the therapeutic success from what it should have been, let us say, the progress and the direction of the cure: to unravel the weave of unconscious phantasies.

What is at stake here, as you may see, is the direction of the cure. Having stated that, according to Freud, the "progress of the analysis" has to do with the operation on the unconscious phantasy (different from the therapeutic success, that is, the elimination of the symptoms), we must therefore include the relation between desire and *fantasme* in the heart of the analysis.

The symptom is located in the graph of desire at s(A), signified of the Other, effect of signification. Within the graph of desire it implies the following articulations:

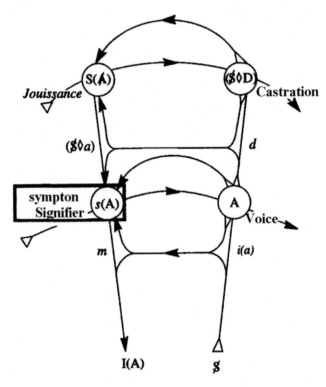

Completed Graph

Schema 1.

Taking into account Lacan's statement in "The agency of the letter in the unconscious ..." that the symptom is a metaphor, it is supposed that—in the graph of desire—the symptom implies the edge departing from S(Ⱥ) (the signifier of the lack in the Other), passing by the *fantasme* ($◊a), upwards towards the symptom s(A), thus inscribing the metaphor as the substitution of one signifier of the superior chain for another of the inferior chain, as the following schema allows us to visualize it:

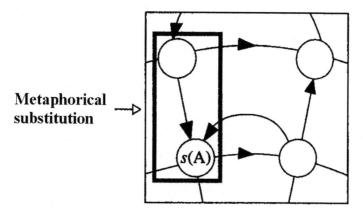

**Metaphorical
substitution**

Schema 2.

However, if we read the graph of desire without prejudices, it indicates that the symptom implies both, the metaphorical and the metonymical slopes:

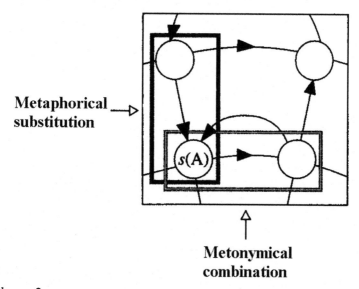

**Metaphorical
substitution**

**Metonymical
combination**

Schema 3.

This is absolutely correct, for it allows us to relate the metaphorical character of the symptom to the hysterical symptom, and its metonymical character, to the obsessional symptom. Let us remember that the hysterical crisis for example, 'kills two birds with one stone' when representing (by means of the same representation) both elements of the conflict. The obsessional symptom tends to a strongly metonymical diachrony, as the: '"I take the stone out", S_1, "I return the stone back", S_2 ...' clearly expresses it. If we review the writing "The agency of the letter ..." with this perspective, we shall see that Lacan is indeed referring to hysterical symptoms, more specifically, conversion ones ("... piece of flesh ...").

That the symptom is not only the articulation of the two chains (the above/below relation, and the one connecting both sides of the graph, left/right relation), but also of the Other (A) is clearly written in the vertex which represents it (schema 4).

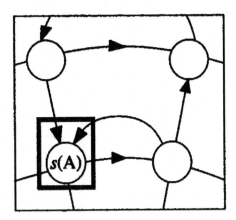

Schema 4.

This can also be perfectly read in the formulae of the *fantasme* for hysteria and obsession from *Le Séminaire, Livre 8, Le transfert*. The metonymical slope is clearly seen in the second part of the formula of the obsessional *fantasme*:

$$Ⱥ ◊ φ (a, a', a'', a''', ...)$$

where the series (a, a', a'', a''', ...) appears. In the formula for hysteria:

$$\frac{a}{(-φ)} ◊ A$$

$\dfrac{a}{(-φ)}$ doubtless inscribes the metaphorical substitution.

In what sense is the symptom 'of the Other (A)'? As Lacan states it in "On a question preliminary to any possible treatment of psychosis"

> "[...] and it should be added, by means of elements of the particular discourse in which this question is articulated in the Other. It is because these phenomena are ordered in the figures of this discourse that they have the fixity of symptoms, are legible and can be resolved when deciphered" (pp. 214–215).

According to psychoanalysis, and unlike philosophy, the subject's question is articulated in a particular way, but it is carried out in the Other. Not only it is formulated in the Other, what we already discussed last week, but it is ordered according to the figures—the figures of rhetoric—received as such from the treasure of the signifier, A, by each subject. It is because figures and tropos are fixed for each language, that the symptom will be capable of making fixed use of them. But it is also because of that that the symptom is decipherable in analysis. For these figures—being the Other's—are shared with the analyst. Let us remember here what Freud used to say regarding the conditions for somebody to become a good recipient of a joke (*Witz*): to belong to the same parish, that is, to share the structure of language. This is truer regarding the figures and tropos of the art of 'well saying', than regarding the set^2 of signifiers.

Let us now begin an analysis of Lacan's conception of the pathway from desire to *fantasme*. I believe this might be hard work. There are many quotations, but it seems to me that it is worth the effort.

In the following quotation, from "On a question preliminary to any possible treatment of psychosis" Lacan corrects himself regarding the use he had made of the Lambda schema; he criticizes himself for having sustained the theory of the subject's recognition by the Other. In order to indicate its impossibility he defines the subject's existence as ineffable (what cannot be put into words) and stupid (a word descriptive of the state of stupefaction). Thus, the subject's existence cannot be put into words and, when it emerges it surprises. Given that the subject is what a signifier represents for another signifier, it always falls in the interval between one signifier and another; so when, unexpectedly, the S_2 re-signifies the S_1, it always produces surprise, stupefaction in the subject.

The word "stupid" that Lacan uses in "On a question pre-liminary ..." is one of the meanings that the term which Lacan uses so often in French has: "*béance*, of which we do not have a translation—and which we had to translate as "gap".[3] For somebody to be "*béante*" means, precisely: flabbergasted, stupefied.

According to Lacan, the problem of the phallic symbol and the function of the father in the Oedipus complex has repercussions for the subject as a question; and this question will be—fundamentally-the question on sex and life. It is unbelievable that the question is about sex and life, for we all think there is nothing as natural for the subject as sex and life.

Lacan states that the question about God's existence (which seems a really human, symbolic problem) is connected precisely to the aspects we believe are more natural, in the sense of biology: life itself and the sexual condition.

Regarding sex the question is, let us say, what is it to be a man—or a woman—? However, things need to be better distinguished when it comes to the question about life. It seems convenient to me—clinically speaking—to clearly highlight, the question which points at the contingency of life.

After this introduction I shall read the quotation to you:

> That the question of his existence bathes the subject, supports him, invades him, tears him apart even, is shown in the tensions, the lapses, the phantasies [*fantasmes*] that the analyst encounters; and, it should be added, by means of elements of the particular discourse in which this question is articulated in the Other (pp. 214–215).

The existence vanishes for the subject due to the incidence of the signifier. What psychoanalysis discovers is precisely that where the lack of existence manifests itself to the subject, there the subject supports, sustains itself—but in the form of a question: I am there, where I ask myself 'who am I?' That which supports me as a subject is the function of the question. The function of the question leads, thus, at the same time towards the lack and to the filling of that lack.

As you can see, the word "*fantasme*" appears in this quotation. This is one of the first times that Lacan articulates the function of the question—support of the subject's existence—to the question of the *fantasme*. I would like you then to keep in mind the following: the question that supports the subject is constituted by means of elements of the discourse. It is already being said that we are not talking of images, but of discursive elements.

And afterwards he adds (what at first sight seems to be contradictory) that it is by means of these elements of the particular discourse that the question is articulated in the Other. The problem is: is it a particular question, of the subject, or a question articulated in the Other? In other words: where is the *fantasme* which supports the subject constituted? On the subject's side or on the Other's side?

There we reach the schema that Lacan introduces in his second class of *Seminar 10*, on "Anguish".

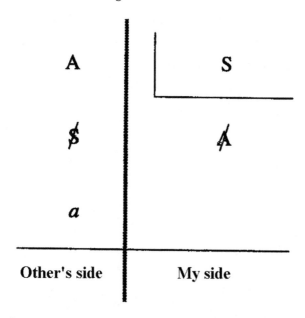

Schema 5.

Lacan states that the question—in so far as particular—is formulated in the Other. From here onwards I would like us to pay attention to the following fact: nobody, ever, could be able to resolve anything regarding his or her *fantasme* without the Other; and this is due to the fact that the *fantasme* is located entirely in the Other. (I know the justification for this statement is still missing; we will introduce it later). Therefore, the invention of a device including the place of the Other will always be necessary in order to account for the relation with the *fantasme*.

We move on to "The direction of the treatment ..." You should not be surprised if I choose this Lacanian writing—which is a pathway itself—in order to work on the problem of the pathway. I want also for you to remember that I will be quoting the last part of the text, from point 14 to point 19. The final part of "The direction of the treatment [cure] ..." has a lot to do with the end of the direction of each treatment [cure].

Although much has been said about the *fantasme*, it remains an especially obscure issue; this is why we will not hurry up at this stage; we will do a meticulous job. The first quotation from this writing:

> 14. The importance of preserving the place of desire in the direction of treatment necessitates that one should orientate this place in relation to the effects of demand, which alone are at present conceived as the principle of the power of the treatment (p. 297).

Lacan establishes clearly that desire is the fundamental motor of the direction of the cure, and he adds that this has to be made explicit, in order to thus rectify a certain current conception of the direction of the treatment. Things can be done through demand, demand has a power, there are no doubts about it, but the true motor of the analysis is desire—and specially desire in the context of the direction of the analytic cure.

> Although it always shows [*transparaître*] through demand, as can be seen here, desire is nonetheless beyond it (p. 298).

Is this metaphor clear—that desire shows, makes itself transparent through demand? One can always lead desire to demand, because behind desire there is always a demand: desire is articulated to demand. Although Lacan immediately adds that desire is nonetheless "beyond", for it is not articulable. If desire is looked at by an observer, let us say, it makes itself transparent in the end, it shows itself, so the observer ends up looking at the demand; but desire always remains, always implies, a field beyond any demand.

On the other hand, every time Lacan uses the notion of "beyond", he is working on the Freudian metaphor of determination: the "beyond" will be determinant. And Lacan says to us, precisely, that beyond demand—even considering its power—desire is determining it.

> It also falls short[4] of another demand in which the subject, reverberating in the locus of the other, not so much effaces his dependence by a return agreement as fixes the very being that he has proposed there (p. 298).

Lacan states that the subject, reverberating between the two demands, tries to fix the being, the being itself that it has been proposed there. Within this 'beyond demand', therefore, in the space we have defined as 'in between' two demands, 'in between' two signifying chains, the problem of the being is posed to the subject. And while trying to solve it, the subject can only "bounce" between them.

> This means that it is only through a word that lifted the mark that the subject receives from his expression that he might obtain the absolution that would lead him back to his desire[5] (p. 298).

If, whenever we enunciate a demand, the beyond demand is produced, then the subject necessitates a word [speech] able to take him out from that dialectic.

> But desire is simply the impossibility of such word [...] (p. 298).

Desire inscribes a certain impossibility. But which one? That a word may efface the effect of speech [word].

> [...] which, in replying to the first can merely reduplicate its mark by completing the split (*Spaltung*) which the subject undergoes [suffers] by virtue of being a subject only in so far as he speaks (p. 298).

By reduplicating the word [speech], aiming at S_2 to rescue it from the effect of S_1, the subject only manages to dig the abyss of its division between them.

Lacan adds, in brackets:

> (Which is symbolized by the oblique bar of noble bastardy that
> I attach to the S of the subject in order to indicate that it is that
> subject, thus $).

The $ is in our algebra the indication of the inexistence of a word
able to erase the effect of speech on the speaking being.

And there is also a note, from 1966, where Lacan adds:

> Cf. the ($◊D) and ($◊a) of my graph, reproduced here in 'The
> Subversion of the subject' p. 315. The sign ◊ registers the rela-
> tions envelopment-development-conjunction-disjunction. The
> links that it signifies in these two parentheses enables us to read
> the barred S: the 'S' fading in the cutting of the demand; S fad-
> ing before the object of desire [...] (p. 308).

He gives then the formulae of the drive ($◊D) and the *fantasme* ($◊a).
The barred S ($) indicates the impossibility of subject finding a word
which takes it outside the effect of speech (the beyond speech).

I would like to give you an indication which—because it is so
obvious—is sometimes forgotten: that Lacan's formulae—for
instance the formula of *fantasme*—are read from left to right, they
have a direction, as in mathematics: $1 + 2 = 3$. In mathematics, such a
pair, where the sequential order is determinant, is called an ordered
pair. This is why regarding the 1966 note, the S fading before the
object of desire, $ → a, must be highlighted. This will be a key for our
reading of the function of the *fantasme* in relation to desire.

I shall continue quoting:

> But identification with the all-powerful signifier of demand, of
> which I have already spoken, must not be confused with identi-
> fication with the object of the demand for love (p. 299).

Lacan posits that there is an identification with the all-powerful
signifier of demand. And what is that all-powerful signifier of
demand? The one we have referred to as I(A). And remember that
in the forgoing paragraph, the problem was that the subject, aiming
at erasing the effects of the first signifier by means of the second,
remained finally between the two of them. Could this identification

with the all-powerful signifier of demand be Freud's primary identification? If that were the case, Lacan posits that there exists a second type of identification, an identification with the object of the demand for love.

> This demand for love is also a regression, as Freud insists, when it produces the second mode of identification, which he distinguished in his second topography when he wrote *Group Psychology and Analysis of the Ego*. But it is another kind of regression.
>
> Here is the exit that enables one to emerge from suggestion. Identification with the object as regression, because it sets out from the demand for love, opens up the sequence of the transference [...] that is to say, the way by which the identifications that, in blocking this regression, punctuate it, can be denounced (p. 299).

Both identifications, with the all-powerful signifier of demand and with the object of the demand for love, are regressive identifications. The difference is that whereas the first one leaves the subject trapped in suggestion (remember the petrifying short-circuit of the identification with I(A)), the second one opens up the way towards transference.

When the subject passes from the dialectic of the all-powerful signifier of demand to the one of the object of the demand for love, at least a possibility of "exit"[6] is presented. This does not mean that it has escaped, but a possible way out has been constituted: transference. It has to be highlighted here that, many times, what we analysts consider as transference, is nothing but suggestion. Many times we believe there is transference when, in reality, it is just the signifier's power effect (and especially that of the all-powerful signifier of demand) which has been produced.

When the function of the Other (A) presents itself, it is not transference that we are facing, but suggestion. Transference, as proposed by Lacan in Seminar 11, is the maneuver made from the place of the Other (A) in order to produce the "enacting of the reality of the unconscious in so far as it is sexual"

> These considerations confirm me in the belief that it is natural to analyze the transference (p. 299).

Lacan is saying that transference has to be followed in the way of the analysis, that there is no other possibility; but he is talking about the transference as we have just defined it, when the dialectic of the object is set into play.

> For the transference is already, in itself, an analysis of sugges-
> tion, in so far as it places the subject with regard to his demand
> in a position that he holds only because of his desire.
>   It is only in order to maintain this framework of the transfer-
> ence that frustration must prevail over gratification (pp. 299–300).

Perhaps we can understand why Lacan proposes that frustration—which is a part of our ethics and not of our *jouissance*—must prevail over gratification within the analytic practice. Because it opens up the possible way out (*exit*). Exit from what? From being captured in the field of the Other. Transference implies by definition the object and the demand, and it produces a field beyond demand, namely that of desire. Therefore the object is determined by desire as a function of the transference. Note that demand annulled (*aufhebt*) the particular object of need, thus producing the object cause of desire.

> It means that interference will occur between the effects that
> correspond in a subject to a particular demand and the effects
> of a position in relation to the other (here, his counterpart)[7] that
> he sustains as subject (p. 300).

And the following paragraph begins with Lacan's self-quotation:

> That he sustains as subject' means that language allows him to
> regard himself as the scene-shifter[8] [...] (p. 300).

Here the scenery is, in itself, the plot (as intrigue, dissimulation, or trickery). The scene-shifter is the one who uses fictions or tricks. The use of the term comes from the theatre (many things regarding the *fantasme* have to do with the theatrical *mise-en-scène*): a machine for figuring transformations or prodigious cases at the theatre.
    The quotation goes on as follows:

> [...] or even the director of the entire imaginary capture of which
> he would otherwise be nothing more than the living marionette
> (p. 300).

Within the context of the *a-a'* dialectic, the subject tries to make a subject of the neighbour. What for? To free itself as a subject. Otherwise it would remain a marionette. The subject postulates the other as subject, becoming itself (by sustaining the other) the scene-shifter or the scene director. This is a very common neurotic fiction (as we have already seen regarding I(A) and i(*a*)) by means of which the subject tries to deny alienation.

> Phantasy [*fantasme*] is the perfect illustration of this original possibility (p. 300).

What original possibility? To sustain the subject. That is what the *fantasme* is: the possibility of sustaining the subject.

> That is why any temptation to reduce it to the imagination, because one cannot admit its failure, is a permanent misconception, a misconception from which the Kleinian school, which has certainly carried things very far in this field, is not free, largely because it has been incapable of even so much as suspecting the existence of the category of the signifier (p. 300).

The problem with the Kleinian school was there consideration of dialectic as if it were a pure and exclusively imaginary matter. And the problem here is how to sustain the subject in the symbolic but not without considering the important role that the imaginary configuration of *fantasmatic*[9] scenes have. What is at stake is the "screenplay", the plot (the same scenery may have a completely different value according to the symbolic context in which it is located).

> However, one it is defined as an image set to work in the signifying structure, the notion of the unconscious phantasy [*fantasme*] no longer presents any difficulty. Les us say that in its fundamental use the phantasy [*fantasme*] [...] (p. 301).

Notice that Lacan is not saying here "fundamental phantasy [*fantasme*]", but that there is a fundamental use of the *fantasme*. We look for the fundamental *fantasme* in a certain subject, when perhaps it is something else which is at stake: a fundamental function of the *fantasme* for each subject. A phrase which seemed to be (at a certain stage of the analysis) the function of the fundamental *fantasme* could change and be taken over by another phrase, which would have the same function, that which made the previous one "fundamental". This is very important in the clinic. What is at stake then, regarding the analysand, is to get to know the function of the *fantasme* has for him or her, but not so much that he or she knows its text.

I repeat:

> Lets us say that in its fundamental use the phantasy [*fantasme*] is that by which the subject sustains himself at the level of his vanishing desire, vanishing in so far as the very satisfaction of demand hides[10] his object from him (p. 301).

Lacan does not use the word "evanescent",[11] and it exists in French. In French they are two different words "*evanescent*" and "*évanouisse-ment*"; the translator into Spanish makes a mistake.

However, before seeing what it means to say that desire is eva-nescent, I would like you to keep in mind that the subject has to be sustained by the *fantasme*, at the level of the evanescent desire, and also that the object of demand is hidden from him. This is why Lacan says that there is a progress when passing from the first mode of identification to the second one. Precisely because the object of demand vanishes in the demand itself, therefore to pass from I(A) to the object (which permanently vanishes) leads one to desire.

Let us take another track for the moment. What is the *fantasme*? To respond in a completely axiomatic way: a way of conceiving the object a, a way of conceiving the barred Subject ($\$$), and a way of conceiving the relation between them, $\lozenge$.

We are permanently working on the relation between the subject and the object. Let us oppose it now to the relation of knowledge between subject and object. In a relation of knowledge, the know-ing subject and the knowable object are simultaneously constituted in the act of knowing. Within the context of the relation that psy-choanalysis posits, both—subject and object—are lacking. On the subject's side there is *fading, Spaltung*,[12] capture in the interval ("in between the two") which produce its ineffable and stupid existence. And on the object's side there is abolition, for it is replaced by the interplay of presence and absence.

Thus, to pass from the all-powerful signifier of demand to the object of demand is a progress in the subject's position, because the object in demand necessarily vanishes. To sum up, we are working on the subject's fading and on the object's fading.

"*Évanescent*" means in French: what gradually diminishes and disappears. The word Lacan uses is "*evanouissant*", which has two meanings: "disappeared" (complete disappearance) and "fainted".[13] In the Robert French dictionary -that usually proposes synonyms- the English word "*fading*" is used to define "*evanouissement*" in its first meaning. Regarding the second meaning, "fainted", this dictionary proposes "*syncope*", which has three meanings; it is the last one of these that will interest us: "suppression of a letter or syllable". You can see that Lacan did not miss these articulations, "*fading*" and "*syncope*" are words that he uses many times.

So Lacan proposes to us that, because of the evanescent desire, there is always certain suppression, both on the side of the subject and on the side of the object, "fading" and "syncope"[14] respectively.

> It is, then, the position of the neurotic with regard to desire, let us say by way of abbreviating the phantasy [*fantasme*], that marks with his presence the subject's response to demand, in other words the signification of his need (p. 301).

Notice what a radical definition of the *fantasme* this is: the position before desire.

We have already said that desire is the recovering of what is lost in need. What Lacan adds is that the *fantasme* is the position of the neurotic with regard to desire, as the response to the demand, which gives a signification to his need. Need is no longer biological, vital, and it acquires a value according to the signification it has for each one. What "I need *x* object" expresses, is for every neurotic subject, the articulation between need (mythical), demand and desire, by means of the formula of the *fantasme*.

> But this phantasy [*fantasme*] has nothing to do with the signification in which it interferes. Indeed, this signification comes from the Other, in so far as it depends on the Other whether the demand is satisfied.[15] But the phantasy [*fantasme*] arrives there only to find itself on the return journey of a wider circuit,

a circuit that, in carrying demand to the limits of being, makes
the subject question himself as to the lack in which he appears
to himself as desire (pp. 301–302).

Pay attention to the fact that Lacan says "in which he appears to
himself as desire", and not "as desiring".

Although we are not commenting on *"Subversion of the subject ..."*
it seems quite obvious to me that Lacan is commenting on the graph.
We can see, indeed, that in the graph the *fantasme* is localized in a
position that has direct effects on signification.

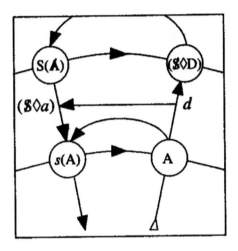

Schema 6.

There is a crossing point (below, left) called "signification of
the Other", s(A), which at the beginning of this class we defined
as symptom. So, first thing: the signification is of the Other. Two
arrows converge at this signification of the Other. The first confirms
that the signification belongs to the Other (from the right inferior circle to the left inferior circle). That is to say, it shows that the subject
always receives the signification of its own message from the other.
And the second arrow comes from the *fantasme* (downwards).

But Lacan states that the signification is not of the *fantasme*, but
of the Other. For only the Other can establish the signification of
what the subject says, and he could even reduce it to nothing if he
wanted to. Therefore, whatever the subject says to the Other carries

the signification of the other. Lacan adds that the *fantasme* interferes with this signification of the Other. How? By being the returning point of a wider circuit.

We have already worked here on a circuit: the imaginary circuit, which has its stopping point in the petrifaction before the signifier of the Other's Ideal I(A), or in the fixation within a never ending circle: the metonymy of the ego's signification. Now Lacan says there is another circuit, the one we have already posited here in terms of the circuit of the question. This is the circuit, says Lacan, that interferes with the signification of the Other. The *fantasme* is posited, in this circuit, as part of the return of the question. He adds that it carries the demand to the limits of being. Can you imagine what demand is in the limits of being? The "what am I?" that we departed from. Lacan states that, with regard to this "what am I?", the subject receives certain signification from the Other, but there is an interference of the *fantasme* with this signification. And the *fantasme* is the return of a wider circuit, in which that question had already been posed. What Lacan is proposing to us, in summary, is that for every neurotic subject there will always be an obstacle inside the circuit where he receives the signification from the Other. This obstacle is indicated in the graph by the *fantasme* itself. It is the *fantasme*, the one which brings down the question embodied above, in terms of the graph's spatiality: it introduces the "beyond the demand" as interference, precisely where the demand of the Other intends to close itself (when the signification is received from the Other, introducing a dimension of the object ($\$ \lozenge a$)).

According to Lacan, the circuit of what the subject is "beyond the demand" is the circuit of the being. There is a 'beyond' that opens up a question. Something of this question returns, amazingly, from the very place where that question is obstructed: the *fantasme*.

Let us go a bit further:

17. Thus, at best, the present-day analyst leaves his patient at the point of purely imaginary identification in which the hysteric remains captive, because her phantasy [*fantasme*] implies its ensnarement.

That is to say, at the very point from which Freud, throughout the first part of his career, wished to extricate himself too quickly by forcing the appeal for love on to the object of

identification (for Elizabeth von R ..., her brother-in-law; for
Dora, M.K ...; for the young homosexual woman in the case
of female homosexuality, he sees the problem more clearly, but
errs when he regards himself as the object aimed at in the real
by the negative transference).

It was not until the chapter on 'identification' in 'Group Psychology and the Analysis of the Ego' that Freud clearly distinguished this third mode of identification that is conditioned by
its function of sustaining desire, and which is therefore specified by the indifference of its object (p. 303).

Lacan criticizes Freud's hurry to indicate the function of this object (the
object of desire) in the *fantasme*. Lacan will point out that the object is
indifferent, that it is not the fundamental thing in the *fantasme*. Given
that the fundamental thing about the *fantasme* is its function of sustaining desire it does not matter what its object is—it does not matter
whether it is or not Herr K. What did matter was to indicate to Dora the
fantasme through which she obstructed her own question: what am I? In
order to be, to be in so far as desiring, Dora needed to indicate an object.
It is not important then, who or which object is it, that is not the fundamental function of the *fantasme*: the *fantasme* is not a device for human
beings to find the object. The fundamental function of the *fantasme* is to
sustain the subject—as desiring subject or as desired object.

> One is aware here of the terrible temptation that must face the
> analyst to respond however little to demand [...] What silence
> must the analyst now impose upon himself if he is to make out,
> rising above this bog, the raised finger of Leonardo's St John, if
> interpretation is to rediscover the disinhabited horizon of being
> in which allusive virtue must be deployed? (p. 305)

Given that he does not respond to demand, what the analyst is left
with is the allusive virtue of the horizon inhabited of being, which
for us is already the disinhabited horizon of being, of the desiring
subject's being, and of the object's being. And there the metaphor
of St John's finger pointing upwards, is presented. According to the
graph's spatiality this above is the upper level, that of the drive and
the signifier of a lack in the Other.

Finally, in the last paragraphs of *"Direction of the treatment ..."* Lacan says while speaking of Freud:

> A man of desire, of a desire that he followed against his will into ways in which he saw himself reflected in feeling, domination and knowledge, but of which he, unaided, succeeded in unveiling, like an initiate at the defunct mysteries, the unparalleled[16] signifier: that phallus of which the receiving and the giving are equally impossible for the neurotic [...] (p. 306).

The object is vanished in demand: it cannot be given nor received. The dimension of impossibility is introduced.

> [...] whether he knows that the Other does not have it, or knows that he does have it, because in either case his desire is elsewhere; it is that of being,[17] and man, whether male or female, must accept having it and not having it, on the basis of the discovery that he isn't it.
>
> It is here that is inscribed the final *Spaltung* by which the subject articulated himself in the Logos, and on which Freud was beginning to write, giving us, at the ultimate point of an *œvre* that has the dimensions of being, the solution of the 'infinite' analysis, when his death applied to it the word Nothing (p. 306).

The allusive virtue of the analyst's intervention, in order to lead the subject to the ultimate *Spaltung*—is that of indicating, allusively, beyond demand, the function of that odd signifier.

We are in the lower part of the graph of desire: the two crossing points on the left side, superior and inferior, and the intermediate point between them, are a combination of the letters "S" and "a". This combination is repeated three times, in different ways: 1st) S($\cancel{A}$), 2nd) ($\cancel{S}\lozenge a$) and 3rd) s(A). There is an arrow going from desire to *fantasme*; this is because regarding desire—considered as the position of the subject and not as an attribute—there does not exist the "I desire", in terms of a being of desire. The *fantasme* sustains me in my being of desire.

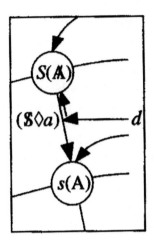

Schema 7.

At this terminal point of the edge of desire on the graph (*d*), the ($◊a)—the *fantasme*—two possible directions are presented. The one going downwards floods the subject: it is the interference of the *fantasme* over the signification of the Other, which in turn goes either to the metonymy of the ego's signification or to the petrifaction of the signifier in the Ideal. The one going upwards (there comes Lacan's metaphor of the raised finger pointing upwards) leads to the odd signifier. This "upwards" is greatly related to sublimation, the direction of the cure and the end of the analysis. At that point Lacan writes: S(Ⱥ). What I am proposing to you is that one of the functions we can give to S(Ⱥ) (the odd, the unparalleled signifier) is that of the phallic signifier.

Do you remember the "*exit*"? This S(Ⱥ) will indicate the way out from the trap of the interference of the *fantasme* over the signified of the Other. It is a way out towards the horizon disinhabited of being, which Lacan articulates to the phallic signifier, Φ. We shall continue with this theme in the next class.

To end our first journey along this subjective pathway, we shall consider now "Remark on Daniel Lagache's Report ..." from Lacan's *Ecrits*.

Remember that we are working on the possible subjective pathway in analysis, which goes from a trapped position to the horizon of a way out, a way of exit, of pass. Regarding the conception of the end of the analysis that Michel Balint has, and the issue of identification, Lacan says:

> That is to say that our model—optical—belongs to a prelimi- nary time of our teaching when we needed to clear out the imaginary as it was too appreciated within technique. We are longer into that.
>
> We being the attention back towards desire, of which is for- gotten that much more authentically than any searching for the ideal, it [desire] is that which regulates the neurotic's signifying repetition as his metonymy. It is not in this remark that we shall say how it is necessary for the subject to sustain that desire as dissatisfied (and it is the hysteric subject), as impossible (and it is the obsessional one).[18]

Hence, if dissatisfaction and impossibility are the support of desire, then they are the *fantasme*. One cannot speak about desire itself. Desire and *fantasme* need to be worked through together.

> Our model does not clarify the position of the *a* object. For one could not describe the function that this object receives in the symbolic by imagining a playing of images.
>
> The same that gives it its use of weapon in the phobic out- post, against the menace of the disappearance of desire; of fet- ish in the perverse structure, as absolute condition of desire.

Not only for obsessional neurosis and hysteria, but also for pho- bia and perversion, the notion of *fantasme* is required in order to account for how desire is sustained in each structure. Dissatis- fied, prevented, impossible or will of *jouissance* are the modes in which desire is sustained in the *fantasme*, through the function of the object *a*.

It is obvious that the object *a* has a singular prevalence both in phobia and perversion, but without it one cannot account for the position of the obssesional or the hysteric subject either.

Notes

1. See note 9, Chapter One.
2. In English in the original.

3. "Hiancia" in Spanish. The word in French combines the meaning of "gap"—as a noun—and "flabbergasted"—as an adjective. The Gaelic part of the slang "gobsmacked" precisely illustrates the gap that is at stake here: the mouth.

4. *"Il est aussi en deça d'une autre demand ..."* (Écrits II, p. 111).

5. Translation modified. *"Ceci veut dire que c'est d'une paroles qui lève-rait la marque que le sujet reçoit de son propos, que seulement pourrait être reçue l'absolution qui le rendrait à son désir"* (Écrits II, p. 111).

6. In English in the original.

7. In the original French *"son semblable"*, meaning "his fellow man, his neighbour". The other in so far as a' (the counterpart of the ego and not that of the subject). As an adjective the word of course implies what is "similar".

8. In French *"le machiniste"*.

9. Of the *"fantasme"*.

10. In French *"dérober "*. Not only "to hide" or "to conceal", but primarily "to steal". Cf. Dicctionnaire Le Micro Robert.

11. Reference to the Spanish translation, *"Escritos 2"*, Siglo XXI Ed., Bs. As., 1988, p. 617.

12. In English and German in the original.

13. A faint or loss of consciousness is called in Spanish *"sin cono-cimiento"*, literally: "without knowledge".

14. Both words in English in the original.

15. See note 26, Chapter Three.

16. Lacan calls the phallus *"sans pair"*. Although one possible meaning of the word is "unparalleled" ('too great to be equalled', according to the English Dictionary), this is an allusive reference to the "pair" in the sense of odd and even numbers. The phallus is one, odd: there is no signifier with which it can make a pair, a couple. It is odd (peculiar, unusual) also because the signifier is itself defined by its relations with others (the pair S_1–S_2).

17. Translation modified. Sheridan translates Lacan's *"c'est à l'être"* by "it belongs to being". Lacan says that the neurotic's desire is that of "being it" as opposed to "having it".

18. My translation.

CHAPTER NINE

Desire and *fantasme*: A pathway (II)

According to Lacan, the fundamental idea that reveals the nature of the relationship between desire and *fantasme* is that the neurotic expects desire to become "I desire this", and the *fantasme*'s maneuver has to do with this purpose. There is no neurotic subject (as such) able to go beyond the question posed to the Other (which is in turn an answer to the Other's question: "*Che vuoi?*"): "What do you want of me? It is a structural limitation.

Through the formula "What do you want of me?", Lacan is telling us two things: first of all, that desire does not belong to the subject, it is not "the subject's". And secondly, that in so far as the subject is desired by the Other (since the desire of the Other is also unconscious) "it (the Other) does not know it". The Other "does not know" what the subject is for it. And if the Other does not know it, the subject is most unlikely to know it.

In the human world—as it is established for the neurotic subject—desire, as a psychoanalytical concept, inscribes the function of lack both at the level of the desiring subject and at that of the desired object.

This is our fundamental line of work.

Today I shall try to investigate a problem on which I only worked succinctly last week: the modes of desire. We can name it: desire as desire for an unsatisfied desire and the desire as desire for an impossible desire. But, are these in fact and in rigor, modes of desire? In other words, does the structure of neurosis imply different forms of desire?

Rapidly, I shall take some quotations from the *"The direction of the treatment ..."* that I have already read last class, and I shall demonstrate to you that the answer is no: that structure does not determine "modes of desire" or "types of desire", at least regarding the obsessional and the hysteric.

> Although it always shows [*transparaître*] through demand, as can be seen here, desire is nonetheless beyond it. It also falls short of another demand in which the subject, reverberating in the locus of the other, not so much effaces his dependence by a return agreement as fixes the very being that he has proposed there. This means that it is only through a word that lifted the mark that the subject receives from his expression that he might obtain the absolution that would lead him back to his desire (p. 298).[1]

If there was such a word able to annul the effects of that word over the subject, then it would allow the subject to encounter his desire. Obviously this is formulated in such a way that we immediately discover that it is absolutely impossible.

Hence, desire is not to desire a certain thing, but the impossibility for a word not to work as a word.

Desire is simply the impossibility of such word[2] (p. 298).

The obsessional uses this structural dimension. The impossible is for the subject to annul, by means of demand, the effect of that demand, what we call "desire", and which is the 'beyond demand'. Because—structurally speaking—every demand produces a beyond demand; there is no demand that exists without its beyond.

So, when the obsessional tries to sustain his desire as a desire for an impossible desire, what does he do in reality? He tries to lead desire back to the field of demand.

Hence the impossible desire is not a type—variety—of desire, it is a subjective attempt at annulling the desire by means of the demand (an attempt which reveals itself as being absolutely not feasible, precisely because desire is the contrary effect to demand, but produced by it).

Let us see now another quotation from *"The direction of the treatment ..."*:

> Let us say that in its fundamental use the phantasy [*fantasme*] is that by which the subject sustains himself at the level of his vanishing desire, vanishing in so far as the very satisfaction of demand hides his object from him (p. 301).

Every time Lacan posits the articulation between desire and dissatisfaction, what sort of dissatisfaction is he referring to? It is not the dissatisfaction of desire, but that of demand. Trying to sustain one's own desire as desire for an unsatisfied desire, then, is to trying to sustain desire within the field of demand. And frustration is precisely the dissatisfaction of demand localized at the level of the subject. It cannot be posited that desire is—as such—impossible or unsatisfied, because both impossibility and dissatisfaction are nothing but attempts at doing as if desire was demand.

> It is, then, the position of the neurotic with regard to desire, let us say by way of abbreviating the phantasy [*fantasme*], that he marks with his presence the subject's response to demand, in other words the signification of his need (p. 301).

Here Lacan is more explicit: it is not enough to articulate desire and demand, a trio is required; it is necessary to articulate need, demand and desire. Then the *fantasme* is indeed the position of the neurotic with regard to desire, which marks with his presence the subject's response to demand. Which effect of the demand is this a response to? It is a response to desire, in so far as desire is the 'beyond demand'.

> But this phantasy [*fantasme*] has nothing to do with the signification in which it interferes. Indeed, this signification comes from the Other, in so far as it depends on the Other whether the demand is satisfied[3] (p. 302).

It will be Other who signifies the demand.

> But the phantasy [*fantasme*] arrives there only to find itself on
> the return journey of a wider circuit, a circuit that, in carrying
> demand to the limits of being, makes the subject question himself
> as to the lack in which he appears to himself as desire (p. 302).

These quotations from "The direction of the treatment ..." seem to
be descriptions of the graph of desire's pathways taken from "*Subversion of the subject* ...".

Every time we read the Lacanian formula of the desiring subject,
we—neurotics—try to use it as a way of solving the problem that
desire represents for each of us. We want to understand "desiring
subject" in the following way: it is the subject in so far as it desires.
We ourselves want to become desiring subjects. And we often go
to see an analyst because sometimes it seems to us that we do not
desire. But the desiring subject in Lacanian psychoanalysis is not
the subject in so far as it desires but the subject as desire. And this
"subject as desire" is a subject, which only localizes itself as lack
with regard to the function of desiring and the function of desired.
The desiring subject, in terms of a formula that is read (we could
say "lived") by the neurotic is indeed a neurotic phantasy [*fantasme*].
"Desiring subject" means, rigorously, a subject for whom the function of lack operates as agent and object.

Therefore, we have a subject as desire and not as desiring.

On this double lack the modern subject operates ceaselessly, for it
is unbearable to him. Why the "modern subject"?, you may ask, and
not just the subject, considering that the structure has always been
the structure.

I will read a quotation for you, from Freud's "*Three essays* ...";
they are only six lines.

> The most striking distinction between the erotic life of antiquity and our own no doubt lies in the fact that the ancients laid
> the stress upon the instinct itself, whereas we emphasize the
> object. The ancients glorified the instinct and were prepared on
> its account to honour even an inferior object; while we despise
> the instinctual activity in itself, and find excuses for it only in
> the merits of the object (p. 149).

My hypothesis is that when Lacan read this quotation he said to himself: when did the break happen? According to Lacan, that moment corresponds to the emergence of courtly love; because for modern society that object is the woman.

Freud is saying that the ancients glorified the sexual act itself, whereas now we dignify the sexual issue through the merits of the object. This is what Lacan writes with his formulae of the *fantasme*, ($\$\lozenge a$): being 'I' vanished as subject—*fading* ($\$$), what rescues me is to desire ($\lozenge$) an object (a).

At the level of the structure an indifference of the object is localized; the lost object, the object cause of desire is never this or that object. The object cause cannot be "that" object. The subject's maneuver then, is to operate on this indifference. At the level of this indifference we localize the position of the ancients. It is the *fantasme* which introduces the "I desire that object".

Let us move to *"Subversion of the subject and the dialectic of desire ..."*, where graph 3 is presented and where this problem is widely developed:

> For in order to rediscover the pertinence of all this, a fairly detailed study is required—a study that can only take place in the analytic experience—that would enable us to complete the structure of the phantasy [*fantasme*] by linking it essentially, whatever its occasional elisions may be, to the condition of an object (the privilege of which I have done no more that touch on above in terms of diachrony), the moment of a 'fading' or eclipse of the subject that is closely bound up with the *Spaltung* or splitting that it suffers from its subordination to the signifier (pp. 346–347).

The link Lacan refers to is inscribed by the rhombus. What Lacan inscribes as a function on the side of the object is "condition of an object": an object that works in the *fantasme* as a condition. This is what the formula of the *fantasme* inscribes ($\$\lozenge a$). The object as such is—we have just said it—indifferent; the object facing desire is indifferent. But what the *fantasme* does, precisely, in order to rescue the subject from the lack that desire constitutes, is to invert the value of the object, turning it into a condition, when in reality it is a cause.

An interesting opposition is produced, in addition, because (in the context of the formula of the *fantasme*) the notion of moment, of time, is left on the side of the subject: "moment of a fading". On the side of the object, the condition. And as the object (the object "of desire", not the cause) is *res extensa*, consonant with Descartes proposal, we can add the notion of space on the side of the object. ($\$\Diamond a$): the subject in a moment of eclipse ($\$$) and the logical relation ($\Diamond$) with a spatial object posited as a condition, which rescues the subject from that moment of eclipse.

The following table sums up these articulations:

($\$	**$\Diamond$**	***a*)**
Fading subject		**Object as a condition**
Moment		**Extension**
Time	**Logics**	**Space**

Schema 1.

From this logic we can now posit a table of the clinical structures: when the subject localizes itself on the side of the subject as time, always a bit early or a bit late, then we talk about hysteria or obsessional neurosis—When the function of space is emphasized in the *fantasmatic* scene, the subject being localized on the side of the object, we talk about phobia and perversion.

A step that I consider as necessary is produced by noting the word 'logics' below the rhombus. It gives us the clue that allows us to reach the logic of the *fantasme*. Let us remember that in his Seminar 11, *The Four Fundamental Concepts of Psychoanalysis*, Lacan proposes that we consider the rhombus, *losange*, as an algorithm.

He continues by saying:

> This is what is symbolized by the sigla ($\$\Diamond a$), which I have introduced in the form of an algorithm; and it is not accident that it breaks the phonematic element constituted by the signifying unity right down to its literal atom.
>
> This algorithm and the analogues of it used in the graph in no way contradict what I said earlier about the impossibility of a metalanguage. They are not transcendent signifiers; they are the indices of an absolute signification, a notion which, without further commentary, will seem appropriate, I hope, to the condition of the phantasy [*fantasme*] (p. 347).

Lacan was saying before (in the previous quotation) that the *fantasme* obstructs the signification of the Other, and he goes to describe how this happens.

How does the *fantasme* interfere with signification? Lacan says it clearly in the paragraph I read to you: by making an absolute signification out of the signification of the Other (A). Notice that the *fantasme* always inscribes the condition. If there is a signification tormenting the subject, it is because the *fantasme* has inscribed it as absolute. The *fantasme* is a machine which inscribes conditions for the subject, which produces absolute significations. This is why Lacan says that he writes the *fantasme* like this ($\$\Diamond a$), like an algorithm made of letters: in order to indicate to us that there is no signification that is absolute by itself, that there is truly none. The *fantasme* as such, then, has no signification. If it was our meta-language, the formula ($\$\Diamond a$) would have a signification and it would be the same for every subject. Given that it is an algorithm made of letters, for each case it must be established which is the signification of the Other that tends to postulate itself as absolute, as an effect of the *fantasme*.

What is the difference between the signification that comes from the Other as such, and the interference produced by the *fantasme*? Through the signification that comes from the Other the axiom that regulates the whole field of significations in neurosis is fulfilled. Every signification leads to another signification. Whereas the signification affected by the *fantasme* postulates itself, precisely, as the interruption of that infinite metonymy, and that is why it is an "absolute signification" (on the side of the subject, the object, or both). It is thus well articulated to desire, given that desire is, as we have already seen, an absolute condition that the *fantasme* substitutes by the absolute signification.

The *fantasme* thus prevents the subject from facing one of the dimensions of castration: the fact that every signification leads to another signification, that is to say, the fact that it does not lead and can never lead to any object.

Let us now analyze the articulation between desire and *fantasme* with the imaginary circuits that we studied last class. The graph of desire allows us to give an extremely clinical version of that relation. Let us see it through the following quotation of "*Subversion of the subject ...*":

> On the phantasy [*fantasme*] presented in this way, the graph
> inscribes that desire governs itself, which is an homologue[4] of

the relation between the ego and the body image, except that is still marks the inversion of the *méconnaissances* on which each is based. Thus the imaginary way, through which I must pass in analysis, and where the unconscious was itself, is closed.

Let us say, borrowing the metaphor used by Damourette and Pichon about the grammatical "I" and applying it to a subject to which it is better suited, that the phantasy [*fantasme*] is really the 'stuff' of the 'I' that is originally repressed, because it can be indicated only in the 'fading' of the enunciation.

So our attention is now drawn to the subjective status of the signifying chain in the unconscious, or rather in primal repression (*Urverdrängung*) (p. 347).

Let us recall the structure of the complete graph (schema 2).

We intend to account for the relationship between the two intermediate floors of the graph, levels that have (for they are 'inter') the greatest importance for structuring and comprehending the graph of desire; but a problem emerges.

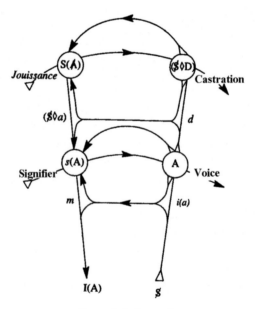

Completed graph.

Schema 2.

Lacan says that as the desire is sustained in the *fantasme*, in the same way the ego is sustained in the other's image or in the body image. The *fantasme* is to the desire what the other's image or the body image is to the ego. Lacan expressed this through the notion of homology. But it occurs that we can no longer visualize this in the graph, because we should go in the same direction from *d* to ($\lozenge a$) than from *m* to *i(a)*, from right to left; but from *m* to *i(a)* the arrow goes in the graph from left to right. These relations, supposed to be homologues, appear inverted in the graph.

$$(\mathcal{S} \lozenge a) \qquad \leftarrow \qquad d$$
$$m \qquad \rightarrow \qquad i(a)$$

Schema 3.

We shall see it through the pathway of the graph. What is the first thing which rescues the subject from its initial position as S-barred ($\mathcal{S}$)? According to the graph's direction, the image of the other –*i(a)*. But it is the image of the other in so far as it allows the subject to establish that this is him, that this constitutes his ego (*m*). There-fore, the ego should be (as desire is) written on the right. However, Lacan highlights that the inversion is on purpose, for in this way it indicates the concealment of determination, one *méconnaissance* on top of the other. The *méconnaissance*—misrecognition—implied by the function of the *fantasme* as a support for desire is the same as the one implied by the image of the other as a support for the ego. Without a psychoanalysis, we cannot discover that the ego circuit is determined by the *fantasme*, the true closing point of the imaginary circuit, which thus includes the function of response to the superior level of the graph, the level of S($\mathcal{A}$) and of ($\mathcal{S}\lozenge$D). And it is so true that we do not see it, that the graph is built up the other way around, "neurotically". The most obvious thing comes across first, the dia-lectics of the ego, and then the fundamental but more obscure deter-minant, the fantasme. This is also the neurotic's view: that he first faces the ego's vicissitudes, and then—if he pursues an analysis—he discovers that it is all determined by the dialectics of the *fantasme* and the desire.

There are thus three things that the neurotic subject does not see, since they are structurally veiled for him: he does not see that the ego is not the ego; he does not see that desire is not the "I desire x" of the *fantasme*; and finally, he does not see that the dialectic of desire and the *fantasme* determines that of the ego and the image of the other.

It is clear that the subject does not see, but we are not referring here to some sort of blindness, we are indicating the pathway for the direction of the cure.

It is due to this double concealment of the *fantasme*'s determinant that Lacan had to do first a whole conceptual route around the mirror stage, in order to establish later another determination function. As you can see, it is a very special case of "over-determination".

When Lacan says that the *fantasme* is properly speaking the 'stuff'[5] of the I (*Je*), he is telling us that the place that the subject has within his discourse as *Je* is what will determine him as imaginary ego.[6] But be let's be careful: the *Je* (I) of discourse is not the symbolic subject; the *Je* is already the 'stuff' offered by the *fantasme*. For at the level of discourse the localization of the subject is the primal[7] repression, pure lack. So that in order to locate itself at the level of discourse (as we have already posited for the level of the imaginary ego), the subject will have to make use of the stuff that the *fantasme* offers as a support for the function of the subject, the subject as "desire".

I want to work on the term Lacan uses in order to account for the function of the *fantasme*: "stuff". Strictly speaking, Lacan uses the French word "*étoffe*". It can be said of a person (in French) that he or she lacks "*étoffe*", but not of an object. I will give you the meaning that this word conveys in French, and you will see how careful Lacan is when choosing this term: "material, in general not only fabric. Material to be worked on in order to stuff, to fill something up". And two more specific meanings: first, "general name of weaves which cassocks are made of". Therefore, if Lacan says that *i(a)* becomes habit[8] (clothing, costume and veil), it is—fundamentally—because the *fantasme* is, contributes with, its material. And the second meaning: "what constitutes or defines (nature, quality, aptitude, condition) somebody or something". This is exactly what the *fantasme* is: that which constitutes or defines the subject's quality, nature, aptitude or condition. We shall see that this has to be worked through within the relationship between the subject (S) and the Other (A). Quality, condition, but, whom to? From whom?

We are going to move on now to *Seminar 10, Anguish,*[9] in order to be able to answer these questions. We find there the formula we commented on last week, that of the subjective division.

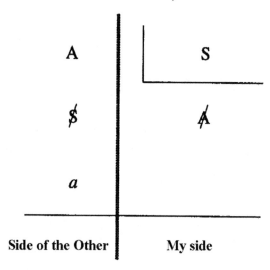

Schema 4.

In the second session of that Seminar, and in the context of his controversy with Hegel about desire, Lacan says:

> For Lacan, because Lacan is an analyst, the Other is there as unconsciousness constituted as such, and he involves my desire in the measure of what he is lacking and that he does not know. It is at the level of what he is lacking and that he does not know that I am involved in the most pregnant fashion, because for me there is no other detour, to find out what I am lacking as object of my desire.[10]

That what lacks me is, precisely, the object of my desire. The subject will only find what comes to occupy this place by exploring the desire of the Other (the Other's desire); without forgetting that in the analytic practice, the Other is the unconscious as such, and that it is inscribed precisely as "it does not know".

But Lacan prefers the formula "it did not know" to that of "it does not know". Because "it does not know" can easily be taken as ignorance, and that is not the problem. It is not that the Other is ignorant, but that the Other is placed in the position characterized as "it did not know" (more ambiguous regarding what he did know and what he did not know). In addition, it is also ambiguous on a temporal level: "it nearly knew it".

What the Other unknowingly lacks, that is what interests me the most, what concerns the most my being of desire. This is why, for me, there is not only no access but no possible support for my desire in terms of pure reference to an object.

The way to access desire, proposed by Lacan, is not and cannot be the reference to an object (no matter which object), but the coupling, the knot, with this necessary relationship to the Other as such. This is not the Other of demand, but the Other from the perspective of the lack and the unconscious—of what it lacks and did not know, the Other of desire.

Let us see some other quotations from *Seminar 10*, which will allow us to understand the formula for the division of the subject in the field of the Other. Via this formula we will continue working through the question of the *fantasme*, to decide whether it belongs to the Subject (S) or to the Other (A). We aim to, departing from there, be able to conceive the analytic practice involving the pathway from the *fantasme* towards desire, that is, psychoanalysis itself.

> If the formula of the *fanstame* is ($\beta \lozenge a$), with barred S (it is needed, for the ones who read me) is written that it refers to A and to $\cancel{A}$. This Other is of course the one that throughout these years I think I have accustomed you to distinguish at every instant from the other, my fellow. It is the Other as locus of the signifier. It is my fellow among others of course, but not simply that, because of the fact that it is also the locus as such at which there is established the order of the singular difference of which I spoke to you at the beginning.

This singular difference that Lacan refers to is the unary trait.[11]

> With respect to this Other, depending on this Other, the subject is inscribed as a quotient, he is marked by the unary trait of the signifier in the field of the Other. Well, it is not for all that, as I might say, that he cuts the Other into slices. There is a remain-

der in the sense of division, a residue. This remainder, this final
other, this irrational, this proof and sole guarantee when all is
said and done of the otherness of the Other, is the *a*. And this is
why the two terms, S/and *a*, the subject as marked by the bar
of the signifier, the little object *a* as residue of the putting into
condition, if I can express myself in this way, of the Other, are on
the same side, both on the objective side of the bar, both on the
side of the Other. The phantasy [*fantasme*], the support of my
desire, is in its totality on the side of the Other, $ and *a*. What
is on my side now, is precisely what constitutes me as unconscious, namely Ⱥ, the Other in so far as I do not reach it.

Lacan does not write in the formula of the division what could
have been added: a rhombus between S-barred and *a*. If we add this
rhombus we will evidently see that the formula ($◊*a*) is entirely on
the side of the Other (see schema 5).

   Division is one of the most interesting mathematical operations.
Division and subtraction are the two basic mathematical operations
which produced a series of inventions in mathematics; it did not
happen with addition and multiplication. Every multiplication and
every addition may be carried out in the field of natural numbers,
whereas this may not always be the case for division and subtraction. For instance, division led to the invention of irrational numbers
and subtraction to that of negative numbers.

   Now I am going to describe the formula: A is the dividend; S is the
divisor—or factor; Ⱥ is the quotient. (Remember that Lacan says that
the subject inscribes itself as a quotient; this implies that the subject
is inscribed in Ⱥ). And the remainder is *a*. Notice that $—the term
that has to be established—is nothing in reality, it only inscribes an
intermediate step in the division.

   The word "quotient", derives from the Latin "*quot*", and it means:
the number that results from the division of a number by another.
And division means: a process or operation that aims at determining how many times a number or quantity is contained in another
number or quantity.

   Therefore, the question Lacan poses is: how many times is S
in A? In other words: how many signifiers fit in the Other? This
hypothetical question is always posed from the perspective of
a subject. It is the subject who has to put into question the structure of the Other.

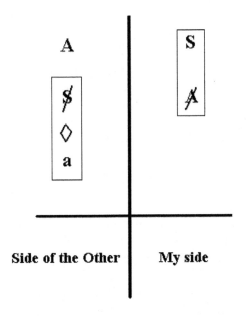

Schema 5.

When the subject asks himself how many times does S fit in A, a result and a remainder are produced out of this operation. This operation can never produce an integer. There is always a remainder. And not because the exact quantity of signifiers (number of times that S goes into A) cannot be determined for a given subject. This is very important for Lacan regarding the end of the analysis: that can be done. The problem, then, not that of what is unspeakable for the subject, the signifier that cannot be captured, the problem is that in the Other there are not only signifiers. That which is not a signifier in the Other, the remainder, is what protects the Other from annihilation. Although an analysis succeeds in establishing an exhaustive list of the signifiers of the Other, the Other is not (through this) annihilated. The Other remains, for this remainder is also a part of it; not everything is signifier in the Other.

That is to say, if ($a), the $ (the fading of the subject in the Other and the a, absolute condition of the object) are inscribed on the side of the Other, it is due to the fact that they come from the Other (from the Oedipus complex, we could provisionally say). And what remains on the side of the subject is the function of the unconscious as such: the interval within the Other, (A).

One should also notice that in what Lacan calls "my side" there is another matheme: S($\cancel{A}$). In effect, the direction of the cure is once again reproduced in this schema—the same direction already inscribed in the graph of desire: instead of the subjective flood by the imaginary circuit, way out towards the matheme S($\cancel{A}$). From ($\cancel{S}\lozenge a$) towards S($\cancel{A}$).

Let us consider *"Subversion of the subject ..."* once again:

> So our attention is now drawn to the subjective status of the sig-
> nifying chain in the unconscious, or rather in primal repression
> (*Urverdrängung*) (p. 347).

Once the subject has discovered this support, this 'stuff' that the Oedipus complex (in so far as structuring of the Other) offers to the *fantasme*, what happens next, how does one continue, where to? It continues towards the subjective status of the signifying chain in the unconscious, or rather, in primal repression. Lacan adds, to elimi-nate any doubts: *Urverdrängung*.

At the level of the originary repression, what happens with the Oedipus complex? This entire level is unfolded beyond the Oedipus complex, beyond the ($\cancel{S}\lozenge a$) inscribed on the side of the Other. This being the case, it does not mean however that the Oedipus complex is no longer a function of the Other for the subject. But the direction of the cure leads the subject to a function of the Other which is beyond the 'stuff' (the weave) in which desire is sustained. In other words: once the subject has been able to go from the ideals, $i(a)$ and I(A), towards the place from where that dialectic is determined, the place of the *fantasme* as a support for desire, once it has been demonstrated that the terms of the *fantasme* are material of the history, of the Other, what remains is the status of the unconscious chain, there where the subject is localized as pure lack, the place where Lacan locates Freud's primal repression. What is at stake there is the pure lack in the Other, not the material of the Other, but what is lacking there.

The crucial and interesting thing is that Lacan does not say that there is nothing beyond this material that the *fantasme* gives to desire. It is not about nothingness. There the subject faces another dimension—much more structural. And it is within this dimension that we must think of the S($\cancel{A}$).

But isn't it amazing that what remains in the formula at the end is still precisely a signifier, S, the signifier of a lack in the Other, S($\cancel{A}$),?

It seems that in the 'beyond' (from which it seemed we were moving away) the signifier returns again in order to determine the subject. We shall make the following classes revolve around this issue.

The thing is that Lacan posits here a signifier that is completely different from all the others; so different that it is not even in the Other. Have a look at the complete graph: there is a place A, the locus of the signifier. So, what is that S, up on the left, showing itself off outside A, and not being barred? This is the key element we must study now, for it is the clue to the way out of the analysis.

But before seeing and analyzing S($\cancel{A}$) we shall see in the next class, as a necessary reference point, the superior right side of the graph, that is, ($\cancel{S}\Diamond$D), the drive. I propose to go from the drive ($\cancel{S}\Diamond$D) towards the signifier of the lack in the Other, ($\cancel{A}$), in the same way we already went from A towards s(A).

The writing *"Subversion of the subject ..."* proposes this pathway. Lacan does it this way, let us follow him once again.

Notes

1. See notes 4 and 5, Chapter Eight.
2. Translation modified. See note 1, Chapter Six.
3. See note 26, Chapter Three.
4. Translation modified. Lacan writes *"homologue"*. (Sheridan translated it as "similar").
5. The French word *"étoffe"* literally means "weave". As in English, it also refers to the material something is made out of, and to the inner quality, the nature of something or somebody. In English it also alludes to the action of filling something up (even obstructing or blocking it completely).
6. The early Lacanian distinction between "ego = *moi*" and "Ego/I = *Je*".
7. Freud's *Urverdrängung*: also called originary, primordial, primary repression.
8. The Spanish word *"hábito"* condenses many different meanings that the author is here playing with: cassock (religious clothing in general); habit (custom) and clothing (costume).
9. Jacques Lacan. *"Seminar 10. Anxiety"*. Unpublished. See note 4, Chapter Two.
10. Jacques Lacan, Seminar 10, Unpublished.
11. See note 5, Chapter Six.

CHAPTER TEN

The formula of the *fantasme*: Introduction to the drive

Today we shall reconsider some aspects of desire and the *fantasme*. Afterwards we shall approach the notion of the drive.

The fact that we posit that there are no types of desire does not imply that no sort of attribution may be given with regard to desire. It is not that nothing can be said about desire; it is not that desire is by itself ineffable.

If I had to choose the most structural attributes of desire, those able to circumscribe it theoretically, within the logic of the case by case, I would propose two: desire is indestructible and desire is unconscious. For every case it can be posited that desire is indestructible and unconscious, whereas "prevented", "impossible", "unsatisfied", etc., are reserved in order to account for the different clinical structures.

If desire is the field, which, as an abyss, is opened up (that is why it implies anguish) beyond any demand for which the function of the limit operates (psychosis is therefore excluded), then it [desire] is indestructible. Therefore, there is no demand that does not carry its "beyond", and the neurotic subject will not be able, when refusing its own desire, to go beyond "to desire not to desire". It is unconscious because there is no demand able to say, to know, about desire. The dialectic between demand and desire always supposes, as we have seen, this "beyond". This is what Lacan's phrase teaches us: "to put it elliptically: it is precisely because desire is articulated that it is not articulable", which we commented on in Chapter Four.

Regarding the relation demand/desire, it cannot be conceived for somebody to go beyond "interpreting" his desire, and in order to do so the function of the desire of the Other will be required. What we may have regarding desire is, in each moment of our lives, an interpretation. This is what justifies the title of Lacan's *Seminar 6: Desire and its interpretation*. The psychoanalyst's tool, interpretation, is demonstrated to be, structurally speaking, the most adequate operation addressed to desire. Let us not forget that interpretation is a figure of rhetoric, as ellipsis is. If psychoanalysis is a device invented with a direction towards desire, it obtains (by means of its articulation to the figures and tropes of rhetoric) a place articulated to the science/art ("*ars*") of the well saying[1] and can thus be considered as a liberal art (as the *trivium* and *quadrivium*[2] ones).

Regarding the *fantasme*, we all depart from an imaginary conception of it, either we want it or not. This imaginary conception of the *fantasme* is mixed up with the phantasy. But Lacan teaches us that this imaginary dimension of the *fantasme*, phantasy, is also determined by the functions of the symbolic and the real. This is precisely what the formula ($\$\Diamond a$) means: it indicates the interrelation of the symbolic and the real, determining the imaginary configuration.

The difference between *fantasme* and phantasy lies in that the latter, although knotting itself to the former and surrounding it, has to be distinguished from it in so far as it does not lead to the structure. Phantasy is correlative to reality, given that reality consists of the assembly of the imaginary and the symbolic. As desire is the real, it is the essence of reality and it receives its support from the *fantasme*. We shall see in what way the *fantasme* works as the frame of reality.

As we saw during the last lecture, Lacan posits that the fundamental function of the *fantasme* is to be an axiom, that is to say, a combinatory of terms which does not require any justification, but which determines and justifies the symbolic and imaginary terms that it engenders. This *fantasmatic* axiom is, doubtless, unconscious. Let us be clear: what does "unconscious" mean? It is no longer something that has no access into consciousness, but the function of something "not entirely known". This is precisely why when in the analytic practice we affect the *fantasme*, one part is always known by the subject, and another one is unknown.

So, the *fantasme* is an axiom; and in order to be able to say that it is unconscious, we say that it is an axiom, which entails a function of misrecognition for the subject itself. This unconscious function is not in the content of the phrase, often known by the subject —as in the famous case of the *fantasme* "a child is being beaten"[3], but in the function that the phrase has for the subject. While working the notion of the drive in the graph of desire, through its formula ($\cancel{S}\lozenge D$), we shall see that this is precisely a point where drive and *fantasme* are articulated. Because the most unconscious part of the *fantasme*, its phrasal structure and its function, are intimately associated with the dimension of the drive, as highlighted in Lacan's teaching: the grammar of the drive. The problem of how to translate correctly the German phrase into Spanish "*Ein Kind wird geschlagen*" (if either "A child is being beaten" or "Somebody beats a child"),[4] clearly indicates that if the *fantasme* is a phrase, it has to be related to the grammar of the drive. What we have to account for is how the drive, according to Lacan, is essentially linked to grammar. We shall try to do so by the end of this class.

I propose we work on the following quotation from *Seminar 11, The Four Fundamental Concepts of Psychoanalysis*, session 14. It is about the partial drive, but it will allow us to better work through these notions and their relations. It says:

> In the phantasy [*fantasme*], the subject is frequently unper-
> ceived, but he is always there, whether in the dream or in any
> of the more or less developed forms of day-dreaming. The sub-
> ject situates himself as determined by the phantasy [*fantasme*]
> (p. 185).

The function of the *fantasme* is, precisely, to determine the subject, the subject as desiring.

> The phantasy [*fantasme*] is the support of desire; it is not the
> object that is the support of desire. The subject sustains him-
> self as desiring in relation to an ever more complex signifying

ensemble. This is apparent enough in the form of the scenario
it assumes, in which the subject, more or less recognizable, is
somewhere, split, divided, generally double, in his relation to
the object, which usually does not show its true face either.

Next time, I shall come back to what I have called the structure of perversion. Strictly speaking, it is an inverted effect of
the phantasy [*fantasme*] (p.185).

We are going to develop the structure of the perverse *fantasme*,
because it throws light on the structure of the *fantasme* in general.
The perverse *fantasme* is an inversion of the direction of the formula
($◊a$). The inversion is what Freud theorized as "perversions being
the negative of neuroses". It is the subject that determines itself as
an object, in its encounter with the division of subjectivity, which
the perverse subject localizes in the other, the *partenaire*[5] (instead of
being the subject the one localized in the division of subjectivity,
and sustained with regard to an object which is desired, as is the
case in neuroses). The perverse subject places himself as an object
before the other's division.

We represent the inversion through the following formulae:

$$(S ◊ a) \qquad\qquad (S ◊ a)$$
$$\rightarrow \qquad\qquad\qquad \leftarrow$$

Direction of the formula   **Direction of the formula**
of the *fantasme*   **of the perverse *fantasme***

Schema 1.

As you can see, I am not proposing that the inversion is:

$$(a ◊ S)$$
$$\rightarrow$$

Schema 2.

Rather, this formula corresponds to the possible formula of the end
of the analysis: the object *a* in its position as the cause of the subject's
division.

This can be clearly seen in the sadist's position: the sadist's arm (in continuity with the whip) works as the object (*a*), instrument of *jouissance*, and the victim's fainting is a way of imaginarising, of putting in scene, the subjective division (*Ø*). Then, the sadist localizes himself in the scene as object: his body in continuity with the instrument, before the *partenaire*'s vanishing, which is not secondary but has a function: it is where the perverse subject, by placing himself as an object, faces a way of imagining the division as contingent, for example as a faint.

The quote continues:

> You see, then, several possibilities here for the function of the *objet a*, which is never found in the position of being the aim of desire. It is either pre-subjective, or the foundation of an identification of the subject, or the foundation of an identification disavowed by the subject [...] But the object of desire, in the usual sense, is either a phantasy [*fantasme*] that is in reality the *support* of desire, or a lure (pp. 185–186).

This quotation has a double virtue: it allows us to revisit the point that we reached last class, and it confronts us with something we had not approached yet, the issue of the *fantasme* as a stage (scenery).

We all know how crucial the notion of scene is in psychoanalysis; from the primordial scene to the analytic experience conceived as a scene. The use of this notion allows us to identify roles and thus to read the transference, with no need for the analysand to say anything in particular, but representing a role and making us represent ours in a certain scenic coordinate. It is enough to understand that roles are being fulfilled in order to determine that—for instance—the role conferred on me as an analyst in this scene is that of the father. The analytic experience has always been conceived as a scene, since Freud onwards.

Lacan says that that which gives, which offers the function of the scene to the human subject, is the *fantasme*. And the scene is, rather than a play of images, disguises or scenery, what the script says they all are. It is important for us to recall at this point Freud's "to unravel this tissue thread by thread"[6] as well as Lacan's "*étoffe*",[7] given that both terms are associated with the plot,[8] the true foundation of the scene.

In order to better understand this issue, we should go back to some of what we have already said. What does Lacan want to represent through the rhombus ($\lozenge$), which he calls "punction" and which he places between the ($\cancel{S}$) and the object (*a*), in the formula of the *fantasme*? (The ($\lozenge$) will be something else in the formula of the drive). The rhombus, considered in its most symbolic way, is a border. It has to be considered as the conjunction of four purely symbolic terms:

<	>	∩	∪
minor	**major**	**and**	**or**

Schema 3.

We usually suppose that the "rhombus", within the formulae, indicates a surface, and what Lacan wants to do is to show us the function of a border. The punction, then, rather that being the definition of a surface, is the circumscription of a void: the one inscribed inside the figure.

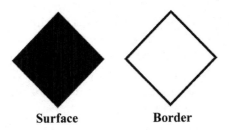

Surface   **Border**

Schema 4.

This is particularly important in the case of the formula of the drive, because we shall compare it to the erogenous zone (defined through the body borders). However, what is the status of the punction in the formula of the *fantasme*? In this case, we shall call this border "the frame of the *fantasme*". "Frame" (as in pictures or windows) leads us, firstly, to the importance of the scopic element for the *fantasme*. This is why we shall emphasize the function of the fantasme as limiting and ordering reality as scopic. Reality (from the point of view of the *fantasme*) is mainly visual reality, and this explains why the imaginary conception of the *fantasme* is so frequent.

In order to fully understand the notion of "the frame of the *fantasme*" and its implications, we must develop the notion of "subtraction of the object *a*".

The frame of reality is what constitutes it as such, and in its scopic dimension the frame will be what is not seen in it. That is why, theoretically speaking, we conceive it as the subtraction of the object *a*. It is that what, being visual, cannot be seen in it. And this is especially interesting: the most hidden of all the modes of the object *a*, the most veiled within reality for the subject itself, is precisely the scopic object *a*.

Magritte is a specialist in artistically representing this function of the frame of the *fantasme* in its scopic dimension, in terms of that which is not seen in the scene. His painting, *The Human Condition*, is perhaps one of the most eloquent regarding this. Here is a copy of it:

The Human Condition (1935)

This painting is the pictorial representation of what is seen through a window frame. We have a representation of reality through a window frame. But notice that Magritte did not add a frame to the canvas imposed over the "hole" of the window, and which reproduces that which is seen through the window. He succeed in getting the represented elements confused with their representation by means of an interplay of frames included in other frames, all of them toned down to the maximum (the painting has no frame, and the window frame is hidden behind the curtains, which take the place of a frame, etc.). That is to say, *The Human Condition* is a painting whose subject is the frame and which, by itself and thanks to the author's excellent understanding of the human condition, takes the frame out of the represented picture. The author only left a small white border with some little nails, a shadow in the superior part, and that which remains visible, behind the easel. But the most important element is the frame of the entire painting, the window frame which circumscribes the border of the represented canvas but which is not painted. The frame of the painted picture is not painted, and Magritte's painting has no frame either.

In order to represent this idea on the *fantasme* more completely at the scopic level, I shall resort to an example, which I think is very eloquent and structural: I am talking of the borders of the eyelids. If our gaze is relatively normalized, it is due to the fact that there is something ruling it, ordering it, determining what we see and what we do not; it is the border of the eyelids that works as a frame for what we see—and which in turn we never see and must never see. On the other hand, this example introduces once again the necessity of articulating what we have been saying about the *fantasme* and the drive.

The problem is what does it mean "to see a border"? There is nothing more complicated than seeing the borders. Despite being that what is not seen, the frame (and moreover that of the eyelids) it is a limit which operates by means of subtraction and organizes the field of what we see.

A certain dimension of the pathology of the scopic structure of reality can be deduced from this point: for instance, those subjects who complain about feeling a gaze in their back. In this case, something that should have accomplished its function by not being there (gaze) bursts into reality, as an excess.

In order to articulate a bit more the function of the *fantasme*, it is necessary to work on the function it has as "veil" or "screen", apart from considering it as the frame of reality. Veil or screen, you can see they are in the same line of the *fantasme*'s strong scopic determination. I say "veil" or "screen" emphasizing the nexus "or", for you to understand that, on the one hand, the *fantasme* veils the subtraction of the object *a*, insofar as it shows (in what is circumscribed by its frame, it conceals the subtraction of the object *a*) what, by structure, cannot be seen. On the other hand, "screen" indicates the projection surface, what allows something to be seen, insofar as it supports what is projected onto it (remember that the topological surface that Lacan articulates to the *fantasme* is the "projective plane"). Saying that the *fantasme* is the support for desire indicates, together with the notions of veil, screen, etc., that the *fantasme* makes that condition of the subject that we call desire to be bearable.[9] Without this function of "support" the border of desire is necessarily experienced as the abyss of anguish.

Thus defined, the *fantasme*'s function as "screen" seems to be in contradiction with its function as "veil". The *fantasme* implies a relationship between the veil, which conceals, and the screen, over which the image is projected. This relationship, which seems to be a contradiction, has in fact a topological structure, where a continuity articulating two heterogeneous surfaces by means of a surface with no cuts is produced. In this sense, that which is moved away (for it is hidden) is at the same time approached, insofar as once the veil is crossed through, that which lacks (and remained hidden) emerges. Being orientated by somebody who knows the structure of the pathway, an analyst, a subject can find the function of the lack precisely there where it is veiled. The metaphor chosen by Lacan in order to account for this relationship which we are articulating, is that of the sceneries called *"practicable"*. These are doors or windows in the scenery of the stage set which are not merely drawn but can be actually used, that is, opened and walked through. They are false because they are part of the scenery, but they are true because they can be distinguished from other openings, which although also painted in the scenery, cannot be walked through. They are false and true at the same time. We are here touching on the logic which is at stake in the Lacanian statement "going through the *fantasme*".[10] It is not about concluding that the *fantasme* is false, but about acknowledging that the truth itself has for the subject the structure of fiction. It is rather about warning the non dupes who dupe themselves (a possible way of reading the title of Lacan's *Seminar: Les non dupes errent*).[11]

I shall propose you now that you consider the notion of drive, in order to pass afterwards towards the upper chain of the graph where we shall localize the subject in the primordial repression. Before doing that, let's try to understand why Lacan affirms, at the beginning of his *Seminar 11*, that the work on the drive cannot be rightly done unless we have previously a good theory of the transference.

We depart then, once again making a step back (it seems that it is always this way), from a good system of oppositions. In this case the required opposition, according to Lacan, to account for the drive is transference vs. suggestion.

In the first part of Lacan's teaching, he posits that transference and suggestion correspond with two dimension of the human bond with the other, one (suggestion) imaginary and the other (transference) symbolic. Thus, suggestion is related to the bond with the other (*a*) and transference is related to the bond with the Other (A). But this notion of transference is not enough, and that is why we need the notion of transference which Lacan elaborates in, for example, "Subversion of the subject ..." and which is definitely established in his *Seminar 11*.

This new theory of transference, specific to Lacan, forces us to distinguish three planes or dimensions: the imaginary other (*a*), the symbolic Other (A) and a third plane that we shall call—provisionally—that of the transference. What I am proposing is that the univocal correspondence between the transference and the Other has been broken; they now belong to different planes, although they are obviously related. Suggestion, in its specifically human sense, will be any word effect that the subject receives from any fellow man (*a*), elevated to the function of the Other (A). This elevation of the other (*a*) to the status of the Other (A) could be called recognition, and recognition is not transference. Despite this fact, as Freud used to say, there can be no psychoanalysis without some suggestion. But, watch out! Precise distinctions do not imply purity in the clinic. Any psychoanalysis includes both transference and suggestion, but they are not the same. And, for the direction of the cure, it is extremely important to distinguish them.

The suggestion involved in taking any other (*a*) and elevating him to the condition of analyst (A) is an obvious condition for the entry into analysis and also, doubtless, an obvious place for the exercise of power, the place of the listener's discretional power,[12] by the analyst. Remember the title of Lacan's writing: "The direction of the treatment and the principles of its power".

Every function of the Other (A) will no longer be considered as specifically transferential, but the transference will be: "the enacting of the reality of the unconscious in so far as it is sexual". This is how Lacan defines transference. Let us go back to the graph of desire in order to bring this definition further.

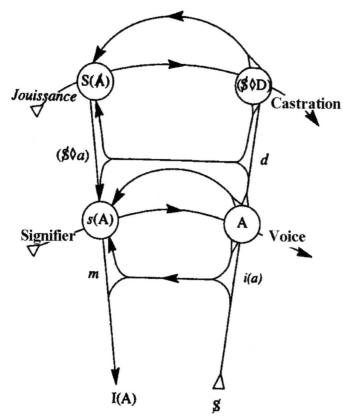

Schema 5.   Completed graph.

Where is the unconscious in it? It is the other chain, the upper one. And which is the place of the transference in the graph? "A"? No, that is suggestion, the power possessed by the Other. In order for the transference to be installed, the analyst must localize himself "between the two chains", in the interval. This maneuver is called: not meeting the demand, not satisfying the demand. To place oneself between the two chains implies to put the yes and the no to work, at the same time. The analyst may accept, "say yes", a demand for analysis, but perhaps formulating an answer for that demand which is not what the subject asked for. This involves a form of "saying no".

According to Lacan, transference consists in sustaining this function of interval. The function that the analyst puts to work is the function "desire of the analyst". Transference no longer means sustaining oneself in the place of A. The analysand's maneuver, consisting of elevating any other (*a*) to the condition of Other (A), will be now named "Subject supposed to Know". The analyst's maneuver is not to localize himself in the place of the subject supposed to know, but to localize himself within the interval, within the "between-two" of both signifying chains.

And what happens if the analyst (instead of opening the interval space) closes it down, joining both chains? The answer of the desiring subject is produced, which is the *acting out*[13] and, for what I have just said, is a responsibility of the analyst.

So, I propose the acting out to be the fall of the analyst's function. But no longer in terms of the fall from his function as Other (A) to that of the other (*a*), rather in terms of remaining trapped in the place of the Other (A) and thus no longer sustaining the place which strictly speaking corresponds to the analyst: the place named by Lacan "desire of the analyst", which is precisely an interval. Thus we can conceive that the analyst is the only one who manages in this way the function of the A, which is a dimension of speech and, therefore, not specific to the analysis. Then, to respond as an analyst to a demand for analysis is to "say yes and no" to the fact of being elevated to the function of the Other (A) by a certain subject.

Remember that in our last class we saw how Lacan proposed, in the direction of the cure, to offer the subject a way out from "the infernal circle of demand" towards the graph's upper chain, where $S(\cancel{A})$ is placed. A question emerges: is it about elevating the dialectics towards the superior chain or to lead it towards the interval? It does not seem to be the same. What happens is that, in order to really elevate the dialectic towards the superior chain, the only existing resource is to posit, each time, the "beyond demand" and, thus, to open the interval able to make possible the "between-two" of the

signifying chains. The peril of supposing that one can directly operate on the upper chain is that it generates the illusion that one would
know or that it is possible to know about that other chain. And to
place oneself in the position of he who believes that he knows about
that "other chain" is the same as meeting the demand. For any
demand essentially demands us (as Other, A) to know. The interval is what posits, for each demand, the beyond itself which is the
beyond of desire.

Once we have reached this point, we shall begin to work on the
graph's superior chain, but from the level I believe is the most structural one. Actually, I propose that you think again about the general
structure of the graph of desire. In order to do so, we shall consider
the mathematical notions of "group", and specially that of the "Klein
group". Have this simple schema in mind:

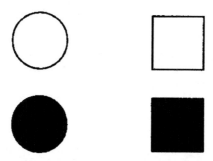

Schema 6.

We must observe, on the one hand , "horizontal relations" (white
figures-black figures) and, on the other, "vertical relations" (circles
and squares). I will read two quotations by Dienes, a famous mathe-
matician who wrote a book called *Geometry through transformations*,[14]
in order to conceptually elaborate this:

> Mathematical groups constitute one of the fundamental con-
> cepts of modern mathematics; it is hardly imaginable how
> could anybody understand that the concepts of modern math-
> ematics have a unity without understanding the structure of
> the group. Essentially, a group is a set whose elements can be
> absolutely anything whatsoever but which must be linked

by an operation, and this operation must determine one particular element of the group given two elements whatsoever of the group[15] (p. 5).

This is an extremely important idea for us, because by delimiting at least two out of the four functions inscribed in the graph of desire we can also progress with the conceptualization of the others. This is valid for groups in general. Groups are ordered according to the quantity of elements, by which they are constituted, and among them, the group of four elements is called "the Klein group". This is the one that specifically interests us, given the quaternary structure of the graph of desire.

Regarding this Klein group, Dienes says:

> This group is very important in many aspects of geometry. Klein group may be applied whenever three defined movements appear, each of one being such that, when applied twice, one returns to the initial position. Also when we apply two of the movements, the result is equivalent to the third movement. Any three movements which fulfill the above, together with the movement "nothing" will always produce the structure of the Klein group (pp. 12–13).

This affirmation can be clearly represented as follows:

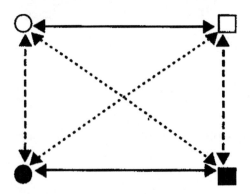

Schema 7.

In this schema every corner represents one of the four elements and each type of line represents the three operations or movements able to be done in the group.

I brought these quotations for you because Lacan uses the Klein group as the fundamental structure for building the graph of desire. This means that the lower functions (black) have to be like the upper ones (white), but with a transformation. It seems to me that this allows an extremely interesting double maneuver over the previously presented schema: by means of a cut we separate circles from squares, and through another cut we separate white figures from black ones. Let's now transfer this same maneuver to the graph, for it has the same structure: a cut between S_1 and S_2, and another cut between one chain and the other. Through those two cuts the two dimensions of the interval we are trying to define—that of the unconscious—have been established.

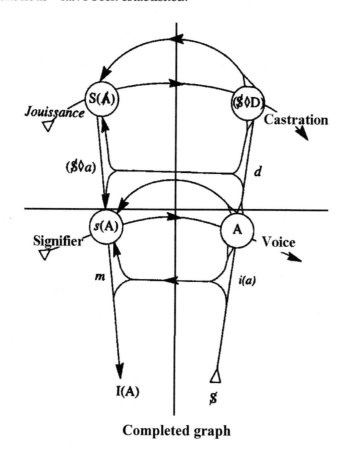

Completed graph

Schema 8.

We would visualize this in the graph in the following way:
However, can these two practicable cuts be reproduced infinitely?
If it was so, a closure would never be produced regarding the subject, and the analysis would be interminable. This is a very important problem for the psychoanalytical theory. According to Lacan, there must be a frame (but functioning as subtracted) that operates as a limit of the analytic experience. This is why I always propose the interior eight in order to account for the closed structure of the graph of desire. The interior eight re-frames this doubly fractured schema, but also articulates the S_1 and the S_2 in continuity with the two chains. To sum up, two pairs are needed as well as the intervals between each of them, that is, their articulation. S_1 and S_2 is one pair; one chain and the other constitute the other pair. Between S_1 and S_2 there is an interval; between one chain and the other there is another interval. We also require a theory able to articulate both pairs and their intervals, and able to put them in continuity within a closed surface. They have to be in continuity but within a closed surface, given that desire is fundamentally finite, limited (although we all fantasize about desire being metonymically infinite). We have already seen, in previous classes, that infinitude only operates, strictly speaking, in cases of psychosis, where desire and *fantasme* do not operate given the lack of extraction of the object *a*.

If the above is in fact correct, we should be able to state that the lower functions are reproduced at the upper level, although not identical, and the same for the functions on the right and on the left.

Let us remember that we took from Jakobson the notions of code (C) and message (M) and we applied them to the analytic experience, then proposing the code to be substituted by the Other (A) as treasure of the signifiers and the message to be substituted by the signified of the Other ($s(A)$). My proposal now is that the drive has to be some sort of transformation of this treasure of the signifiers (lower chain) in the upper chain.

I will now present you with a quotation from Lacan's "*Subversion of the subject* ..." so you can trust a little bit more this pathway I place before you:

> But although our completed graph enables us to place the drive
> as the treasure of the signifiers [...] (p. 347).

Lacan performed exactly this maneuver: he put the treasure of the signifiers below right in the graph, but as he is working using the logic of Klein group, then the drive is also in a certain way the treasure of the signifiers in the upper chain, which is not the same.

What has to be justified now (and I warn you: this is even more difficult and even more incredible) is that the signified of the Other $(s(A))$ agrees in a certain way with $S(\cancel{A})$, the signifier of a lack in the Other.

Let us begin with the relation below right/above right, (A) with $(\cancel{S} \Diamond D)$. If there is a formula in the graph that appears to us, by itself, surprising and complex, it is that of the drive. Precisely there where we were sure of knowing what was at stake, in the drive: what was at stake was the body. But Lacan decides to write there, instead of the body, the demand (D).

I shall return to "*Subversion of the subject ...*":

> So our attention is now drawn to the subjective status of the signifying chain in the unconscious, or rather in primal repression (*Urverdrängung*).
>
> In our deduction it is easier to understand why it was necessary to question oneself regarding the function that supports the subject of the unconscious, to grasp that it is difficult to designate that subject anywhere as subject of a statement, and therefore as the articulator, when he does not even know that he is speaking. Hence the concept of drive, in which he is designated by an organic, oral, anal, etc., mapping that satisfies the requirement of being all the farther away from speaking the more he speaks" (p. 347).

The first problem we face regarding the graph's upper chain is: how is the subject sustained in it? A logical question, for it is about the subject at the level of the upper chain. But the problem is that the subject cannot be localized at this level, because the subject—in the upper chain—is primordially repressed: there is no particle able to indicate the subject in the superior chain. How can the subject be localized, then, within the "other chain" where he cannot be? It is at this point that Lacan proposes that we name "drive" any localization of the subject in any part of the body. He no longer says (as most of the post Freudians do) that the drive is the hinge between the body and the psychical activity. He defines it the other way around, by saying that we talk about drive when the primordially repressed subject (a subject that can never be present either in the statement nor in the enunciation due to the problem that statement and enunciation open up in terms of an interval) is localized in the body. But why ought we name this localization as "drive"? Precisely because the drive is that localization in which, the more one speaks, the less it is considered that it is the subject speaking there.

The most typical example is where there is suffering, where there is pain linked to a drive exercise. Whenever there is pain connected to the exercise of a drive function, the subject may ask himself: what does *this* mean? And what is the virtue of this question? To reveal that the presence of that "this" says that the subject is saying something without being the one who says it, without even knowing that it is being said. Notice that this is a logically adequate localization for the subject in the unconscious enunciation.

Lacan is asking himself how the subject is localized in the unconscious enunciation, and he answers: through the drive. Obviously because when the drive speaks it is about an organ that begins to send a message to the subject. Lacan says that it is this organ or this set of organs speaking, what corresponds to an unconscious localization. But the fact that "it" speaks does not mean that it is the subject who is speaking. Lacan will call this function of the body "drive", and he will say that it is through this function that the subject obtains another localization.

Because the subject is primordially repressed in the structure, we are all the time asking ourselves about its localization. During our last class we found a first localization for it: that the subject—as desire—is localized as desiring in so far as the *fantasme* supports it by giving it a function as desired object. Now Lacan is asking himself: what is it that supports the subject at the upper chain level, at the unconscious level? And he answers: when it is no longer localized as desiring but within a corporal organ. Which corporal organ? The organ that speaks for the subject without the subject speaking there. We now have a new localization for the subject of the unconscious.

It seems now more coherent that Lacan writes, regarding the function of the drive, $ and not Ego: the subject cannot be localized there as subject. When the body speaks, the subject is represented, and with regards to this speech it is not him who speaks. Therefore, there is a fading of the subject, and there is also a function of the demand (D), that is, the speech we are talking about. Hence, we have here a first justification for the formula of the drive ($0D).

I would like to quote again from "*Subversion of the subject ...*":

> But although our completed graph enables us to place the drive as the treasure of the signifiers, its notation as ($0D) maintains its structure by linking it with diachrony (p. 348).

We said that, in the Klein group, if there was a square below there had to be a square above. But there had also to be some transformation in it. Which is this transformation in the case of the Other (A) and the drive? It is a temporal transformation. The (A), treasure of the signifiers, has a fundamentally synchronic structure: when the subject comes out, the Other is already entirely there, once and for ever. This implies synchrony. But Lacan is telling us that it is the transformation of the treasure of the signifiers of the lower chain into the upper chain which inscribes the diachrony.

I shall continue quoting:

> It is that which proceeds from demand when the subject disappears in it. It is obvious enough that demand also disappears, with the single exception that the cut remains, for this cut remains present in that which distinguishes the drive from the organic function it inhabits: namely, its grammatical artifice, so manifest in the reversions of its articulation to both source and object—Freud is unfailingly illuminating on this matter (p. 348).

Let us remember what we have said: that we exited the imaginary circuit in the lower floor and we rose upwards to the unconscious level, beyond the infernal circle of demand, which also disappeared. And if the organ (whenever the drive is involved in it) says something, that which it says is ciphered for the subject itself. The message, then, also vanishes. What remains? The cut, says Lacan. And what does it mean that the cut remains? Firstly, that if the organ is something that the body offers to the subject for him to localize there the drive at the unconscious level, it is as a cut that it will do so.

Let us think about it. When we say "oral" ("oral erogenous zone"), we are obviously thinking of the nourishing function. The nourishing function supposes the functioning of a number of organs, but we circumscribe—among them—the one that corresponds to the oral drive. Which one is it? The organ that works for us as a border: the border of the lips or teeth, or (as with Dora's cough) the throat. Every time we get close to the oral erogenous zone, we find a border, and not the set of organs or the surface of the organ. The same can be said about all the other erogenous zones. Remember how we defined, at the beginning of the class, the "punction" in Lacan's formulae.

This means that what is offered (of the body) as real for the unconscious localization of the demand, is that what (as body) has the structure of the cut.

Psychosomatic lesions are very interesting in this respect, for they introduce a failing function of the cut, outside the zones offered by the corporal real: the border of the mouth and psoriasis in the elbow are not the same. You have there the introduction of a cut in an anomalous place, which indicates the failure in the function of the interval, and which leads us to the notion of holophrase.[16]

What kind of organs are specially designed for embodying the function of the cut of the demand? To begin with, those whose real structure is a true cut. But also those that have been selected from a certain conjuncture of the Other's demand. Because of her particular history, Dora's throat is a good example of what I am trying to say.

Finally, if we localize the treasure of the signifiers (A) below right, what of this treasure is kept above right, in ($\lozenge$D)? The grammatical artifice. There exists a popular or vulgar theory of language, placed for us in the inferior floor of the graph. It is the conscious theory, which supposes that the treasure of language resides in the words of that language and in their meanings. So, what other form may the treasure of language take in the upper chain? Grammar. But let us think about it, for it is an extremely interesting case of the treasure of the signifiers. Grammar is a knowledge that we constantly apply, in fact, to our discourse, but that we forget we do: there you have an aspect of language that can be localized in the superior floor of the graph.

When one knows well the grammar of a certain language, one is able to better manage that language. Through understanding the ways in which phrases are built up, even the meaning of the words can be better understood. And this is due to the fact that this is another dimension of the same treasure. And this is a dimension which, as well as the treasure of the signifiers, has to be shared by the speakers of the language (this does not happen with rhetoric, whose objectives are better produced if the receiver does not know its figures and tropes).

We shall place therefore, above right, the treasure of the signifiers: grammar as the remainder of demand, left once that demand is vanished. That is to say, it does not matter what message this demand is emitting, what matters is its structure—and its structure is fundamentally grammatical.

Concerning the drive, and in order to anticipate the theme of our next class, Lacan says that in relation to the breast the activity is suction. Therefore, to be suctioned (the vampire's *fantasme*) will be its opposite. Do you realize that the logic of the drive (active voice, passive voice, reflexive voice) has to be necessarily supported by grammar, for this is the only one which functions as its support?

Drive is a localization of the subject which has to articulate the treasure of the signifiers as grammar with the diachrony, articulated to the corporal organ as a cut.

This development that I propose to you (and on which we shall continue working next week) implies the following schema, which represents the structure of the graph of desire as a Klein group:

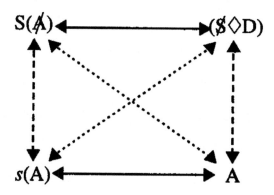

Schema 9.

Notes

1. "*Bien-dire*" is one of the French expressions that Lacan uses in order to define the ethics of psychoanalyisis.

2. *"Trivium"*: The lower division of the seven liberal arts in medieval schools, consisting of grammar, logic, and rhetoric. From Latin: "crossroads". *"Quadrivium"*: The higher division of the seven liberal arts in the Middle Ages, composed of geometry, astronomy, arithmetic, and music. From Latin: "where four roads meet".

3. See Freud's article "A child is being beaten", SE 17.

4. This paragraph presents the problem of the different uses that the passive voice has in Spanish and English, and also the fact that in Spanish the subject can be "tacit". This is why the second option does not make much sense in relation to the English translation of the German phrase.

5. In French in the original.

6. See the author's reference to Freud's case of the Rat Man. Chapter 8.

7. See Chapter 8 for a definition of the French word and the context in which Lacan uses it.

8. In Spanish *"trama"* means both "tissue" (more technically "weft") and "plot" (in the sense of a "script").

9. In Spanish the same word is used to say "to support" and "to bear".

10. Also "traversing the fundamental phantasy". In French *"traverser le fantasme"*.

11. Jacques Lacan, *Seminar 21* (1973–1974), unpublished.

12. See note 3, Chapter Four.

13. In English in the original.

14. Zoltan Paul Dienes. Geometry through transformations. Education Supply Association in association with Hutchinson. 1967.

15. My translation.

16. Holophrase: Late Lacanian notion that aims at accounting for psychosomatic disorders and other psychopathological phenomena. See, for instance, Jacques Lacan. "Seminar 11. The Four Fundamental Concepts of Psychoanalysis".

CHAPTER ELEVEN

The drive (I)

In order to continue working on the notion of the drive, as Lacan does in his *Seminar 11*, I think it is very convenient to depart from the following question: what is *Seminar 11* about? It seems to me that the function of this seminar is not clear yet. *Seminar 11* is Lacan's response to his expulsion from the International Psychoanalytical Association. A peculiar expulsion, for it was formally established that, according to the Association, his teaching and his analytic practice would be considered forever null in relation to the formation of analysts ever since.

In the first class of this seminar, Lacan makes a diagnosis of the IPA, taking the opportunity that, by chance; he was expelled from the IPA on the same date that Spinoza had been excommunicated from the Jewish faith. He says: "I have been also excommunicated". Lacan's diagnosis is the following: the current structure of psychoanalysis is equivalent to that of a church. I—says Lacan—have been punished, like a heretic; I am a heretic according to the international organization of psychoanalysts.

However, this had already happened with Melanie Klein. Melanie Klein was about to be expelled in exactly the same way as Lacan was expelled: because of heresy. The difference is that Melanie Klein avoided the expulsion. Let's say that she made a vote of credibility for the church: the presentation, at an international IPA congress, of a paper entitled "On observing the behavior of young infants". Those psychoanalysts who read Melanie Klein's work at the time had the feeling that her theoretical building was absolutely fantastic, inconsistent. She was asked to demonstrate that her statements were the product of empirical observation. You can grasp the point that psychoanalysis had reached by then.

Lacan always considers problems from an interesting angle. He posed the following problem: the question is not why I was expulsed, but why psychoanalysis, institutionally speaking, became structured like a church. *Seminar 11, The Four fundamental Concepts of Psychoanalysis,* is an attempt to answer that question; it is the attempt at producing the necessary theory in order to avoid such a fate. It is produced in order to avoid psychoanalysis being sustained on the structure of a church. Lacan's stake is, I posit, that the only option psychoanalysis has in order to not become a church is its articulation with science. This is the way out for psychoanalysis, its future, the psychoanalytical perspective of psychoanalysis. It seems to me that Lacan's work around the fundamental concepts is done from this perspective: to found them in the way science founds its notions. To sum up, the aim is to re-find the scientific basis of the psychoanalytical notions.

In this context Lacan elaborates a fundamental notion (notice that I use "fundamental" in its double meaning of base and foundation): the notion of the drive.

We shall work today, then, on the notion of the drive from *Seminar 11,* taking these remarks into consideration. However, and retaking our pathway, I must warn you that the graph of desire is not external to *Seminar 11.* In this sense, our work maintains its continuity. At the same time, we ought to find what is absolutely new in Lacan's re-conceptualization.

Two of the basic notions by means of which Lacan presents the concept of the drive are that of *montage* and deconstruction of the drive.[1] I propose to use these notions in order to approach the four themes with which I divide this issue. I chose three themes. The first one: the formula of the drive. I am referring to the formula itself: ($\$\Diamond D$) and what it means within the context of *Seminar 11.* The second one: the deconstruction of the drive into its four elements. The third one: the four drives that Lacan distinguished: oral, anal, scopic and invocatory. However, there is a fourth element, which I decided not to consider: the four vicissitudes—destinies—of the drive.

Let us go to our first subject: the formula of the drive ($OD). Lacan works on this formula using the following postulate: drive is by no means something natural in Freud's work. While reading "Drives and their vicissitudes" one cannot be completely sure that Freud is not talking sometimes about something natural; one cannot determine whether Freud is trying to articulate (in some particular way) the natural, in the sense of biology, with the psychical. Lacan says that he is not, that the text is full of references indicating that Freud's concept has nothing to do with nature. This implies that two things are rejected: firstly, that the drive belongs to the organic register, and secondly, that it represents the manifestation of the organic life in the psychical order. Among us, drive is usually thought of as the hinge between the organic order and the psychical one, but Lacan says it is not like that: there is nothing natural in it.

Let us go to the positive formulae of the drive, so we shall know what it is:

> [...] sexuality as such comes into play, exercises its proper activity, through the mediation—paradoxical as that may seem—of the partial drive (Lacan, 1998, p. 193).

This "seeming paradoxical" refers both to the theoretician who studies the problem and the neurotic who suffers it. To sum up, everyone who approaches the problem of sexuality faces the paradox that it introduces its own activity through the partial drive. So Lacan articulates the sexual to the drive, and not to the organic.

Second formula:

> The drive is precisely the *montage* by which sexuality participates in the psychical life, in a way that must conform to the gap-like structure that is the structure of the unconscious (p. 176).

This formula has such an extension that Lacan does not hesitate to use the Freudian expression "psychic life". Evidently, Lacan is trying to place this formula at the level of the Freudian formula.

Sexuality participates in psychic life through the montage of the drive: but this participation has to tune with the fact that in the subject's psychic life, the most important thing is the structure of gap [b¬ance], precisely where the unconscious is localized. Notice that we are putting together not only drive and psychic life, but also drive and unconscious. Hence, if the drive has to face these gaps in its representation of sexuality, the rhombus in the formula ($◊D) will therefore imply the structure of those gaps.

We are already taking the opportunity to use these formulae from *Seminar 11* in order to read the algebraic formula of the graph of desire: if the rhombus, the punction, is placed in the middle of the formula, this is because these gaps are intervallic ones. It is the gaps of the interval between signifiers which are at stake.

Third formula:

> The drive represents the curve of fulfilment of sexuality in the living being (p. 177).

Obviously, Lacan is considering sexuality from a broader perspective, not limited to sexual copulation. He is placing in sexuality the entire perspective of the species' progress and future. That is the curve represented by the sexual drive.

Two notions regarding this last formula will specially matter: curve and representation. The notion of "curve" interests us due to the pathway that Lacan inscribes in the partial drive, and that of "representation" due to the particularities it takes when it is a living speaking being which is at stake: it is a representation that will be affected by the legality of signifier.

One more quotation:

> All subjects [...] they deal only with that part of sexuality that passes into the networks of the signifier (p. 177).

Remember that in mathematics the notion of the network is equivalent to that of the graph. Although this is not a graph of Lacan's psychoanalytic theory, but each subject's graph, which is the articulation of his or her particular signifying system. So that which of sexuality is not represented in the nets of signifiers, will be the lost sexuality. For us, there is no possibility of natural sex; it will always be via the signifier.

And he adds:

> Sexuality is realized only through the operation of the drives
> in so far as they are partial drives, partial with regard to the
> biological finality of sexuality (p. 177).

Given that what we know about sexuality is only what is brought
in by the net of signifiers, the first thing that is lost, says Lacan, is
the total drive. Only partial drives remain, because the net of signifiers is precisely characterized by the fact that it lacks the "all"
("whole"). This means two things: firstly, that the "all" of sexuality—
that would be its biological aim—cannot be inscribed; and secondly,
that sexuality is not inscribed as a total drive. I am saying this for
us to begin thinking about the psychoanalytic problem of genital-
ity, posited by the post-Freudians as the subject's complete sexual
development. Lacan sustains that this "complete", "all", is impossible, because sexuality—via the drives—is a signifying representation that renders impossible the complete representation, but which,
at the same time, produces its ideal.

Lacan warns us that, in "Drives and their vicissitudes", Freud
mainly speaks about two themes: one is the mechanism that Lacan
calls "deconstruction of the drive" and the other one is love. It is
Freud who says that love does not fully represent the sexual impulse.
Why is love linked with sexual drives? Given that neither there is a
total drive nor a total representation of the man's biological aim, it
is via love (which is an effect of that lack) that the subject tries to
recover the lost totality. This is why the letter D is included in the
formula ($D), for the demand is always a demand for love, for the
Other's love (A).

To sum up: the sexual drive only represents sexuality within
psychic life; it does not represent the biological body. Because the
drive "represents", we are immediately led to the field of the signifier. This is why the drive has the structure of a montage: it shows
the solidarity with the montage that the net of signifiers imposes on
it. This net affects, at the same time, the drive itself, and causes the
four elements to be knotted in a net. The sexual drive, then, does not
present but represents, and it does it in a partial way, what leads us
to the notion of not-all. Finally, the other side of the not-all is love,
which is thus also articulated to the drive.

In *Seminar 11* Lacan works on love in terms of narcissistic love, that is to say, love in relation to the ideal of completeness: the Other's omnipotence. It is apparent that we are commenting on the function of demand, D, within the formula of the drive.

Lacan considers Heraclitus in order to explore his own thesis about the sexual drive as representation of the curve of the human being's sexuality; Heraclitus says:

The bow[2] has the name *bios*, life; its work is death.

What is at stake—as Lacan says—is an arch that necessarily ends up in death. Why does the sexual drive curve end up in death? Try to take into account, at the same time, that in the analysis of the famous forgetfulness of the name Signorelli, Freud posits that it always concludes with the duo: sexuality and death. Until here, Lacan—like Freud—seems to us capricious when supposing this articulation.

Throughout this Seminar, Lacan gives a logical reason for the articulation between sexual drive and death. He posits that the sexual condition of the human being (in terms of species and not of speaking being) implies the articulation with death; given that we are sexual reproductive animals, for reproduction to occur, for a new generation to exist, the previous has to die. It is not the symbolic death but the real death that is at issue.

Let us pass to the term $\bar{S}$ (barred S) in the formula of the drive:

This articulation leads us to make the manifestation of the drive the mode of a headless subject [...] for it has no relation to the subject other than one of topological community (p. 177).

Lacan is working here with the topological notion of community; he is positing that the function of the subject in the drive has a relation of topological spatial community with the function of the subject outside the drive.

Let us observe the graph on page 348 (schema 1). Lacan says that between $\bar{S}$ (S barred), which is a departure point of the pathway, and the $\bar{S}$ (S barred) of the formula of the drive, there is a topological community. This does not mean that they are the same, but that there is a coincidence between them at a very peculiar spatial dimension. And this spatial community is one of a topological structure. He has not told us yet what sort of topological coincidence is at stake, but he has already said that the subject in the drive functions as a headless subject. We shall return later to this point.

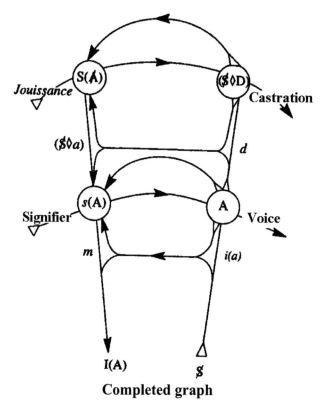

Completed graph

Schema 1.

Let us have a look at the following quotation:

> I have been able to articulate the unconscious for you as being situated in the gaps that the distribution of the signifying invest-ments sets up in the subject, and which figure in the algorithm in the form of a *losange* [◊], which I place at the centre of any relation of the unconscious between the subject and reality (p. 181).

The rhombus, the punction (◊) is always considered as an opera-tor between the subject and reality, any subject and any reality whatsoever. It is placed in the middle, representing the gaps that exist in the distribution of the signifying investments, whose structure always implies them. The unconscious happens to be localized in these gaps. We must articulate, once again, the gaps with the unconscious, but we must not get them confused:

> It is in so far as something in the apparatus of the body is structured in the same way, it is because of the topological unity of the gaps in play, that the drive assumes its role in the functioning of the unconscious (p. 181).

I ought to warn you: the "apparatus of the body" does not match the biological body. In other words, the drive is regarding the instinct, what the body as apparatus is regarding the biological body. An apparatus is an artificial instrument that involves a set of parts or system. And if Lacan states that something is structured in the same way, that is because the apparatus of the body is a system of parts with gaps, like the ones we find in the networks of signifiers.

A superimposition is thus produced: there are holes in the nets of signifiers, and there are gaps that belong to the apparatus of the body: the drive (which is lodged there) represents gaps inside other gaps. In other words: the rhombus [losange] ($\lozenge$) represents both the border structure of the erogenous zone, the apparatus of the body's gaps, and also the gaps of the interval between S_1 and S_2. This allows the drive to be articulated from a different perspective than the one we worked on last week, the grammar of the drive.

Another quotation from *Seminar 11*:

> [...] radical structure in which the subject is not yet placed. On the contrary, what defines perversion is precisely the way in which the subject is placed in it (p. 182).

The notion of headless subject implies that, in the drive, the subject is not placed *yet*. When the subject *is* placed in a drive, it is perversion. But notice that the "yet" in this quotation is a structural one, there is no "after" regarding it, no evolution to be considered. Structurally, and when we are not referring to perversion, the subject is always *not yet* localized in the drive.

Thus, the $\$$ (barred S) in the formula of the drive tells us that the subject is not yet placed. Where is the subject placed in perversion? In *a*, necessarily, he is placed as the object, instrument of the Other's *jouissance*. The D of demand in the formula of the drive has to be substituted, of course, by the *a* of the object. The $, then, will have as many meanings as it does positions. One thing is the $ within the *fantasme*; another thing is the $ as starting point in the graph of desire, and another one is the $ within the drive.

Let us change now the usual use of the terms: when has perversion to be diagnosed? When the subject places itself as an object within the dialectic of sexual drives. Briefly, in the formula of the drive the subject is not localized; and when it is, it has to be as *a* and never as $. Obviously, a transformation in the formula of the drive is produced: it becomes the formula of perversion.

However, the transformation of the formula of the drive into the formula of perversion (due to the subject's localization) does not imply a change in the formula. It is in both cases ($◊a). The difference is that whereas in neurosis the subject is localized in $, in perversion it is localized in the only other possible location: *a*.

Here we can see what was just said in a schema:

($◊D)	**($◊a)**
$	***a***
Subject's position in neurosis: it is not localized	**Subject's position in perversion:** localized in *a*

Schema 2.

Through this structural difference, posited by Lacan, we are able to account for the difference between neurosis and perversion. Freud had stated that perversion was the negative of neurosis. Here "negative" becomes an inversion in the formula of the *fantasme*. When I highlighted, during past classes, that we should not forget that the formula of the *fantasme* has a direction, a sense,[3] an orientation "→" I did it in order to account for the opposition that interests us now. The *fantasme* in perversion has the following direction: "←", for the perverse subject, as object *a*, postulates itself as the contingent cause of the *partenaire*'s[4] division ($).

We should not confuse the inversion in the perverse *fantasme* with the following formula: (*a*◊$) which I believe has to be kept in order to account for the end of the analysis: an object that, from the position of cause, divides the subject.

The perverse *fantasme*

$$(\$ \lozenge a)$$
$$\leftarrow$$

Schema 3.

with its inverted direction, accounts for the difficulty in the analysis of subjects who are in this position: they do not cede[5] to the analyst the possession of the object *a* that is required for the analysis of the function "desire of the Other".

If in *Seminar 11*, as we have just seen, Lacan accounts for the perverse manoeuvre, in *"Subversion of the subject ..."* he enunciates in a very precise way that of the neurotic:

> Indeed, the neurotic, whether hysteric, obssesional, or, more radically, phobic, is he who identifies the lack of the Other with his demand, Φ with D.
>
> As a result, the demand of the Other assumes the function of an object in his phantasy, that is to say, his phantasy (my formulae make it possible to know this fantasy immediately) is reduced to the drive ($\$ \lozenge D$). That is why it was possible to draw up the catalogue of drives in the case of the neurotic (p. 355).

Regarding the inversion in the formula of the *fantasme* within the perverse structure, we can now state the following: a) in perversion, the formula of the drive becomes the formula of the *fantasme*, because the subject places itself in it as object; b) in neurosis the formula of the *fantasme* becomes the formula of the drive, for the neurotic substitutes the *a* object with the demand (D), in so far as he demands to be demanded. So we have:

Neurosis:	Perversion:
Fantasme: ($\$ \lozenge a$)	Drive: ($\$ \lozenge D$)
↓ (becomes:)	↓ (becomes:)
Drive: ($\$ \lozenge D$)	*Fantasme*: ($\$ \lozenge a$)

Schema 4.

THE DRIVE (I)   215

Thanks to Lacan's formulae we have been able to give the Freudian affirmation ("perversion is the negative of neurosis") an extremely formalized character that has great articulation with the psychoanalytic clinic.

We have to pay attention to Lacan's use of the formulae. They can become or be transformed one into another, but these are the formulae and there are not others. Their structure and their number are closed, unless the contrary is demonstrated. They are not open to a personal consideration.

Let us go further into the issue of the drive through another quotation:

> The object of the drive is to be situated at the level of what I have metaphorically called a headless subjectification (p. 184).

"Acephalia" (headlessness) is a metaphor and not algebra. Do you realize which the paradox is? Headless subjectification, that is: with no subject. Subjectivity without subject.

I shall repeat the quotation:

> The object of the drive is to be situated at the level of what I have metaphorically called a headless subjectification, a subjectification without subject, a bone, a structure, an outline, which represents one side of the topology. The other side is that which is responsible for the fact that a subject, through his relations with the signifier, is a subject-with-holes [sujet troué]. These holes came from somewhere (p. 184).

Lacan has given us two different dimensions, two topological facets of the subject: firstly, when he directly called it object; and secondly, when he called it subject-with-holes. The subject is both on the surface where the holes are as well as in the holes themselves.

> At this level, we are not even forced to take into account any subjectification of the subject. The subject is an apparatus. This apparatus is something lacunary, and it is in the lacuna that the subject establishes the function of a certain object qua lost object (p. 185).

These are the two dimensions: there is a surface with holes; that surface is called "the subject", and in the hole we localize the object, the lost object: but Lacan also says that this is another dimension of the "subject".

The quotation goes on:

> It is the status of the object *a* in so far as it is present in the drive (p. 185).

How is the object *a* present in the drive? As lost object. Here the Lacanian myth of the lamella takes its place. What is it the lamella? It is the lost object as a part of one's own body. Lacan considers the placenta as a metaphor of this object-lamella. This is the myth that Lacan builds up in order to say that the lost object is a part of the subject and not of the Other.

The placenta is a foetus' differential tissue; it is not of the mother. When Lacan elaborates the loss in the Other's body, he does it trough the expired membranes (*decidua*). Where is the lamella (the object as a structurally lost part of the subject's body) placed? Within the body's holes, within the gaps.

The articulation between the subject's condition as being a surface with holes and the subject's conditions as being an object has crucial importance, and it will have a more and more fundamental place in Lacan's teaching.

Let us go now to the deconstruction. What we must take into account is that the deconstruction is a decisive consideration in order to establish that the drive is not natural; it is the deconstruction of a montage that accomplishes no biological function.

Regarding the montage's structure, we have to consider that the drive is not the *"drang"*[6] (pressure, push, effort). The first thing that Lacan warns us about is not to confuse this *drang* with the drive. What has to be taken into account (in order not to confuse drive with nature) is that this *drang* corresponds to a constant pressure; it is thus different from the biological function, which always has a rhythm.

Lacan adds that the four terms of the drive have to be distinguished. They can only appear disjointed, never in such a relationship that they would constitute a unity. Partial drive and conglomerate of parts. Lacan revisits the notion of the "Freudian field" in order to go further in relation to the drive's structure of montage. The notion of Freudian field allows him to oppose the structure of the biological organism to that of the nervous system. The opposition is between the organism as a complete three dimensional body (the real of the species) and the nervous system as plane subject, the subject designed in a two dimensional plane. If the nervous system has the structure of a plane, it is then homologous to a topological surface. Remember when we worked on the nets and graphs structures in relation to the two or three dimensionality of the space that is at stake. Freud had already said it in *"The Ego and the Id"*: the ego is the psychical representation of the corporal surface, a "signifying" representation (clarifies Lacan) of the corporal surface. So Lacan, honouring Freud, calls this plane, this topological surface, the "Freudian field". And why is the nervous system a topological surface? Because the length, the shape or the three dimensionality of the connections do not matter: what matters is the system itself, the connections and the intervals that constitute them. The "Freudian field" refers to a field which includes a function of lack, a hole, and which is, therefore, opposed to the notion of a "unified field".

Another quotation:

> In the drive, there is no question of kinetic energy; it is not a question of something that will be regulated with movement (p. 165).

Strictly speaking, for us to be able to conceive the psychoanalytic notion of *jouissance*, it is necessary first to get rid of the notion of "psychic energy". We cannot do that today. That is why the notion of *jouissance* barely appears in my class. It is necessary first to find a pathway which closes the history of the function of energy in psychoanalysis, given that energy is opposed to *jouissance*. None of the properties that physicists assign to energy can be applied to the Lacanian notion of *jouissance*. If you are interested in this topic, you can find precise conceptualizations in *Television*.[7]

Ziel: the aim. We know that according to Freud the aim is satisfaction. Lacan sustains that the notion of drive in psychoanalysis allows us to put into question what this satisfaction is. It is enough to consider sublimation, where there is satisfaction without the aim being reached. The problem is that if we state that sublimation is satisfaction without aim, and also that the aim is satisfaction, then we are stating that sublimation is a satisfaction without satisfaction.

What Lacan proposes is that, in psychoanalysis, satisfaction and dissatisfaction are a continuous series. It seems to me that this is an absolutely fundamental operation that practically distinguishes psychoanalysis from any philosophical approach to the problem of satisfaction and the Supreme Good. It is the same problem that Freud posed in relation to the preliminary pleasure, which appeared as excitatory (that is—in the Freudian system—as displeasure) and pleasure at the same time. The logic of the symptom inscribes the same problem: that what in it is satisfaction becomes dissatisfaction and vice versa; if only one of these terms was at stake, it would not be a symptom.

Within this context and regarding the problem satisfaction/dissatisfaction, Lacan states that the subject's pathway passes through two walls of the impossible. One impossible is that of satisfaction: because the notion of drive with which psychoanalysis works implies that satisfaction is impossible, for it always ends up being dissatisfactory. Satisfaction as such is impossible because going along the pathway it defines always implies that it will become dissatisfactory. The other impossible is the pleasure principle. How is this proved in Freud's work? By the fact that satisfaction is achieved by means of hallucination. If satisfaction is hallucinatory it means that it is impossible. Because there is no object of the need able to satisfy any drive, the pleasure principle is impossible.

Therefore, to ask ourselves what distinguishes satisfaction from dissatisfaction (given that there is continuity) would be akin to asking ourselves what distinguishes one side of the Möbious strip from the other one: absolutely nothing, because, strictly speaking, there are not two sides. What happens is that, according to different moments in the pathway of the strip itself, one may have the illusion that it is composed of two sides, and that one could cross through one side of the strip to the other and thus be "on the other side". The same occurs for every moment of the subject. But within the structure, it is impossible to distinguish satisfaction from dissatisfaction. This is a fundamental function of the drive: to inscribe that, for the human being, satisfaction and dissatisfaction are indistinguishable.

The question of the relationship between the *jouissance* of the drive and the ethics of desire emerges here. The limit has to be sought somewhere else and not within the drive itself. The limit is in the field of ethics.

The question is now a clinical one: if, structurally, every satisfaction becomes dissatisfactory, when must we, psychoanalysts, intervene? Lacan introduces here the notion of *"trop de mal"*, which in English means: too much effort, too much suffering, an excess of suffering. Lacan says that the moment for intervening is only when this balance between satisfaction and dissatisfaction implies an excess of suffering for the subject. Psychoanalysis as such does not attack the civilization's discontent, it is a product of this discontent, and it only intervenes when there is an excess for somebody with regards to this discontent.

In relation to the aim, Lacan says:

> If the drive may be satisfied without attaining what, from the point of view of a biological totalization of function, would be the satisfaction of its end of reproduction, it is because it is a partial drive, and its aim is simply this return into circuit (p. 179).

The aim is to get out and to come back into a circuit. What does that aim look for? Lacan uses the term *"tour"* in French, and he detaches it into the English *"turn"* and *"trick"*. "Turn" defines the turning around the object, and "trick" refers to the magician's trick, which always involves an object. Therefore, in order to elaborate the notion of the aim, the notion of drive object is required.

Lacan says:

> The *objet petit a* is not the origin of the oral drive. It is not introduced as the original food, it is introduced from the fact that no food will ever satisfy the oral drive, except by circumventing the eternally lacking object (p. 180).

The oral drive is satisfied within a circuit, in a "circumventing". We already have there the logic of satisfaction and dissatisfaction: it will be—let us say—satisfactory when going and dissatisfactory when returning. And, regarding the object *a*, he adds:

> The object that we [must not] confuse with that upon which the drive closes (p. 180).

This is the trick. Do you realize now what the two functions of the object are? The first one, a lacking object around which one revolves; and the second one, an object by means of which the drive closes itself up. This is the trick of satisfaction, which strictly speaking, conceals the fact that satisfaction—for example, oral satisfaction—is only reached by means of a lacking object; and this can only lead to dissatisfaction. The trick, in other words, aims at hiding this dialectic. Lacan proposes the NASA schema in order to represent this functioning of the object *a*:

Schema 5.

The object is closing the hole. On the contrary, in the following schema the object *a*, as a lack that is equivalent to the hole itself, is circumvented by the pathway of the drive.

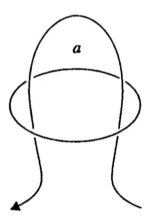

Schema 6.

At this point, I propose to introduce the following deformation, into a continuous shape (that is, a topological one) in order to see the problem in a clearer way:

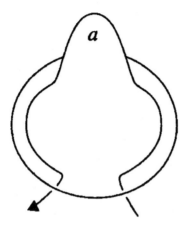

Schema 7.

And then:

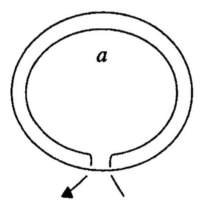

Schema 8.

Through the transformations of these schemata I am trying to account for:

1) Regarding the two dimensionality of the erogenous zone, a third dimension is not introduced in Lacan's schema, which could

be metaphorized as "going outside to look for the object *a*", and 2) the going and returning of the drive fits with the fact of circumvent-ing the hole of the erogenous zone. The transformation of Lacan's schema that I am proposing is, finally, nothing less than to incline the schema in order to avoid the supposition of the third dimension, which is so negative for the conceptualization.

In the schema I called 7 it is apparent that the erogenous zone in continuity with the drive pathway, establishes the topological struc-ture that Lacan calls the "interior eight".

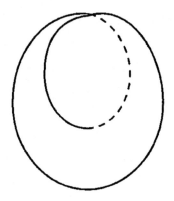

Schema 9.

Finally, the remaining element which we must consider is the source, the erogenous zone, as we conceive it in psychoanalysis. We shall only say that its border structure has to be emphasized, its structure of corporal hole. Localization determines there the offer of the real of the body. However, we must not forget that for each case, the border as such may be displaced to the zone of the body which has been better taken by the dialectic of demand, especially the Oth-er's demand. Thus, the oral zone may be for example, the borders of the lips, of the teeth, the hole of the throat, etc., depending on how this is determined by each subject's history.

At the beginning of this course I emphasized how the graph of desire should be closed up, as an interior eight, and how its pathway implied an interior hole which gives us the structure of the graph itself. Now that we have worked on the notion of the drive, I think these articulations may be justified for you. We shall reconsider these elaborations of the drive at our next meeting.

Notes

1. I follow A. Sheridan's translation. Cf. The Four fundamental Concepts of Psychoanalysis. The Seminar of Jacques Lacan Book XI. Norton. New York. 1981. p. 161.
2. In Spanish the word *"arco"* means both "bow" and "arch", which, at the same time, can be used as a synonym for "curve" in geometry.
3. As it is the case in French, the word *"sentido"* in Spanish means both "direction" (orientation) and "sense" (meaning).
4. In French in the original.
5. This is the verb that Lacan uses when referring particularly to the object *a* (in French *"céder"*) Literally, the "giving of property, land or rights".
6. Term used by Freud when referring to the *"Trieb"*, the drive.
7. Jacques Lacan. Television: A Challenge to the Psychoanalytic Establishment, ed. Joan Copjec, trans. Jeffrey Mehlman, W.W. Norton & Co., New York, 1990.

CHAPTER TWELVE

The drive (II)

Today we shall resume our elaboration of the notion of the drive. We shall also return to its articulation with the concept of perversion, as you seemed particularly interested in it. This, however, is not unusual: perversion is always an interesting theme. At this point, there exists a fantasy: that the perverse enjoys (*jouit*). Departing from *Seminar 11* we are going to put into question the idea—neurotic idea *par excellence*—that the perverse subject enjoys. We shall see that nobody else is as limited, regarding *jouissance*, by the *fantasme*, as the perverse subject is.

Last class we said (following Lacan) that the subject is "headless" in the drive. "Headless subjectivity" means that, in the drive, the subject is not yet placed. Let us stop for a moment in this "yet". It is a complex notion which Lacan studied and to which he even dedicated the title of his seminar: *Encore*.[1] What is Lacan trying to tell us through this "yet"? It is by no means an evolutionary or developmental notion, it is not "not yet, maybe later".

We also began our work on the drive by saying that the more the drive speaks, the less the subject speaks there. In 1966, in an addition the *Seminar on the purloined letter*, Lacan talks about the "silence of the drive"; we can understand that the drive, although it is silent, it is not mute: it is precisely the other way around. The more "it"[2] speaks, the more the subject remains silent.

If the subject abandons this position—"not placed yet"—and places itself in the drive, then we are faced with a case of perversion.

Perversion is—let us highlight it—an inverted effect of the *fantasme*. In order to understand this it is necessary to remember that the formulae have a direction: from left to right, that is, the direction that writing has both in French and Spanish.

> I shall come back to what I have called the structure of perversion. Strictly speaking it is an inverted effect of the phantasy [*fantasme*]. It is the subject who determines himself as object, in his encounter with the division of subjectivity.
>
> I will show you [...] that the subject assuming this role of the object is precisely what sustains the reality of the situation of what is called the sado-masochistic drive [...][3] (Lacan, 1993, p. 185).

We also said last week that we must be careful regarding the way we understand the fact that in perversion the subject localizes or places itself. It places itself, yes, but the question is where or how does he do it. The perverse subject always places itself as object. This is why the formula of the *fantasme* and the formula of the drive match in perversion: because the subject places itself as an object, as an object of *jouissance* in the drive.

$$(\$ \quad \Diamond \quad D)$$
$$\downarrow \quad \text{(becomes)}$$
$$(\$ \quad \Diamond \quad a)$$

Schema 1.

This proves that the idea that the perverse enjoys is merely a neurotic fantasy: there is no other case where the satisfaction of the drive is more limited by the structure of the *fantasme* than in the case of the perverse. I repeat: because in perversion the formula of the *fantasme* and that of the drive, coincide.

Lacan says that, in the case of the perverse subject, the formula of the *fantasme* becomes inverted.

Schema 2.

What does "becomes inverted" mean? It means that the direction has changed. That is to say, the subject—by placing itself as object *a*—sustains the following fiction: that it is he who produces, who causes (as an object) the other's division, making the *partenaire*[4] represent the division—the $\bar{S}$ (barred S).

Let us analyse how the perverse subject locates himself, as object *a*, within each of the four types of perversion described by Freud: exhibitionism, masochism, sadism and voyeurism. I deliberately leave aside fetishism because it presents more than one anomaly regarding this point. I even think it is not possible to say that it is one more in relation to these four. It cannot be put directly in series with the other four.

We shall try to establish how the perverse subject localizes himself as object *a* with regards to the *jouissance* of the drive within the *fantasmatic* scene: the exhibitionist exhibits, shows the object as a part of himself to the other's gaze. The masochist offers himself, the whole of himself, as an object (an object in the most radical sense of the term, a contractual object, for instance). In the case of the sadist, a part of his body—his arm, for example—acts as a torture instrument, as an instrument for *jouissance*. His victim represents, in the scene, the fading—in our algebra: $\bar{S}$—whose contingent cause the sadist precisely tries to make believe is him. And finally, the voyeur, a darker case of perversion with regards to the localization of the perverse subject in the place of the object. The voyeur seems to be fascinated by the object that the other possesses and which he stares at. We could even read symbolically the formula of the *fantasme*: the rhombus would be the lock through which the subject's eye $\bar{S}$ (barred S) looks at the object which the other has. However, if we describe thus the scene, the voyeur would be in the place of the desiring subject; it is of no use, since two essential elements of the voyeuristic scene are missing: 1) It is produced in a public place (in private there is nothing less perverse than voyeurism) and 2) there is always a third party—at least indicated—in the scene who looks at the voyeur, or who could at least see him. That is why a public place is needed. The scene is complete once the voyeur stops spying through the lock, through the hole, in order to see whether he is being seen as he spies. The $\cancel{S}$ (barred S) then, is neither him looking nor that at which he is looking, but he who looks at him looking. Why do we state that his position is that of an object? Because through looking, he becomes the object offered to the vision of a third party. It is only in this way that the position of the voyeur is defined as perverse.

The perverse fiction is that he is, as an object (*a*) the cause ($\leftarrow$) of the other's division ($\cancel{S}$), trying to hide that the lack in the Other, $\cancel{A}$, is a structural one.

In the perverse drive, the subject (in so far as he is placed as an object) is the support of the scene, that is to say, he is the *fantasme*. That is why drive and *fantasme* are so closely linked in perversion.

Let us leave perversion and now return to our theme. In the drive (within neurosis), ($\cancel{S}\Diamond D$), the subject is both the body in the form of a montage with holes, and the holes themselves; this might be the most amazing thing we worked on last week.

A double localization is possible for the subject: the body as a montage with holes, and the holes themselves. You could say: but does not the object *a* localize itself in those holes? Well, yes, but what is it the object *a* in *Seminar 11*? It is, metaphorically speaking, the lamella. And what is the lamella? The subject's lost part (not the Other's lost part).

Within this context, the schema of the erogenous zone of *Seminar 11* makes sense (schema 3).

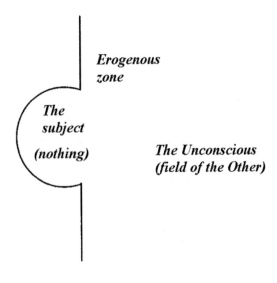

Erogenous zone

The subject

(nothing)

The Unconscious (field of the Other)

Schema 3.

The erogenous zone is thus schematized as the border of a hole, and in the hole itself Lacan writes "the subject", namely: "nothing". Notice that the subject is localized precisely where we would have, intuitively, placed the object *a*. What happens is that, that which for the subject is the object, as a lost part of its own body, is in reality the lost part of the subject.

This is very close to what Freud postulates in those magnificent pages published after his death entitled *Conclusions, ideas and problems*. Freud sustains there that:

> To have" and "to be" in the child. The child tends to express the object link by means of identification. "I am the object". "Having" comes afterwards, it comes as a counterpart to the "being" after the object loss. "The breast is a part of me, I am the breast". Later, just: "I have it, that is, I am not [...][5] (p. 299).

What has to be distinguished is the lost part of the object which, coming to that place, conceals by means of its existence the loss itself.

Let us go further with this notion of the object. Lacan says that the object is that around which the drive does the *"tour"*. But he warns us that we must differentiate between the drive object as "turn" and the drive object as "trick".[6] He plays with two English terms that are close (homophonic) to the French word. Therefore, the object is both the revolving around a nothingness[7] and the trick, as a device, required in order not to see that one is revolving around a nothingness.

> The *objet petit a* is not the origin of the oral drive. It is not introduced as the original food, it is introduced from the fact that no food will ever satisfy the oral drive, except by circumventing the eternally lacking object.
>
> [...] Do not confuse it with that upon which the drive closes—this object, which is in fact simply the presence of a hollow, a void ... (p. 180).

The object by means of which the drive closes itself has to be differentiated each time; that is, the trick of the eternally lost object around which the drive revolves.

Regarding the erogenous zone, it is essential that we know that it has the structure of a border. This implies that it has to be differentiated from a surface (the digestive system, for instance). The erogenous zone has no extension, it is just a border.

Let us now posit the pathway, or better, its logic. In order to do this Lacan proposes to think of the creel. The creel is a fishing device that consists of a rush cylinder with a sort of funnel, pointing at the inside in one of its bases, and closed with a lid in the other, to be emptied. Remember what Lacan says in "Subversion of the subject ..." while introducing graph 1, in relation with the retrograde vector: "... the fish it hooks ... in its free movement ...". The creel is a fishing device which implies a closed surface, like a very special container.

The schema that appears in *Seminar 11* is:

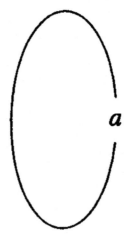

Schema 4.

This schema has to be considered in opposition to that of the subject inside the hole of the erogenous zone, and both have to be understood as being seen from the side. It must be remembered that the creel closes itself over the object, the fish. While one schema indicates that there is an object *a* working as a trick, the creel, the other indicates a circuit always reproducible around a hole (close to what the expression "vicious circle" means).

In order to advance further we shall work on the pathway by opposing the schema called by Lacan "the partial drive" to that of the "interior eight".

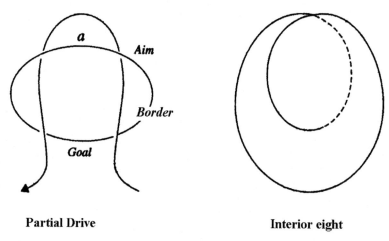

Partial Drive   **Interior eight**

Schema 5.

When opposing these two schemata we have to consider: 1) that regarding what Lacan calls the "partial drive" (and given that every drive is partial in relation to the biological finality) "aim" and "goal"[8] have to be distinguished. It is not the same to hit the blanc (aim) than to convert a goal (both English terms correspond to the German "*ziel*"); and 2) as we have just said, to hit the target or to convert a goal without leaving the return circuit of the drive.

Every time the drive is produced, we might say, "downside up", then its inversion cannot be avoided, for it to become "upside down". Here we have the structural effect of the demand (D)—always returning in its inverted form—in the field of the drive. It is always partial then, because it is a to and for movement, coming and going, and its only aim is to reach again the place from which it departed. The interior eight is another way to represent this.

This must be distinguished from what is represented, the same but through another logic, in the optical model by means of the vase embracing a bunch of flowers. Lacan states that it is by no means a vase because there is no relation container/contained. This is why Lacan so radically rejects Freud's "ovum schema",[9] for it is founded on the distinction container/contained, conceived three-dimensionally. The interior eight, precisely and in opposition to the ovum, allows us to conceive the inside and the outside in continuity. The name "interior eight" already indicates an operation by means of which the exterior is included in the interior. Thus, the circuit of the drive has the structure of an interior eight: it implies a circular border in relation to which a circular pathway will not ever be closed, fulfilled. The circuit will not generate the object able to obtrude it because the object is forever lost.

We have already seen, in our last class, how the circuit of the drive could be transformed from a continuous shape into an interior eight. The interior eight is a structure which, as such, is repeated a lot of times in the most diverse human situations; and this is because, due to the law of the signifier, every time there is redoubling in life, there is also antinomy. Every time a circuit tries to be repeated, the impossibility of its repetition is produced, and also, the impulse for reencountering it. This is one of the most important dimensions of what psychoanalysis calls the discontent of civilization.

The interior eight is the Möbius strip's border; it is also the knot that structures the torus. So its structure is to be found in places that are extremely important for psychoanalytical theory. In fact, the interior eight is a fundamental structure for human subjectivity. It is the psychoanalytical notion of repetition *par excellence*: a failed but repeated attempt at reproduction.

The theory of demand included in the formula of the drive (D) allows us to conceive the journey of the drive and its return Then, the effect of the signifier over the body is to highlight the erogenous zone as a border, and afterwards, the demand will define there another space. What is it the relationship between these two defined spaces? It is that of difference, for within the human world the possibility of repetition is always failed.

The basic problem to understand these considerations is that we are accustomed to departing from a false point: perceptive identity as one of the species of the psychical functioning; and that is a Freudian idea. This is the true problem: perceptive identity is impossible because every perception, determined by the function of the signifier, is characterized by the formula of the interior eight. This schema of the partial drive creates the illusion that the drive sweeps the field of the Other. But the drive as such does not go into the field of the Other. The circuit of the drive (its always impossible satisfaction of the drive) is not knotted to the Other. What in the exercise of the drive is knotted to the Other then? We know it: no Other is needed for the satisfaction of the erogenous zone, but it is indeed needed for love and for desire. There the dimension of the Other is included, not in the pure drive but in the knotting of the drive with desire and love.

Before finishing I shall make a comment on the four drives: oral, anal, scopic and invocatory. The important thing here is to work on how, at the level of the four drives, could we convince ourselves again that they are not natural. And this is necessary because, involuntarily, we still believe sometimes that "it is very natural".

What can explain why the oral always comes first, followed by the anal, and then, we cannot establish the order that corresponds to the scopic and the invocatory? The order oral-anal, can it be explained via nature? Lacan affirms:

> There is no relation of production between one of the partial drives and the next [...] there is no natural metamorphosis (p. 180).

The drive dialectic passing from oral to anal can by no means be understood as a natural metamorphosis. It is a metamorphosis, but not a natural one. However, there is still a problem: despite this fact, the oral continues being first and the anal second. The passage from oral to anal is due to the intervention of demand and not due to any dimension of the body conceived as natural. The order oral-anal is an effect of the presence of the function of demand. Oral implies the "demand of the Other". This dialectic begins with orality, not because of the predominance of sucking in the beginnings of life, but because in the beginnings of life the cry is interpreted by some Other as a call addressed to it; this is the logical beginning of human life: the transformation of the cry into call. And because the Other makes a demand out of the cry, the inevitable follows, the inverted effect: "one receives from the Other one's own demand in an inverted form", "demand of the Other", that is: sphincter control. Sphincter control is what inscribes the inversion of the demand. Now it is the Other who demands. So the sphincter control does nothing but metaphorize an effect of the structure: that the subject is demanded something only because somebody—Other—took his cry as a demand and then the structural inversion of demand is unavoidable. This is another justification for the presence of demand (D) in the formula of the drive, which is initially surprising.

It is the object of gift that the subject offers to respond to the demand of the Other. This is how the series (uite mysterious) laborated by Freud, may be understood: excrement-money-gift: they are all objects offered by the subject as a gift to the Other's demand.

The scopic object and the invocatory object remain. They are characterized, precisely, for being more linked to the object of desire than to the object of demand. This is what excludes them from the series. Due to the structure of the speaking being, the voice and the gaze tend to appear as lacking objects: the object gaze is precisely that which is not seen in the scopic field; and the voice is what is forgotten always in the field of speech.

Notes

1. English version: On Feminine Sexuality. The Limits of Love and Knowledge: The Seminar of Jacques Lacan, Book XX Encore 1972–1973. Ed. J-A Miller. Trans. B. Fink.
2. *Es* in German, Id.
3. Jacques Lacan, Seminar XI, p. 185.
4. In French in the original.
5. My translation.
6. In English in the original.
7. The original text says *"una nada"*, as a countable noun. I decided to retain the definitive article in order to maintain the implicit reference to the object.
8. In English in the original (both words).
9. Introduced by Freud in *The Ego and the Id* and in conference 31st of the *New introductory conferences to psychoanalysis*, "The decomposition of psychic personality" (1933). See also Chapter Two.

CHAPTER THIRTEEN

S(Ⱥ): Being, *jouissance* and desire

The subject for this class—and the following—will be S(Ⱥ); an arduous, an extremely difficult theme to work on. I propose to you that we begin by entitling it: "Being, *jouissance* and desire" (this title could make the bravest back down).

Let us start by departing from this quotation from *"Subversion of the subject ...":*

> What the graph now offers us is situated at the point at which every signifying chain prides itself on looping its signification (p. 349).

Once again we have the code (C) and the message (M), but elaborated as treasure of the signifier, A, and the signified of the Other, s(A). Lacan states that the last floor of the graph posits again a circle: the circle of the completed graph. And he also posits that this circle closes itself (loops itself) upon a signification which, passing by S(Ⱥ), flows into s(A), which—actually—is the closing of signification.

$$\begin{array}{ccc} \textbf{(M)'} \ \text{---} \ \textbf{(C)'} & \quad \textbf{s(A)'} \ \text{---} \ \textbf{A'} \\ | \qquad | & \quad | \qquad | \\ \textbf{(M)} \ \text{---} \ \textbf{(C)} & \quad \textbf{s(A)} \ \text{---} \ \textbf{A} \end{array}$$

Schema 1.

More radically, Lacan states that it is at S(A̸) that the signification closes itself at the unconscious level; thus, S(A̸) has the function of s(A) at the level of the unconscious. This seems to be, at first sight, contradictory.

Second quotation:

> If we are to expect such an effect from the unconscious enunciation, it is to be found here in S(A̸),[1] and read as: signifier of the lack in the Other, inherent in its very function as the treasure of the signifier (p. 349).

Therefore, the closing of this circle is produced from the unconscious enunciation. We must be careful here, for it is here—precisely—that one tends to get lost.

Regarding the opposition: lower chain/upper chain, I have already proposed to you another opposition: statement/enunciation. We shall posit it today in these new terms: the content of what is said/the act of saying it. It is the unconscious enunciation that is at stake, which we will consider as the act of unconscious saying—leaving the contents aside.

Immediately after that Lacan adds:

> And this is so even though the Other is required (*che vuoi*) to respond to the value of this treasure, that is to say, to reply, from its place in the lower chain certainly, but also in the signifiers that constitute the upper chain, in terms of drive, in other words (p. 349).

The Other is asked to respond to the value of the treasure, which is localized in (A). Notice that "value" and "treasure" are very similar words. Later on, Lacan will define Other as the battery of the signifier, and this is not the same; we shall further establish the difference between treasure and battery. The Other is then required to respond to the value it has as a treasure. This is a question posed to the Other, A, that receives its answer at the level of the unconscious enunciation, of the unconscious act of speaking.

One more quotation from "*Subversion of the subject ...*":

> The lack referred to here is indeed that which I have already formulated: that there is no Other of the Other. But is this a mark made by the Unbeliever of the truth[2] really the last word that is worth giving in reply to the question, 'What does the Other want of me?', when we, the analysts, are its mouthpiece? Surely not, and precisely because there is nothing doctrinal about our office. We are answerable to no ultimate truth; we are neither for nor against any particular religion (p. 349).

Thus, at the level of the unconscious enunciation, the Other is interrogated about its value as treasure of the signifier. Remember that when we worked on the term "treasure", we said that it was applied to both valuable objects and to the place where these objects are kept, but we also said that the notion of treasure itself necessarily implies incompleteness. What does this lack in the value of the treasure imply at the level of the Other? Lacan says that there is no Other of the Other.

In the Other, there is no function, which can guarantee it; and what happens is that the subject demands from him a guarantee. If we call this function of guarantee 'the Other', then there is no function in the Other of Other to itself. That is how we can affirm that there is no Other of the Other. If we go to the field of formal logic, this lack should be enunciated: there is no meta-language. That is to say, there is no language able to logically "make coherent" another language considered as object-language, given that the former, being a language, could never guarantee the latter (because, strictly speaking, it could not guarantee itself).

We know that we are slaves of the punctuation of our message made by the Other, and we know that the signification is of the Other, s(A). In this sense, we already find here a lack of power at the level of the speaking being, who cannot produce his own message without the Other. But despite this, we keep on trusting in the guarantee of the Other: it is thus the Other who imposes the message (given that I, the subject, am impotent for it). What Lacan posits is that this Other, who we suppose is a guarantee, lacks himself a guarantee.

The problem deduced from this lack of guarantee of the Other of guarantee, is what Lacan calls "No-Faith" [see note 2]. We lack the guarantee for the true of the truth. This can also be considered in relation to formal logic, given the use it makes of truth, for instance, in the tables of truth. When what is at stake is language, signifiers, a table of truth cannot be made out of what a subject says, for the proof of the presence of the subject is that he can lie. If you recall the Krakovia and Lemberg joke, it showed how the subject can lie, and that he can do it in the most subtle ways, for example, by telling the truth.[3]

However, given that we (psychoanalysts) are the mouthpieces of the locum of the Other in the analytic experience, how do we manage to make the ultimate true word, the ultimate word, work? There is no guarantee, then there will not be ultimate truth. There is no ultimate word that the analyst may enunciate from the place of the Other, for analysts do not sustain any doctrine, in the sense of religious doctrines. How is it that, at a religious or a philosophical level, the fact that there is no guarantee of the Other is enunciated? God has died. This is, doubtless, a very complex issue. Everything seems to indicate that the fact that there is no Other of the Other is the ultimate truth that the analytic experience, and especially, the Lacanian orientation, can offer to the subject. We might suppose that "God has died" is precisely the "beyond the Father" that the right direction of the Lacanian cure implies. However, Lacan says it is not; he says this is nothing but a form of religion, and not of the analytic practice.

Lacan asks us not to forget that, in terms of the graph, it is only by means of the drive that we get out of the Other, A, arriving at this point where the circle is closed, through S(A̷). If this pathway implies that we pass through the drive, it therefore introduces the issue of the body (schema 2).

Schema 2.

It is already quite enough that at this point I had to situate the dead Father in the Freudian myth. But a myth is not enough to support a rite, and psychoanalysis is not the rite of the Oedipus complex—a point that I shall develop later.

No doubt the corpse is a signifier, but Moses's tomb is as empty for Freud as that of Christ was for Hegel. Abraham revealed his mystery to neither of them (Lacan, 2006, p. 350).

We were on the right pathway when distinguishing psychoanalysis and religion in relation to the S($Ⱥ$). Abraham is the father who founded the three monotheist religions: Islamism, Judaism and Christianity. Lacan says that the dead Father is a signifier. This is no surprise for us, we (in psychoanalytical theory) have always given it this status and we speak of the Name-of-the-Father. Every time we conceive the paternal function through the signifier, we associate it with the death of the Father, both on the side of the common myth and on that of the neurotic's individual myth. But Lacan adds that although it is true that the corpse functions as a signifier, this does not solve another problem: that of the empty tomb.

In order to understand what Lacan is referring to, it is necessary, I think, to recall the conditions of Moses's and Christ's deaths. Moses was not allowed to cross the Jordan River: God decided that he had to die on this side of the river. But not only did he decide this, he also stated that the location of his grave was to remain forever unknown. His tomb is not known. On the other hand, the grave where Christ was buried, the Saint Grave, had a very different fate. However, they have one thing in common: it is an empty grave. Christ was buried and the following day the grave was empty (although a big rock covered its entrance). It is in this sense that Lacan says that both graves are empty. Moses and Christ were two big legislators (unlike Abraham). Lacan states that their corpses worked as signifiers of the dead Father both for Freud and for Hegel. But what they both missed in their respective analysis was the fact that the graves were empty. And Lacan adds that this omission results from not having taken into account the mystery of Abraham.

I do not know exactly what Lacan is referring to, but fortunately the text goes on and we can take the opportunity to establish the connections, able to throw light on this point. A few paragraphs ahead, Lacan introduces the formula: $\sqrt{-1}$, and he highlights that this formula is produced whenever the proper name appears. But before thus introducing the issue of the proper name, Lacan presents the question of the inherence of the "–1".

Taking into consideration the question of the proper name and its relation with the logical problem of the "–1", I would bet that the mystery Lacan is referring to with regards to Abraham is that of the pact, Abraham's pact with God. This pact is at the origin of what later happened to both Moses and Christ. We shall take two elements of this pact into consideration: first, the practice of circumcision is founded there (which will automatically lead us to the problem of the phallus) and, second, from this pact comes the transformation of the name "Abrám" into "Abraham", as well as his wife's name, "Saray", which becomes "Sarah". The pact that is at stake involves circumcision and changing one letter of the name.

We should take Lacan's indication regarding how both Freud and Hegel missed this problem of the function of the names and the phallus, both issues being beyond the legislative function of the Father. It is not the pact related to giving somebody a name and the castration threat (both themes on the paternal side) that is at stake, but the function of the proper name and the phallic signifier within the structure of the signifier. Both functions, extremely close to the S($\cancel{A}$), are localized, given their place within the structure, beyond the Father.

Therefore, what is at stake in the analytic practice (especially on the analyst's side) is not to embody, like a mouthpiece, an ultimate truth (as the castrating truth "the Father has died" could be), because as Lacan proposes, neither is there an ultimate truth nor, consequently, is there any possibility of embodying it. And as no "ultimate" one exists, the opposition that Lacan proposes is: the hole (the empty grave) or the corpse (considered as a signifier).

This leads us to posit what you already know as the development and progress of Lacan's teaching: to go beyond the Father. But going beyond the Father does not mean that the analyst has to incarnate the function of the dead Father; it is not about that. Going beyond the father is the way in which psychoanalysis distinguishes itself from any religion, and is also the way of the direction of the cure.

Personally, I will begin [...] (p. 350).

How is it that Lacan says "I will begin" when "*Subversion of the subject ...*" is almost finishing? Far from arriving at an ultimate, or final truth, what Lacan proposes is "to begin", he proposes a way that begins.

> [...] I will begin with what is articulated in the sigla S(Ⱥ) by being first of all a signifier. My definition of a signifier (there is no other) is as follows: a signifier is that which represents the subject for another signifier. This signifier will therefore be the signifier for[4] which all the other signifiers represent the subject [...] (p. 350).

What is at issue here is, not to arrive at an ultimate truth because there is no such thing, but to go on, to retake, to begin, according to each case, departing from the hole that the structure presents to the subject. We ought to do it, both in the conceptualization and in the practice, by means of S(Ⱥ). In the quotation Lacan states that S(Ⱥ) represents the subject for another signifier, for "another signifier" in the sense of "any" other signifier.

> [...] that is to say, in the absence of this signifier, all the other signifiers represent nothing, since nothing is represented only *for* something else.
> And since the battery of signifiers [...] (p. 350).

Here Lacan calls the (A) "battery", whereas before he had said treasure; and he had also said that the Other had to respond to the value of the treasure. A battery (kitchen utensils or guns, for instance) is always complete, no matter how many pieces it contains. There could exist another battery with a different number of elements, but nothing is lacking from either one of the different batteries. On the contrary, the treasure is never complete, all. If there was a treasure which contained "all" the gold in the world, it would be worth nothing (for the gold would automatically loose its exchange value).

> And since the battery of signifiers, as such, is by that very fact complete, this signifier can only be a line [*trait*][5] that is drawn from its circle without being able to be counted part of it. It can be symbolized by the inherence of a (–1) in the whole set of signifiers (p. 350).

The problem is not that the Father cannot be trusted anymore; the question is how to go from the Father towards the signifier. But, towards which signifier? Towards the signifier which allows all the other signifiers to represent the subject, and this signifier is not that of the Father.

We face now a logical problem. Lacan speaks here once again of the circle. I shall suggest that we consider the battery of signifiers to be located on the right side of the graph. We shall include in that battery, obviously, all of the signifiers. But the problem we face now is that one signifier is left on its own on one side, and all the rest are on the other side. Therefore, if all the signifiers are on one side, the signifier that remains on the other side should also be on the right side. Thus, this S($\not{A}$) is a signifier that is not in the locus[6] where all the signifiers are. In other words and to be more precise: it is a signifier which is not in the locus of the signifiers. But if it is not in the locus of the signifier, is it actually a signifier? The problem is that Lacan calls it "signifier" and not "incognita", "lack", "hole". Let us see it in a schema.

S($\not{A}$)	$\leftarrow$	($\$ \lozenge D$)
Signifier of a lack in (A)	$\rightarrow$	**(Treasure of the unconscious signifier)**
$\downarrow$		$\uparrow$
s(A)	$\leftarrow$	A
Signified of the Other	$\rightarrow$	**Battery of the signifier**
		(all of the signifiers)

Schema 3.

We began by substituting (A) to Jakobson's code (C). (A) is the treasure or battery of signifiers, the locus where all the signifiers are lodged. But it happens that there is now one signifier, S($\not{A}$), which is excluded from this locus of the signifier and which is, moreover, the point where the circle of signification is closed. This is the logical problem that we must approach first.

We face a signifier which is outside the locus of all of the signifiers; it is what it is not being what it is: a signifier. The problem is, in sum, that we keep on calling it "signifier".

And even more, if the graph has the structure of the Klein group (as we constantly state) how come Lacan places a signifier, S($\not{A}$), on the side of the signification, s(A)? The seems to be a total anomaly.

What is the other anomaly already discovered by Lacan, the other signifier which was different from all the rest? The one of the Name-of-the-Father. And why was it different from the others? Because it was the signifier of the Law in the Other. And why does that make it different? Because it is the signifier that legislates all the others. Now Lacan is positing that, despite inscribing particular differences in (A) and despite being the signifier of the law, the Name-of-the-Father is a signifier like the others. Remember that when postulating the Name-of-the-Father as a signifier with a structure different from the others, the problem was that it became or functioned as the Other (A) of the Other (A), (AᴬA), which contradicts our: "there is no Other of the Other". There is only one signifier which is truly different from all the others: S(Ⱥ).

Lacan states that this signifier cannot be but a line[7] which is drawn from its circle without the possibility of being counted as part of it. Let us recall the following quotation from "The agency of the letter in the unconscious ...":

> [...] rings of a necklace that is a ring in another necklace made of rings[8] (2006, p. 169).

Here Lacan is giving us the structure of the signifying chain. These rings, in topology, are called torus. Lacan says, then, that the signifier that is at issue in S(Ⱥ), this line, this trace (a signifier), is like an extra turn that will never be counted together with the other turns of the demand; there is a structural difference there.

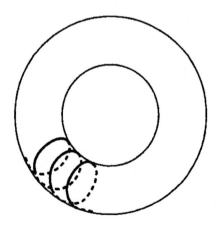

Schema 4.

If we conceive the torus as being constituted by the coiling around a void of the failing repeated turns of the demand, as the schema represents them, we can notice that after an x number of turns we have either done one extra turn or counted one less turn. This turn is the one whose mark we are talking about when referring to S($\cancel{A}$).

In order for this problem to become more intuitive, think of the movements of the Earth around the Sun. Each time the Earth rotates fully around its axis we call this a day and there are 365. There is also turn around the Sun (translation), which is an extra one, but which—in relation to the 365 ones—is a turn in less, for it cannot be counted as another day. So, the Earth turns 365 times plus one. The translation turn is an extra circle. It is a turn (metaphor for a peculiar signifier) which can never be counted together with the other turns, together with the other signifiers; it is of a different nature, despite being a turn. This turn qua signifier is that which allows all the other signifiers to represent the subject.

In order to account for the operation required when conceiving this signifier which is different from every other signifier, Lacan proposes that we work with $\sqrt{-1}$.

> As such it is inexpressible, but its operation is not inexpressible, for it is that which is produced whenever a proper noun is spoken. Its statement equals its signification [...] namely:
>
> **S (signifier)**
> ----------------= **(the statement), with S = (–1), produces:**
> **s (signified)**
> $s = \sqrt{-1}$

Lacan states that this signifier is inexpressible because, in fact, it is the inherence of a –1; but its operation is not, and it is present each time, in every act when, for instance, a proper name is spoken. This is an interesting case, since the subject supposes, every time the proper name appears, that it represents him in a special way. Remember that this issue is being posited in relation to the unconscious enunciation, in relation to the act of saying rather than to the content of what is said.

To speak someone's name—to speak our own name—implies an operation. This operation is that of this signifier that we must conceive. But this signifier cannot be spoken. This is why, if one said: "one signifier is lacking", one would strictly speaking be saying: "I deny that such a lack of the signifier exists", since what I say occupies the empty space of the one that is lacking. This is why the signifier of the Name-of-the-Father is of no use for this function, on the contrary, it conceals it. This is why Moses and Christ conceal (for Freud and Hegel respectively) the mystery of Abraham's name transformation: they did not take into consideration the act of pronouncing that name. Now, I easily say "the pact between Abraham and God", but that pact implies God's name, which is also inexpressible (unpronounceable). The same problem is found on both sides of the pact.

Which is the shortest formula to write the operation of the signifier? The Saussurean algorithm, as Lacan does it: S/s, the signifier on top, a bar that resists signification, and the signified below. But in the case of our signifier S(A̶), what would we put on top? The inherence of a −1, namely: we cannot write anything because it is inexpressible. Otherwise, it would be the replacement of the lack, its obstruction.

But in the cases of proper names, something different happens: its statement becomes equivalent to its signification; as happens with the signifier we are working on.

Let us go to the book by Kasner and Newman, *Mathematics and Imagination*, where they teach the problem of the π number, imaginary numbers (i) and the number e. What they posit there is amazingly close to what Lacan requires at the level of the concept. The first thing they do is to write it in such a way that the word "pie" is formed (πie), a great joke, whose sense, obviously, cannot be fulfilled.

So, we know that π is 3.14159265 ..., and e is 2.718281 ... The three points mean three different things: 1) that the decimals are not periodic; 2) that the numbers which follow are infinite; and 3) the most interesting bit, that although an infinite series of numbers follow, each number added will never be surpassed by the those which come afterwards. Example: 3.14, no matter how many other decimals we add to it, will never become 3.15. Therefore, numbers like π are made equivalent by means of an operation, "jump to the limit", but we will never be able to fully speak them, because they do not exist as numbers. We then write a part as if it was a number, but it is not a number. The same happens with e.

So, neither π nor e are numbers. In consequence, whenever we work with them, there is a jump, a cut.

Let us think of this equation:

$$X^2 + 1 = 0$$

Can you see any anomaly in this formula? Apparently there is none. But if you analyze it, you will soon notice it is a monster: something that when squared and added 1 produces 0. It has to be something that when squared produces –1. And we know that no number squared produces a negative number.

Let us consider now the following triangle:

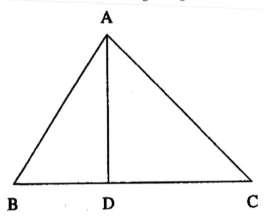

Schema 5.

The AD line is called the geometric mean, and it is calculated: $\sqrt{BD \times DC}$. That is to say:

$$AD = \sqrt{BD \times DC}$$

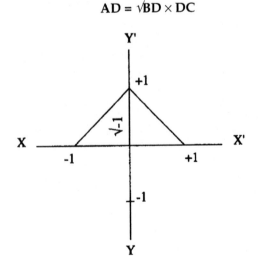

Schema 6.

We shall now consider the Cartesian plane, but as Gauss proposed it:

On the left of Y–Y' the negative X are written, and below X–X' the negatives Y are written. Let us draw a triangle going from –1 to +1 over XX', and from there towards +1 over Y', and coming back to –1 over Y. Let us calculate now the geometric mean of this triangle: it is obviously, 1 divided Y, (1/Y). Given that it is the same case as in the previous triangle, which would be the formula of its geometric mean? The formula is:

$$S \text{ (geometric mean)} = \sqrt{-1} \times +1 = \sqrt{-1} = i$$

As the square root of $\sqrt{+1}$ is 1, then $S = \sqrt{-1}$. The geometric mean of this triangle is then $\sqrt{-1}$: an imaginary number, i.

Kasner and Newman[9] (2001) say in their book:

> The two systems of logs to the two bases, 10 and e (the Briggs and the natural base respectively), are the principal ones still in use, with e predominating. Like π, the number e is transcendental ad like π it is what P. W. Bridgman names a "program of procedure", rather than a number, since it can never be completely expressed [...] (p. 84).

This is what Lacan calls "inexpressible". π and e can never be completely expressed.

The quotation follows:

> [...] in a finite number of digits, (2) as the root of an algebraic equation with integer coefficients, (3) as a nonterminating but repeating decimal. It can only be expressed with accuracy as the limit of a convergent infinite series or of a continued fraction.
>
> [...] $\sqrt{-1}$ is the best known imaginary. Euler represented it by the symbol "i" which is still in use. It is idle to be concerned with the question, "What number when multiplied by itself equals –1?" Like all other numbers, i is a symbol which represents an abstract but very precise idea. It obeys all the rules of arithmetic [...] Its obedience to these rules and its manifold uses and applications justify its existence regardless of the fact that it may be an anomaly (Kasner and Newman, 2001, p. 93).

It is pointless to ask oneself which numbers correspond to π or to e because they are not numbers; they are symbols which represent an abstract but precise idea.

> Extension of the use of imaginaries has led to complex numbers of the form $a + ib$, where a and b are *real* numbers (as distinguished from imaginaries). Thus $3 + 4i$, $1 - 7i$, $2 + 3i$ are examples of complex numbers.
>
> By virtue of the peculiar properties of i, complex numbers may be used to represent both magnitude and direction. With their aid some of the most essential notions in physics such as velocity, force, acceleration, etc., are conveniently represented.
>
> Enough has now been said to indicate the general nature of i, its purpose and importance in mathematics, its challenge to and final victory over the cherished tenets of common sense. Undaunted by its paradoxical appearance, mathematicians used it as they used π and e. The result has been to make possible almost the entire edifice of modern physical science (Kasner and Newman, 2001, pp. 95–103).

Lacan took a mathematical development of the time that completely breaks with common sense: A number with the property of not being any number, and on top of which nothing less than the whole edifice of modern physics lies.

> This is what the subject lacks in order to think himself exhausted by his *cogito*, namely, that which is unthinkable for him (2006, p. 350).

That the subject can finally localize himself in the Being as "I think", is prevented by the S($\cancel{A}$), for it is the absolutely unthinkable, the turn beyond any demand.

> But where does this being, who appears in some way defective in the sea of proper nouns, originate?
>
> We cannot ask this question of the subject as 'I'[*je*]. He lacks everything needed to know the answer, since if this subject 'I' was dead, he would not, as I said earlier, know it. He does not

know, therefore, that I am alive. How, therefore, will 'I' prove to myself that I am? (2006, p. 350).

The problem for the understanding of this paragraph is that we do not know of whom Lacan is talking about, since he speaks not only of the subject. The particle that leads us to confusion is 'I'; what happens is that Lacan cannot help, in so far as he is a speaking subject, that every time he talks about the Being of the subject, the unconscious enunciation appears—with regard to himself. This is the logical foundation of the *"etourdit"*;[10] we have no time to consider this more fully during this course.

What does that 'I' indicate? A shifter: the particle indicating who speaks in what is said; the particle which indicates who the subject of the enunciation is in a particular statement. Lacan is not doing philosophy here; he is in the middle of the problem about the Being of the subject, the speaking subject; and in such a way that it is not possible to talk about it without talking; but while talking, he falls into the same problem he is trying to solve.

> For I can only just prove to the Other that he exists, not, of course, with the proofs for the existence of God, which over the centuries he has been killed of, but by loving him, a solution introduced by the Christian *kerygma* (p. 350).

The problem is not the existence of the Other; the problem is our own existence.

> Indeed, it is too precarious a solution for me even to think of using it as a means of circumventing our problem, namely: 'what am "I"?' (p. 351).

Lacan is not asking "who am I?", in the sense of the recognition; he is neither asking "who loves the Other?", although the Being of the subject can already be localized there. He is asking: "what am I [*Je*]?". And he answers:

> 'I' am in the place from which a voice is heard clamouring 'the universe is a defect in the purity of Non-Being' (p. 351).

I am in the place where a voice clamours, where it is as an object that the voice counts, that it matters, and not due to the content of what is spoken. And those clamoured sayings[11] affirm, not that there is Non-Being in the universe, but that the universe is a defect in the purity of Non-Being. It is there that I am: where, in respect to the Non-Being, effect of emptiness of the signifier, there is an impurity, where in the non being of the signifier appears the impurity that the object, the voice, for instance, introduces.

> And not without reason, for by protecting itself this place makes Being itself languish. This place is called *Jouissance*, and it is the absence of it that makes the universe vain (p. 351).

What is it that Lacan calls *jouissance*? It is not a pleasure activity; it is not even suffering, but an empty place. Let us go back. Lacan states that the voice in which I am says that there is impurity in the Non-Being, that there is no ultimate truth, and that there is impurity even in the mortifying effect of the signifier. And then he adds: "and not without reason". It is not without reason that I am in the place where a voice is heard clamouring. So what happens is that the signifier kills the thing, but that there is a mark saying that it does not kill it entirely; the object remains, for instance, the voice accompanying the enunciation. Then he says:

> [...] for by protecting itself this place makes Being itself languish (p. 351).

Which place? Precisely, the place from where it is clamoured that the universe is a defect in the impurity of Non-Being. That place is called *jouissance* and its absence would make the universe vain. So it is the lack of this place, and not that of *jouissance*, which would make the universe vain. In French, *vain*: vain. It leads to the vain graves, the empty graves, of which we have talked enough. It has a second meaning: "lacking consistency". The following paragraph refers, precisely, to the inconsistency of the Other. Also a third one (literary): "with no value, useless, insignificant, and frivolous". And a fourth one: "with no foundation".

What Lacan proposes is, then, that *jouissance* is the place of the subject. And what is it that place? It is the inherence of a "−1" implied in the unconscious enunciation. Every time one clamours [articulates] something is produced which annuls the whole Non-Being,[12] an impurity, from where we extract the theory of the Superego. Every time a certain drive satisfaction is forbidden for the Subject (S) by the Other (A), the subject will inevitably localize itself in this clamour of the prohibition, as *jouissance*. Remember that in French, *jouissance* is homophonous to "I hear". Wherever I hear that a certain drive satisfaction is forbidden to me, I will localize myself exactly there as *jouissance*.

My Being is placed in the place where something disturbs in the Non-Being, which says no to the whole Non-Being. And this place of the Being of the subject is called "*jouissance*". In the graph:

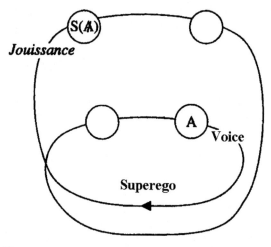

Schema 7.

Notice that (A) and S(Ⱥ) are in continuity if you accept that we close the graph of desire as an interior eight, as I have proposed several times, and also notice that this pathway leads to *jouissance*.

In previous classes we stated that the subject as desire is a remainder, a sprout of that which of the need did not pass into demand; the remainder of that subtraction as a lack is the subject as desire. *Jouissance* will be the localization of the subject, which implies the body. The body no longer as lack but as that which, out of the nothingfication[13] of the signifier, remains as satisfaction. On the side of desire, lack of being [*manqué-à-etre*], on the side of *jouissance*, the Being as what resists the "nothingfication" by the signifier.

Notes

1. A. Sheridan writes S(Ø).
2. Lacan says « *ce trait du Sans-Foi de la verité* ». Literally « Without-Faith ». See Écrits II, Éd. Du Seuil, p. 299. The Spanish version translates it as "*No Fe*", literally "No-Faith". See Escritos 2, Siglo XXI Ed., p. 798.
3. See Chapter Six.
4. I would suggest the following translation of Lacan's sentence: "this signifier will therefore be the signifier thanks to which [or due to which] all the other signifiers represent the subject ...". The meaning changes: it is not that all the other signifiers represent the subject for this signifier, but that without this one "all the others [would] represent nothing".
5. The French word "*trait*" can also mean "trace" and "trait".
6. See page 336, Ecrits. A selection.
7. See note 4 above.
8. See note 7, Chapter Two.
9. See note 2, Chapter Five.
10. Reference to Lacan's writing "L'étourdit", published in 1973 in Scilicet, 4, Le Seuil.
11. See note 19, Chapter Three.
12. "Whole Non-Being" or "Non-Being all". Alludes to the logic of the Not-All.
13. In Spanish "*nadificación*". It refers to the act through which something becomes a "nothingness" ("*néant*" in French).

CHAPTER FOURTEEN

S($\overline{A}$): "Being (Res), *jouissance* and desire" (II)

Today I will propose to revisit the logic—rather than the quotations—of what we discussed in our last class. In this sense and regarding the suggested title: "Being, desire and *jouissance*", I shall propose a slight variation: "Being (*res*), desire and *jouissance*". Without doubt I am thus introducing the Cartesian opposition *res cogitans / res extensa*.

Despite what I have just said, I will present to you some statements (as few as possible), taken from Lacan's texts, and which I will use as the steps for my argument—except the first one, which has the structure of an axiom-, they can all be found in "*Subversion of the subject ...*"

> [...] every signifying chain prides itself on looping its significa-
> tion (p. 349).

Every signifying chain—from the moral perspective of values—prides itself on looping its signification. And, obviously, every chain honoured with that pride will as a result, be finite, for it is honoured precisely in so far as its loop [circle] is closed. This is what we call "message": when a chain loops on its signification. However, the point is that, in the context of Lacan's teaching, that signification is of the Other, $s(A)$. Nevertheless, we tend to conceive signifying chains as being infinite. I believe that almost all of us think that "S_1-S_2" is a formalized reduction of "S_1-S_2-S_3...S_n". So we must go slowly through this statement that I am proposing to you as an axiom.

The closing point is there where the message is produced, and this message is the Other's. But where in the graph does this occur, at what level? We, psychoanalysts, count at least two chains: one, that of what the subject says (the statement), and another one, supposed by the psychoanalyst: the enunciation. We have already worked on how the inferior chain circle, although it tends towards the infinite metonymy, closes itself up at $s(A)$. On the contrary, in the case of the unconscious enunciation, the superior chain, the message closes itself up at $S(\cancel{A})$.

A noticeable conceptual disparity appears here, for we are stating that the closing up of signification is produced at a signifier. This seems to be contradictory. But do not forget that we are working with the "other scene"[1] supposed by the psychoanalyst: the unconscious. Freud clearly indicated that there are only representations in the unconscious. No affects, no values, no significations will be found there. The unconscious chain closes its message up at a signifier. It could not be otherwise because, as such, significations do not participate of the unconscious. But the signifier at which the superior chain closes itself up is $S(\cancel{A})$, which is the signifier of the lack of a signifier in the Other.

It is important for you not to forget that, according to Lacan, the operation of the unconscious as such, and also the operation of the psychoanalyst on the unconscious, is reading, and not listening. It is "agency of the letter" and not of the signifier. So, how do we read the point where the message of the unconscious loops on itself? It is read: signifier of a lack in the Other. And Lacan clarifies that this lack in the Other is a specific one, it is not any lack whatsoever. Something lacks which is inherent to the function of the Other: being, below and right, treasure of signifiers, A. When demanding of the Other, when asking the Other about the value of that treasure, we find out that one term is lacking. That is the one that corresponds to the subject, in so far as it (the subject) must discount himself from the signifying count. The signifier that the Other lacks is precisely the one that corresponds to me as a subject, in so far as it is me who poses the question.

The Other, A, has the function of representing the treasure of the signifier, but when asked to account for the value of that treasure, in relation to one particular subject, he who poses the question (to himself and to the Other), it is impossible to avoid the evidence: that one is lacking. But we have to remember that this lack in the value of A, which affects the inferior chain, is only registered in the superior chain. It is in the "other chain" that the problem of the inherence of the lack of a signifier in the Other, S(Ⱥ), is posed and dealt with. However, in so far as it is the upper chain that is at stake, it automatically relates to the drive. If we say "drive" then, we must not forget that we are saying that it has repercussions in the body.

I would like to make a clarification here. You might have noticed that neither the dreams, nor the slips of the tongue, nor the jokes have—or seem to have—anything to do with this inherence of the lack of at least one signifier in the Other. The particularities of every subject's unconscious, let us put it this way, appear in them. In order to understand Lacan's ideas, we have to understand that the message that we have just defined serves as a message of the unconscious for every subject. At this level we do not find the particularity of each case. What Lacan is inscribing here is what each of the messages deciphered at the unconscious level (in any analysis) have in common with every other message at that same level (in any other analysis whatsoever). This is equivalent to the point reached by Freud in the analysis of the forgetting of the name "Signorelli": sexuality and death. The inherence of a "–1" presented by the signifier of a lack in the Other, S(Ⱥ), is what every message of the unconscious has in common. This is a property—the only Lacan gives us, together with the incidence over the body—that characterizes every message of the unconscious. Every message of the unconscious will always have this property: every signifier representing the subject will do so with regard to S(Ⱥ); and this independently of the differences of each particular case and moment, which—by definition—cannot be inscribed in S(Ⱥ).

This lack, which inscribes the signifier of a lack in the Other, means, precisely, that there is no Other of the Other. However, by inscribing it, by marking it as a signifier, S(Ⱥ), it affirms the function of the Other, not an omnipotent Other, but a lacking one. Through S(Ⱥ), Lacan is not positing that there is no Other, no A, because indeed, not only does it exist but it operates in all of us. Subjectivity, if I may say so, is founded on it: the existence of an Other is a condition of the existence of the subject. What Lacan states is that there is no A of the A; that is to say, A is not identical to itself. The A = A identity is interdicted in the symbolic order. Strictly speaking, we cannot write any letter that is identical to itself.

Thus, the lack does not appear when we try to apply the function "A" to the subject, but when we try to apply it to itself. In the same way, there is no S = S either, for when the S looked for the identity with itself, it founded (without wanting it, we may say) the S_2.

The same structure applies to the case of the truth: there is no truth able to articulate itself as true (this is why we cannot say that the truth is true). Every truth, in order to postulate itself as true, has to say about itself that it is not lying; the same applies to every lie.

This is the point of Without-Faith[2] of the truth, the point where there cannot be truth of the truth. But Lacan states that the truth has the structure of fiction. This can be understood within the context of bivalent logic: truth does not get truth value by itself, but through falsity. Therefore, every truth operates in relation to a possible lie. Then, the fact that there is no truth of the truth, by no means implies that there exists no truth; we are completely affected by this issue of truth.

Science works with the notion of exactitude; magic and religion, as well as psychoanalysis, work with the notion of truth. And what is the difference between the use we make of the notion of truth and that of religion or magic? That the statement "there is no truth of the truth" does not operate or function, for us, as an ultimate, last truth. That is not the last thing that can be said. In other words, "there is no Other of the Other", "there is no truth of the truth", these statements do not close the message up. And this has, precisely, the following virtue: that our knowledge does not become a doctrine affirming that there is no ultimate truth (because in that case the message of psychoanalysis would be in respect of the Other and not of the Subject).

Concerning God, the message of psychoanalysis is neither negative nor positive; neither is it the religious doctrine of God's omnipotence nor the philosophical doctrine of God's inexistence (God is dead). What interests us as analysts is how that lack of the Other of the Other affects the subject, which is our true object. Psychoanalysis analyzes the structure of the Other in so far as it determines the subject's position—and not in itself. In other words, we depart from the Other, but in order to take that dialectic to the side of the subject.

Thus, this inherence of the "–1" in the Other has, for us, the status of what the subject lacks in order to think himself exhausted by his *cogito*. If we knot the function of thinking to the signifier, we can then affirm that at the level of the thinking there will always be a lack. No subject can exhaust himself by his thinking, in the sense of finding himself in the Being. Given that the subject has to think of himself with the Other, and given that there is an inherence of a lack in the Other, we can deduce that the logical mechanism of the *cogito* ("I think, therefore I am") is falsely posited. The subject cannot find his being by means of thinking; via his thinking he will always be led to a point of lack (any obsessional thinking will show you this).

Now that we have affirmed that neither the Other nor the truth can guarantee themselves, the problem becomes that of the subject's Being. In order to advance in the analysis, at this point, we need to knot the upper level: the drive ($ \$ \Diamond D $) and the body. The question is then: where does the Being come from, if it does not come from thinking?

This is, according to Lacan, the departure point (of psychoanalysis, of its practice and, why not, of the entry into analysis): What (Being) am I?

Given that there is no Other of the Other, but there is indeed Other of the Subject, what Lacan posits is that we have to go back to the structure of the Other as such, in order to see how the question of the subject's Being is solved.

Let us reconsider the following quotation from "Subversion of the subject ...", which we worked on last class:

> I will begin with what is articulated in the sigla S(Ⱥ) by being first of all a signifier. My definition of a signifier (there is no other) is as follows: a signifier is that which represents the subject for another signifier (p. 350).

I shall propose that you "read" this formula, for it may be saying: "the signifier is that which represents the subject for another signifier", but also: "the signifier is what represents the subject for an Other, whenever this Other has the status of a signifier". S(Ⱥ) is the signifier by which all the other signifiers represent the subject. This signifier, in its second function, inscribes the particularity of the Subject in relation to the Other. And that particularity, being the subject's particularity, corresponds to every subject and not to each subject. Each subject's particularity, the "case by case", is not our theme today.

Lacan says that this is not the way Claude Lévi-Strauss believes: it is not the function of zero in arithmetic what is at issue but, precisely, the lack of the zero symbol.

Let us make one more step by means of the following quotation:

'I' am in the place from which a voice is heard clamouring 'the universe is a defect in the purity of Non-Being' (p. 351).

"I am in the place": we have passed from *res-cogitans* to *res-extensa*. The Being of the subject is produced in a place. Which place is that? This might be complicated, because it is obvious. It is obvious that the universe is the failure of the Non-Being, since the universe is what it is. If the Non-Being was pure, what would there be? Nothingness.

Now, what is it that establishes the lack-of-Being [*manqué à être*]? The function of the signifier, if I may say so, is to nullify[3]. Let us remember the famous statement "the signifier kills the thing". Everything that exists is an impurity of that nullification by the signifier. Try to follow the argument: the signifier has the virtue, let us say, of producing the dimension of the Non-Being; but this Non-Being is impure.

The function of the cry appears here; the cry as a function adhered to the signifier without signified. The signifier has the power of transforming the cry into a call, but it cannot make the presence of the cry, as such, disappear from the human world. So Lacan states that what exists—the universe—is the impurity of Non-Being. We are not ideas and we do not live in a world of ideas.

Lacan names "the voice" the line in the graph going out from A. Therefore, we not only obtain the treasure of the signifier from the Other (treasure that will nullify the universe), and the lack of being of desire (the beyond any demand of the Other), but we also obtain the voice: a dimension accompanying the signifier which, as such, has no signification and has the property of escaping, as an object, the nothingness produced by the signifier in the world of the objects.

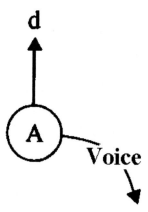

Schema 1.

Please notice that Lacan is not postulating the lack; he is not a philosopher of the Non-Being. What he is positing is that the point from which the problem of the being of the subject departs is the point where the Non-Being fails, the point of the impurity of the Non-Being. It is when the Being inlays like a chip in us, through an object, in the lack of Being. It is the wooden reel in the *Fort-da*. Where is the Being produced? Where is its impurity produced in that dialectic of the lack of being, created by the signifier? In something that does not allow itself to be reduced, nullified by the signifier, something that resists. And what is that? For instance, in speech it is the voice. The voice is that which, in the entire function of speech, resists the nullification by the signifier. What a fate, that of the signifier! To nullify everything but the place where it is produced as such: the voice. It is like if we said: "Do not try, my lord, to localize your Being at the level of the signifier; you will only find lack there. Rather try to face the problem of that which, in your relationship with the Other, did not allow itself to be reduced to the lack of Being". Lacan's manoeuvre is brilliant; he inverts the terms: the Being occupies now the place of that which (in the signifier) had not allowed itself to be nullified, the lack in that which makes something lack.

That place is called *jouissance*, but not in the sense of 'enjoying'. It is a place, a place which is absolutely determined by the symbolic. And what do we know about this symbolic place? That the "nothingness" of the signifier fails there. *Jouissance* is the point where the symbolic, by structure, fails.

And what are the attributes of the voice? To be a place of defect in the purity of Non-Being. Something remains: a core, a bone; and it is precisely there where the subject is.

We have also worked on the fact that the Lacanian notion of desire—different from the Freudian one- does not match with the neurotic's psychological theory on desire. It is necessary to go from the neurotic "I desire something", ($\lozenge$a), towards the "I am caused by a lack", "(a$\lozenge$$)". Now we find ourselves facing the same problem with regards to the notion of *jouissance*. One thing is the neurotic, vulgar notion about enjoying, and another very different is the Lacanian notion of *jouissance* that we have just exposed. From the neurotic "I enjoy with this", we must pass to the Lacanian notion of *jouissance* as a place.

The universe, what exists, is that which says no to the Non-Being. And the place from where this is clamoured—*jouissance*—is what gives meaning to the universe (which would be vain without it). The neurotic theory is that the universe becomes vain if one does not enjoy. It is the neurotic subject who raises the imperative of enjoyment to the status of being the support of the universe; psychoanalysis does not do that. This is why the neurotic subject clings to his symptom—one of his ways of enjoying. If this would be what psychoanalysis sustained, then we should keep our patients' symptoms—in order for their universe not to become empty. However, it is not about that. That which would make the universe empty, valueless, meaningless and with no basis, would be the absence of that place where it is clamoured that the Non-Being is not pure.

If we further analyze the problem of enjoying in the neurotic, Lacan asks himself: where does the voice come from? And he answers: from the Other. Am I in charge, then, of this empty place that we call *jouissance*? Am I responsible for it? Yes, he answers; I am in charge of the *jouissance* whose lack makes the Other inconsistent.

In logic, some properties of the symbolic orders need to be distinguished. Logicians are very careful when it comes to the confusion between incompleteness and inconsistency. They notably distinguish them. Inconsistency is thus defined: there exists at least one formula for which A and not A can be simultaneously demonstrated. That is to say, it is a case for which we cannot affirm that A is identical to A.

Lacan answers that "one has to take responsibility". But he asks himself afterwards: is it mine? Is it my *jouissance*? One can take responsibility for something that is, however, not ours.

Let us quote him:

> Am I responsible[4] for it, then? Yes, probably. Is this *jouissance*, the lack of which makes the Other inconsistent[5], mine, then? Experience proves that it is usually forbidden me [...] because of the fault [*faute*] of the Other if he existed; and since the Other does not exist, all that remains to me is to assume the fault upon 'I' [*Je*] [...] (p. 351).

So, is it mine? Lacan says it is not; it cannot be mine, thinks Lacan, since it is forbidden to me. My problem is now that, since there is no A of A, I cannot make the Other take charge for that prohibition, since its structure has no guarantee. It is not he Father, as you see; it is not the interdictory Law which is at issue. But neither is my *jouissance*, because (as Lacan says) it is forbidden to me. And it is forbidden to me because of the fault of the A, if it existed. Now, as it does not exist (there is no Other of the Other) it is my fault.

This is where the logic of the original sin is grounded. Which is the "original sin"? the empty place from where it is clamoured that the Non-Being is impure. And we have to make ourselves responsible for this place, because there is nobody on the side of the Other to be responsible for it. This is an effect of the structure that falls on the side of the subject, on its account. If there is a bone which may not be nibbled by the Other of the signifier, then it will imply my fault; moreover, if there was no subject implied, there would be no faults to be distributed.

Here we require the notion of the castration complex, which is (says Lacan) at the origin of desire, the major lever of the subversion of the subject. Why? Because this well founded lack in the Other founds (since it falls on the side of the subject) a lack in the subject, desire. "Lack" in French is "*faute*", which means both that something is lacking ("lack"), and also "fault", as "sin". What Lacan proposes to us is that the function of the superego and the unconscious feeling of culpability are effects of determination in the subject, since the lack of a signifier on the side of the Other is inscribed not only in terms of desire but also in terms of sin on the side of the subject.

Another quotation:

> [...] *jouissance* is forbidden to him who speaks as such, although
> it can only be said between the lines for whoever is subject of the
> Law, since the Law is grounded in this very prohibition (p. 352).

We face, therefore, an effect of the structure that determines the speaking subject, and not the paternal interdiction; that interdiction—if it can be written somewhere—operates at a place where there is, for the subject, a sin. It is thanks to the fact that this lack in the Other is inscribed in the subject as a fault in the moral sense, that the Law operates. It is because we are sinners (originally sinners) that the Law has for us a function, an anchoring point. It is only by means of the guilt (culpability) created by the original sin, that the Law efficaciously fulfils its interdictory function.

It is not the Law, then, that closes the access of the subject to *jouissance*. On the contrary, it is due to the fact that there is a certain closing of the access to *jouissance* and a return, that there can be a moral Law for us. This is precisely the opposite to the Kantian logic of the categorical imperative. If there is a categorical imperative, it is due to the fact that there was previously a primordial fault.

Lacan founds all this on the following logic: even if the imperative was: 'Enjoy!', even if the Law itself ordered to enjoy, it could not be prevented for the subject to respond: 'I hear'[6]; in other words, it could not be avoided that the subject interposes the function of the signifier to his *jouissance*. The function of the signifier will necessarily nullify this *jouissance*, implying its loss. So we have to remember that every time we tell the subject to listen, we must calculate that, at a certain point, he enjoys. It is impossible to impose *jouissance* by means of the Law; as it is also impossible to impose the interdiction of *jouissance* by means of the Law. This is why *jouissance* is unpronounceable; it can only be said between the lines.

What does it mean that *jouissance* is interdicted[7]? That it cannot be said, articulated, since if it was said it would be nullified by the effect of the signifier. There is *jouissance* because it can only be said between the lines, and it is on this "interdict" of the "between the lines" that the interdiction, the forbidden, the paternal law is grounded. If there exists an operative interdictory Law, that is due to the failure in the structure and not due to the function of the Father.

Last quotation:

> For it is pleasure that sets the limits on *jouissance*, pleasure as
> that which binds incoherent life together[8], until another, unchal-
> lengeable[9] prohibition arises from the regulation that Freud
> discovered as the primary process and appropriate[10] law of
> pleasure (pp. 352–353).

First of all we must distinguish that that which establishes a limit to
jouissance is the bond we maintain with life. That limit is imposed
by the body and it is a dimension of the not-all of the signifier operating on itself. But Lacan adds that there is even another prohibition, a second one, which is unquestionable. Lacan uses the word
"contestable", which means disputable and doubtful. Thus, this other
prohibition—says Lacan—cannot be doubted, cannot be the object
of the methodical Cartesian doubt.

The question is: how far can one take the doubt?, that is to say,
where is the limit? In the locus of this question (never too well
answered by the body) Lacan introduces another prohibition:
the indisputable one, that of the primary process and the pertinent Law of pleasure. And why does this one stop the doubting
process? Because it has a signifying text: "You shall not covet your
neighbour's wife". It is indisputable since it is enunciated in terms
of a Law. The obscure, always doubtful, questionable, is that which
remains as a bond with life, precisely because it cannot be proc-
essed [worked through] by the signifier. Limits imposed by the
body are always doubtful. Let us think of the always new Olympic
records, the question is always renewed: how far will the body go?
Is there no limit?

Thus, on the one hand, *jouissance* is that which escapes the nullification by the signifier—as a bone, as a core. And, on the other hand,
which is the limit of that *jouissance*? Pleasure is, to a certain extent,
another function of the same place from where the bone, namely,
the body emerges (although this function is always doubtful). But
fundamentally, the limit is constituted by this other definitive prohibition: that which is grounded in the signifier which is the primary
process and the pertinent Law of pleasure.

Once again we face two dimensions of pleasure, well distinguished by Lacan: the limit imposed by the scarce bond with life that

is left, and the pleasure which constitutes itself as a limit to *jouissance* by means of the Law of pleasure.

To conclude, let us remember what we did in previous classes when positing the relations among need, demand and desire as structured like a Möbius strip. In the same sense, it becomes apparent that the trio that has to substitute the previous one—demand, *jouissance* and desire, also has this structure. Regarding the letters we should write Demand (D) with capital letter and desire (*d*) and *jouissance* (*j*) with lower case letters, since they are both inverse varieties of what escapes the signifier: desire (*d*) as lack of being; and *jouissance* (*j*) as that which, of the body, is not nullified by the signifier. If we consider the schema that we previously used, we would have:

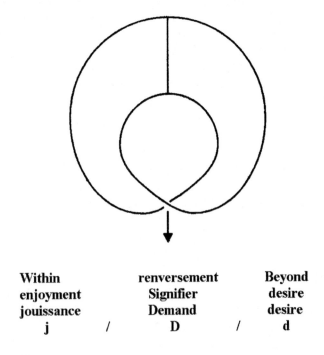

Within		renversement		Beyond
enjoyment		Signifier		desire
jouissance		Demand		desire
j	/	D	/	d

Schema 2.

Notes

1. "The other scene", in Lacan *"l autre scène"*; reference to Freud's *"eine andere Schauplatz"*, in The Interpretation of Dreams.

Cf. Jaques Lacan, "The Direction of the Treatment and the Principles of its Power", and also "The Signification of the Phallus". In Ecrits: A selection. Trans. A. Sheridan. Routledge.

2. See note 2, Chapter Thirteen.

3. The verb that the author uses in Spanish is *"nadificar"*, literally 'to transform something into a nothingness'. I will translate it as "nullify" in what follows. See note 10, Chapter Thirteen.

4. Lacan says « *En ai-je donc la charge?* ». Literally: « Do I have the charge? Should I take charge for it? » He does not use the word « responsible ». And he answers: *"Oui, sans doute"*, that is "Yes, without doubt", and not "probably", as translated by A. Sheridan.

5. Lacan writes *"inconsistent"*. A. Sheridan changes the meaning completely (and the entire theory behind it) when writing "insubstantial". It is precisely not a substance but a logic what is at stake.

6. See "Subversion of the subject ...", p. 352.

7. See notes 18 and 19, Chapter Four.

8. « *Le plaisir comme liaison de la vie* ». Literally: pleasure as the bond with life.

9. *"Non contestable"* in French.

10. Lacan uses here the word *"pertinente"*, which means "appropriate", but has another meaning in sciences: "able to account for the structure of an element or a set of elements".

CHAPTER FIFTEEN

The castration complex in Lacan's teaching

I shall dedicate this last chapter, predictably, to the final pages of *"Subversion of the subject ..."*. The title I propose to you as a framework for our work is "The castration complex in Lacan's teaching".

This outline will be supported, as has been the case during this course, by a series of quotations. The first one has already been presented to you during the last class:

> But it is not the Law itself that bars the subject's access to *jouissance*—rather it creates out of an almost natural barrier a barred subject. For it is pleasure that sets the limits on *jouissance*, pleasure as that which binds incoherent life together,[1] until another, unchallengeable prohibition arises from the regulation that Freud discovered as the primary process and appropriate law of pleasure.
>
> It has been said that in this discovery Freud merely followed the course already being pursued by the science of his time, indeed, that it belonged to a long-standing tradition. To appreciate the true audacity of his step, we have only to consider his

> recompense, which was not slow in coming: failure over the
> heteroclite nature of the castration complex (pp. 352–353).

The first thing we shall take into account is that Lacan sustains that
the castration complex is, in Freud, a heteroclite response to what
had been enunciated so far with regards to the Law of the Pleasure
Principle. The unheard of Freudian answer to the question of the
Pleasure Principle, which in a way inaugurates psychoanalysis as
such, is the castration complex.

We shall pose some questions about the clinical structures starting
from the value and properties of the castration complex in Lacan's
teaching. What is Lacan's conception of the castration complex?

Let us resort to some quotations in order to answer this question:

> It is the only indication of that *jouissance* of its infinitude that
> brings with it the mark of its prohibition, and, in order to con-
> stitute that mark, involves a sacrifice: that which is made in
> one and the same act with the choice of its symbol, the phallus
> (p. 353).

Lacan states that the castration complex is the mark, the trace of
interdiction over the infinite *jouissance*. In the Spanish version it says
"prohibition" instead of "interdiction". The translation is right from
the semantic point of view, but the translator misses the point: the
interdiction over the infinite *jouissance* is not only the prohibition of
that infinite *jouissance*, but also what we worked on last class: *jouissance* can only be said between-the-lines, in the inter-said [*inter-dit*].[2]
Therefore, it is not the mere prohibition of infinite *jouissance*; it is the
fact that it receives a mark. Doubtlessly, if we talk about a mark, we
are at the level of the signifier, of the signifier of the lack in the Other,
S($\cancel{A}$). First knotting: between the castration complex in Freud and
the signifier of the lack in the Other in Lacan.

We shall begin to surround the theory of *jouissance* by means of
taking the signifier of a lack in the Other as the mark [trace, trait] of
the interdiction of the infinite *jouissance*. We shall now go a little bit
further, in order to establish its relation with the castration complex.

Lacan states that the constitution of this mark implies a sacrifice,
that this sacrifice corresponds to the act of the choice of its symbol,
and that this symbol is the phallus.

This act of choosing its symbol is presented by Lacan in "The signification of the phallus" as "rising"—*aufhebung*[3]—: to raise the phallus to the category of symbol. But that what we gain as a mark implies a sacrifice, a loss.

Regarding the choice of the symbol that corresponds to the castration complex, what is it that justifies our calling it "castration"? We must take into account that this is not a particular choice, case by case; it is, if I may say so, a cultural choice: in the history of humanity, the phallus has been (and still is) the prevalent symbol for a lot of human societies. Hence, it is a choice determined by the structure. We ought to establish why.

Another quotation:

> This choice is allowed because the phallus, that is, the image of the penis, is negativity in its place in the specular image. It is what predestines the phallus to embody *jouissance* in the dialectic of desire (p. 353).

The choice of the phallus as the symbol of the mark of the interdiction of infinite *jouissance*—which implies its sacrifice as an organ- is authorized by the fact that the phallus itself (that is, the image of the penis) is negativity in its place in the specular image. What is it that authorizes, facilitates for the phallus to be chosen as mark and to be sacrificed? That the phallus is negativity in its place, in the specular image. That is to say, that in the specular image—where the phallus should be seen- it is not seen. And this due to the fact that, in the specular image—in the identification with the other's image *i(a)* in relation to which the alienating identification is produced- the phallus cannot be present, precisely, because the phallus is that which in the body is the object of the desire of the Other.

To say it in Freudian terms: the equation "penis-child" cannot be seen in the mirror, because in the mirror the subject cannot see the "wonder" that means, to the mother's eyes, the child's body. The metaphor coined by Lacan is very eloquent: for the child to be able to see the value that his own image has for his mother, he must necessarily loose sight of the specular image, take the look—his own look- out from his own image in the mirror, and go seeking in the maternal Other the value that this image acquires.

This notion of the non-specularity of the phallus is completely different from that of the object a. The phallus is a hole, a void, a blind spot in the mirror; the object a, on the contrary, can be seen in the mirror. So, what does it mean that the object a is not specular? The non-specularity of the object a lies in the fact that what appears in the mirror as an object, always implies a radical change of structure with regard to the object a cause of desire. In order to account for this difference (that the non-specularity of the phallus is different from the specularity of the object a), the topological notion of specularity is required. This notion is related to that of symmetry. For instance: a Möbius strip is not specular given that if we place a strip with a left torsion in front of a mirror, we will obtain the image of a strip with a right torsion, and both strips are structurally different, that is to say, it is impossible to transform one into the other by means of a continuous transformation (a topological one, with no cuts or glued parts[4]).

In this sense, we may try to correct a certain misunderstanding of some post-Freudians with regards to the Freudian: "*His Majesty the Baby*".[5] Some people understood that it referred to the child enunciating "*I'm the Majesty*", but this is not the case. The parents are the ones giving this majestic place to the child. Due to this equivocation, some post-Freudian analysts believed that it was the subject's narcissism that had to be attacked in the analytic experience—and it is not the subject's narcissism that is at stake, but that of the Other.

This is precisely what predestines the phallus to embody *jouissance* in the dialectic of desire. What is it this "this"? To be a blind spot, a void, in the place, which corresponds to it in the specular image: this is what predestines the phallus to embody *jouissance*. But it embodies it precisely in the sacrificed part of the body, namely, in the dialectic of desire.

Let us continue with Lacan's text:

> For desire is a defence (*défense*), a prohibition against going beyond a certain limit in *jouissance* (p. 356).

Every time *jouissance* articulates itself to desire, the phallus will embody it by means of the sacrificed part and, if *jouissance* does not articulate itself to desire, what will embody it is the erogenous zone—which has a completely different structure. Whenever desire intervenes and *jouissance* is knotted to the sacrificed part, desire becomes a defence against *jouissance*. In French it says *"défense"*, and the translator correctly clarifies that it is on the one hand prohibition—desire as prohibition—and, on the other hand, defence.

Therefore, *jouissance* can operate as a defence against desire, as desire can operate as a defence against *jouissance*. Although both defences are of a very different nature, each of them conceals a point of castration. *Jouissance*, by means of its object, may be a defence with regard to the object cause of desire, as well as by manoeuvring with the lack that desire implies, the interdiction of the infinite *jouissance* may be concealed.

I shall propose now to oppose once again the structure we have just analyzed: *jouissance*-demand-desire, to the ternary: need-demand-desire; as we did last time: to oppose jouissance (*j*)—demand (D)—desire (*d*) to need-demand-desire. I shall schematize it thus for you, taking advantage of the structure of the graph:

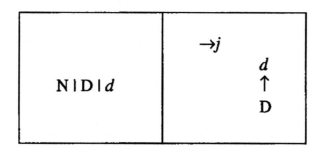

Schema 1.

Regarding this issue, Lacan states in "The signification of the phallus":

> One can see how the sexual relation occupies this closed field of desire, in which it will play out its fate. This is because it is the field made for the production of the enigma that this relation arouses in the subject by doubly 'signifying' it to him: the return of the demand that it gives rise to, as a demand on the subject of the need [...] (2006, p. 318).

We said it thus: in the passage from need to demand there is a loss, and that loss (rest) is called desire. If the sexual relation falls into the field of desire, then desire via the demand goes back to the need. How? Simply as a demand on the subject of the need, in the sense for instance, of the requirement of the erection.

> [...] the return of the demand that it gives rise to, as a demand on the subject of the need—an ambiguity made present on to the Other in question in the proof of love demanded. The gap in this enigma betrays what determines it, namely, to put it in the simplest possible way, that for both partners in the relation, both the subject and the Other, it is not enough to be subjects of need, or objects of love [see how Lacan is articulating need and demand], but that they must stand for the cause of desire[6] (p. 318).

It is not enough that love operates correctly, as a dimension of demand (every demand is demand for love). It is not enough either that, at the level of need, the bodies are ready; it is necessary to become the cause of the desire of the Other; that each of the *partenaires*[7] manages, if I may say so, to get the Other's body ready through the causation of his desire. This is how we posit that human sexuality requires the articulation of the ternary: need, demand and desire.

Thus, what Lacan is positing is that, within the context of the structure need-demand-desire, the triple articulation is bidirectional, going left to right and right to left: from desire to need passing through demand and from need once again to desire—via the "need" for becoming the cause of the Other's desire. You may recall that I proposed a structure in the form of a Möbius strip to account for the relation of continuity/discontinuity between need and desire, through the field of demand (the left-right orientation as opposed to the right-left orientation). Now we have added, to what we said at that time, the links between need and demand.

The theoretical step made by Lacan between "The signification of the phallus" and "Subversion of the subject ..." is enormous. In "Subversion of the subject ..." the triad "need-demand-desire" is substituted by the triad "*jouissance*-demand-desire". Instead of taking the call made from desire via demand over the body, considered as need, we now work on the corporealisation of *jouissance* via the phallus (as that which does not appear in the specular image). This has no longer anything to do with the body that corresponds to the need, at least the biological need. It will be, thus, a logical need (a necessity), which is at stake.

Through this passage, the conception of the body changed: in "need-demand-desire", the body is the biological body (although mythical), whereas in "*jouissance*-demand-desire" the body is that which the desire of the Other inscribes in one's own body, insofar as phallus, as the lacking part in the specular image (–φ).

I shall go on with the series of quotations I selected from "*Subversion of the subject* …:" in order to develop our theme:

> We must distinguish, therefore, between the principle of sac-
> rifice, which is symbolic, and the imaginary function that is
> devoted to that principle of sacrifice, but which, at the same
> time, masks the fact that it gives it its instrument (p. 353).

First of all: the principle of sacrifice is not imaginary. If it were imaginary, it would be the absence of the specular image of the phallus. But Lacan states that it is not, that the principle, in the sense of the origin and the legality (as in pleasure Principle, reality Principle) is indeed symbolic. We must clarify that it is not imaginary because, for every neurotic, the absence in the specular image is lived and understood, as such, as being imaginary. Secondly, it is to that symbolic principle that an imaginary function is given. At the same time that it is given it, it veils it. On the one hand, the imaginary is determined by the symbolic, but, on the other hand, the imaginary can veil the symbolic; the idea of a hierarchy between the registers has almost no use. A certain imaginary function, the image of the penis and all of its equivalents, is ruled by the symbolic legality. At the same time, the symbolic operation receives its instrument from the imaginary, and that is why it is the symbolic "phal-lus", Φ, and, finally, what closes this dialectic up in the form of a loop [*boucle*] is the fact that the imaginary veils (t the phallic level and in so far as it lends the instrument) that the legality is symbolic.

The relation between the registers is conceived of as a knot. We shall see that this function of the knot established with regards to the phallus, also implies taking into account the relations of the symbolic and the imaginary with the real. Lacan formulates this in the following way:

> The imaginary function is that which Freud formulated to
> govern the investment of the object as narcissistic object. It

was to this point that I returned myself when I showed that the specular image is the channel taken by the transfusion of the body's libido towards the object. But even though part of it remains preserved from this immersion, concentrating within it the most intimate aspect of autoeroticism, its position at the 'tip' of the form predisposes it to the phantasy[8] of decrepitude[9] in which is completed its exclusion from the specular image and from the prototype that it constitutes for the world of objects (p. 353).

This imaginary function (which is subsumed to the symbolic legality, which it veils and to which it gives its instrument) is in Freud nothing less than the investment of the object as narcissistic object, that is to say, narcissism. According to Lacan, he says it himself, it is the specular image that functions as the channel of transfusion of the body's libido towards the object. Precisely there we find the following problem: according to Freud, the ego is an object, whereas according to Lacan, it is an image. In Lacan's work, then, $i(a)$ is the channel through which the body's libido passes into the objects.

At this stage Lacan adds an extremely important notion, by saying that a part (of the ego's and the object's image) is preserved from immersion in the mirror, concentrating the most intimate aspect of autoeroticism. Immersion is a topological notion. The word "immersion", in topology, implies a certain metaphor; it means: to take an object which has a certain spatial legality and to transport it to another spatial legality—this is absolutely unthinkable for us, given that the space has always, for us, the same three-dimensional structure. In topology, for example, to submerge a two dimensional object in a three dimensional space, would be the equivalent of making a volumetric model of certain planar surfaces. But we must not limit ourselves to this case; topologists are also interested in thinking what would happen—for instance—if we submerged a three-dimensional figure in a space of more than three dimensions (four, for example). This is absolutely unthinkable for us, because we do not have an intuition of it. If a three-dimensional cube is submerged into a four dimensional space, a hypercube is obtained, something that escapes completely our intuition. The immersion in the mirror, thus, implies a change in the structure of the object in question. As we have already said in relation to the Möbius strip, when accounting for the respective specularities of the phallus and the object, we know that a scar on the right cheek becomes a scar on the left cheek in the mirror image. That is the sort of immersion that is at stake here.

Lacan states that there is a part that is always preserved in the mirror-immersion, and in it the autoeroticism is concentrated. Many of you must be thinking of the "Achilles' heel", which was preserved from its immersion in the waters of the river Styx. Do you recall that Achilles' mother was a Goddess, Thetis, daughter of the Ocean God? This idea goes completely against our intuition: that which is not on the mirror knots itself, in the most intimate way, to the subject's autoeroticism. Hence, Lacan localizes the autoeroticism in that of the body, which has been lost in the immersion in the mirror. This idea is a contradictory one, if we take into account what we were saying before, namely, that what is not present in the specular image is the object of the Other's desire. But notice how notable Lacan's manoeuvre is. It is precisely in the autoeroticism, he says, that the subject searches in his body for that which escapes to the imaginary capture of the body. Lacan is stating that there is nothing more "marked" by the "alloerotic" ("allo" from "alienation") than the autoeroticism. Think of the "Rat Man", for instance, showing to his dead Father's ghost his erected penis, that with which the masturbatory manipulation was produced.

You can then realize how human masturbation can be distinguished from animal masturbation. In the animal, masturbation is the pure and simple manipulation of an especially sensitive part of the body, in the human being it is the inscription in the body of a certain function of the Other, which is veiled for the subject himself.

I shall give you one more argument before we can say—and justify—that autoeroticism is the inscription of (–φ) (minus phi, lower case) which implies the desire of the Other.

The "at the tip" position of the penis in the subject's body (I am quoting Lacan) predisposes to the phantasy [fantasme] of decrepitude in which its exclusion from the specular image is completed, and from the prototype that it constitutes for the world of objects. Because the phallus is, in relation to the penis, the lost part of the body at the imaginary level, is it not by chance that the phantasy [fantasme] of decrepitude (lapsing) emerges precisely there. The impotence that falls over it, due to the real shape that characterizes it. So the fact that it is not visible in the specular image and its "at the tip" position in the real image, are articulated in favour of their knotting in the phantasy [*fantasme*] of decrepitude in which its exclusion from the specular image is completed. Lacan will sustain that every object conceived by the subject according to this dialectic of the exclusion from the image will be due to the transference of the function of the phallus. That it is not seen in the mirror will mean that it is the lacking part of the image.

"Decrepit" ("expired") is that which falls, and also that which is old-fashioned. But it has one more meaning: in zoology, the *decidua*[10] is the epithelial lining of the endometrium that is expulsed together with the placenta during the birth. This decrepit *fantasme* is closely linked to the lamella. However, we must not forget that the lamella refers to one's own body's lost part, whereas the *decidua* has to do with the part of the Other's body that is lost during one's birth.

> Thus the erectile organ comes to symbolize the place of *jouissance*, not in itself, or even in the form of an image, but as a part lacking in the desired image: that is why it is equivalent to the $\sqrt{-1}$ of the signification produced above, of the *jouissance* that it restores by the coefficient of its statement to the function of lack of signifier (–1) (p. 353).

What is then the phallus within this dialectic? Three things: the lacking part of the desired image (–φ) (minus phi); the lack of a signifier (–1), and the interdiction of infinite *jouissance*. Thus, we have written the phallus as the articulation of the Symbolic as (–1), the Imaginary (as –φ), and the Real (as the interdiction of infinite *jouissance*).

The Spanish translation of the following paragraph contains a mistake: where in French it says "*nouer*", which means "to knot", they wrote "to annul". The phallus is a knot.

> If its role, therefore is to bind[11] the prohibition of *jouissance*, it is nevertheless not for these formal reasons, but because their supersession (*outrepassement*) signifies that which reduced all desired *jouissance* to the brevity of auto-eroticism: the paths laid out by the anatomical conformation of the speaking being, that is, the already perfected hand of the monkey, have not, in

effect, been ignored in a certain philosophical ascesis as paths
of a wisdom that has wrongly been termed cynical [...] The
fact remains that analytic experience demonstrates the original
character of the guilt that its practice induces (pp. 353–354).

It is not thanks to its erectile shape that the phallus knots the interdiction of *jouissance*, for when we try to access this *jouissance* in an
autoerotic way ... there Lacan comes across with his joke about the
'man's hand as the monkey's hand has not been perfected yet'. I think
he is referring here to the expression 'spanking the monkey'. And
after that he says: every autoerotic masturbatory act will end sooner
or later, that is to say, it will not lead to an infinite *jouissance*. If the
phallus implies an interdiction of *jouissance*, it is—essentially—in the
sense of culpability: the structural guilt produced by masturbation.
The knotting between the phallus and the interdiction of *jouissance*
is not due to its shape, but due to the symbolic principle, given that
interdiction as prohibition is inscribed through culpability, caused
by masturbation. In the clinic of the obsessional, the male obsessional, this culpability or guilt is often "typical". He posits: "I harm
nobody by doing this". But he who complains is not "nobody", but
that which Freud calls "the voice of conscience".

> Guilt that is bound up with the recall of *jouissance* that is lack-
> ing in the office rendered to the real organ, and consecration of
> the function of the imaginary signifier to strike the objects of
> prohibition (p. 354).

This guilt regarding the masturbatory *jouissance* has—frankly- the
structure of a knot between the real organ, the function of the signifier and its imaginary use. The phallus implies the real organ but as
imaginary signifier. I believe what Lacan is trying to say is that we
cannot forget what the phallus carries in terms of (-1), the mark of
the interdiction, and in terms of $(-\phi)$, what is not seen of the specular
image.

> The passage from the $(-\phi)$ (small phi) of the phallic image from
> one side to the other of the equation, from the imaginary to the
> symbolic, renders it positive in any case, even if it fulfils a lack.
> Although a support of the (-1), it becomes ... Φ (capital phi),

the symbolic phallus that cannot be negated, the signifier of *jouissance* (p. 354).

The (–ϕ), the phallic image as lacking, passing from the imaginary to the symbolic, becomes Φ. And Φ will never be (–ϕ), but the signifier of *jouissance*. We have come back to the dialectic of the signifier of a lack in the Other, Sʄé ʃᴇ And it is important not to loose sight of our departing point: that this dialectic does not end up in what the Other is lacking, but in the positive mark of that lack in the Other. Hence, Phallus will not be the lack at the level of the Other; symbolic phallus will not be the (–1); it will be the mark of that (–1): the signifier of *jouissance*. Signifier of *jouissance* in so far as it inscribes the interdiction of infinite *jouissance*, and also in so far as it inscribes the lack at the signifying level, which inscribes something of *jouissance*.

The symbolic phallus, Φ, as the positive rendering of (–ϕ) will be a mark. Of what will it be a mark? On the one hand, of the fact that *jouissance* is no longer infinite *jouissance*, and, on the other hand, of the fact that the mark of jouissance establishes a limit to the function of the signifier. There is no "all signifier", which would be "nothingness", for *jouissance* has been inscribed. And this is a positive mark.

Notes

1. See notes 8, 9 and 10, Chapter Fourteen.
2. See note 20, Chapter Three.
3. See J. Lacan, The signification of the phallus, in Ecrits. A selection. Routledge. Trans. A. Sheridan, p. 319.
4. See note 3, Chapter Two.
5. In English in the original.
6. Lacan says here: *"ils doivent tenir lieu de cause du désir"*, indicating that "they must serve, be, function as cause of the desire".
7. In French in the original.
8. *"Fantasme"*. See note 9, Chapter One.
9. "Decrepitude" only translates one of the possible meanings of the word that Lacan uses here: *"caducité"*, and its adjective *"caduq"* which also means "old, expired, transitory, brief, precarious, impotent, ruined, old-fashioned". It is the word used for "sell-by date" for food, for instance. That is why the author refers below to *"decidua"* or "expired membranes".
10. Also "expired membranes". See Chapter Eleven.
11. In French *"nouer"*, literally, "to knot".

REFERENCES

Aleksandrov, D. Kolmogorov, M.A. & Laurent, E.V. (1962–1963). *Mathematics: Its Content, Methods and Meaning.* American Mathematical Society: Providence.

de Saussure, F. (1983). *Course in General Linguistics.* Open Court Chicago and La Salle: Illinois.

Dienes, Z.P. & Golding, E.W. (1967). *Geometry of Congruence.* McGraw-Hill Book Co.: New York.

Eidelsztein, A. (1992). *Modelos, Esquemas y Grafos en la Enseñanza de Lacan.* Manantial: Buenos Aires.

Eidelsztein, A. (2006). *La Topología en la Clínica Psicoanalítica.* Letra Viva: Buenos Aires.

Flament, C. (1963). *Applications of Graph Theory to Group Structure.* Prentice Hall, Englewood Clis, New Jersey.

Fréchet, M. & Fan, K. (2003). *Invitation to Combinatorial Topology.* Dover: New York.

Freud, S. (1905d). *Three Essays on the Theory of Sexuality.* The Standard Edition of the Complete Works of Sigmund Freud, vol. 7. Hogarth Press and the Institute of Psychoanalysis: London.

279

Freud, S. (1915e). *The Unconscious*. The Standard Edition of the Complete Works of Sigmund Freud, vol. *14*. Hogarth Press and the Institute of Psychoanalysis: London.

Freud, S. (1920g). *Beyond the Pleasure Principle*. The Standard Edition of the Complete Works of Sigmund Freud, vol. *18*. Hogarth Press and the Institute of Psychoanalysis: London.

Freud, S. (1923b). *The Ego and the Id*. The Standard Edition of the Complete Works of Sigmund Freud, vol. *19*. Hogarth Press and the Institute of Psychoanalysis: London.

Freud, S. (1933a). *New Introductory Lectures on Psycho-analysis*. The Standard Edition of the Complete Works of Sigmund Freud, vol. *22*. Hogarth Press and the Institute of Psychoanalysis: London.

Freud, S. (1941f). Moses and Monotheism. The Standard Edition of the Complete Works of Sigmund Freud, vol. *23*. Hogarth Press and the Institute of Psychoanalysis: London.

Freud, S. (1950). *A Project for a Scientific Psychology*. The Standard Edition of the Complete Works of Sigmund Freud, vol. *1*. Hogarth Press and the Institute of Psychoanalysis: London.

Kasner, E. & Newman, J. (2001). *Mathematics and the Imagination*. Penguin classics: New York.

Lacan, J. (1988). *The Seminar, Book I. Freud's Papers on Technique*. Norton & Co.: New York.

Lacan, J. (1988). *The Seminar, Book II, The Ego in Freud's Theory and in the Technique of Psychoanalysis*. Norton & Co.: New York.

Lacan, J. (1988). *The Seminar of Jacques Lacan, Book I, Freud´s Papers on Technique*. Norton & Co.: New York.

Lacan, J. (1991). *Le Séminaire, Livre VIII, Le transfert*. Éditions Du Seuil: Paris.

Lacan, J. (1992). *The Seminar, Book VII, The Ethics of Psychoanalysis*. Norton & Co: New York.

Lacan, J. (1993). *The Seminar, Book III, The Psychoses*. Routledge: London.

Lacan, J. (1998). *On Feminine Sexuality: The Limits of Love and Knowledge*. Norton & Co.: New York.

Lacan, J. (1998). *The Four Fundamental Concepts of Psychoanalysis, Book XI*. Norton & Co.: New York.

Lacan, J. (2004). *Le Séminaire, Livre X: L'Angoisse*. Seuil: Paris.

Lacan, J. (2006). *Kant with Sade, Ecrits, The First Complete Edition in English*. Norton & Co.: New York.

Lacan, J. (2006). *Metaphor of the subject, Ecrits, The First Complete Edition in English.* Norton & Co.: New York.

Lacan, J. (2006). *Remarks on Daniel Lagache's presentation: "Psychoanalysis and personality structure", Ecrits, The First Complete Edition in English.* Norton & Co.: New York.

Lacan, J. (2006). *Seminar on "The purloined letter", Ecrits, The First Complete Edition in English.* Norton & Co.: New York.

Lacan, J. (2006). *The direction of the treatment and the principles of this power, Ecrits, The First Complete Edition in English.* Norton & Co.: New York.

Lacan, J. (2006). *The instance of the letter in the unconscious, or reason since Freud, Ecrits, The First Complete Edition in English.* Norton & Co.: New York.

Lacan, J. (2006). *The Seminar, Book XVII, The Other Side of Psychoanalysis.* Norton & Co.: New York.

Lacan, J. (2006). *The subversion of the subject and the dialectic of desire in the Freudian unconscious, Ecrits, The First Complete Edition in English.* Norton & Co.: New York.

Lacan, J. (unpublished). *Le Séminaire, Livre VI, Le désir et son interprétation.*

Plato, (2003). *The Symposium.* Penguin classics: New York.

Real Academia Española, (1991). *Esbozo de una Nueva Gramática de la Lengua Española.* Espasa-Calpe: Madrid.

Stewart, J. (1995). *Concepts of Modern Mathematics.* Dover: New York.

Toranzos, F. (1976). *Introducción a la Teoría de los Grafos.* Secretaría General de los Estados Americanos: Washington D.C.

Wilson, R.J. (1990). *Graphs: An Introductory Approach—A First Course in Discrete Mathematics.* Wiley: New York.

INDEX

Abolishment of repression 62
Abraham's pact with God 240
    name transformation 245
Absolute sufficient condition 65
Acephalia 215
Achilles' heel 275
Aires, Buenos 43
Ambiguity 47
Analysand's maneuver 194
Analyst
    desire of 194
Anchoring point 74
Androgynous 37
Anguish 129, 151
Anticipation-retroaction 77
Antigone 52
Argentine 43
Aristophanes' intervention 36
    symposium as illustration
    of ancient roots 36–37

Balint, Michel 165
Biunivocal relationship
    23
Bivalence, principle
    of 42

Cartesian notions 20
Cartesian opposition
    6, 253
Castration 34
Christ 239
Circumventing 219
Comb schema 28–30
Comte, Auguste 97
Consciousness 2, 117, 166
Convenient marriage 78
Crossing point 160
Crusoe, Robinson 105
Current conception 152
Cytoplasm 83

Deception 105
Demand 45–68
    as signifying chain 66
    beyond 169, 194
    dissatisfaction of 169
    unconditional regarding
        need 63
Demand's effect 63
Demand-desire relation 60, 184
Departure point 109
Desire 45–68
    dialectic 144
    jouissance and 235
    modes of 168
    pathways 170
    subject 170
    types of 168
Desire and *fantasme*
    articulation between 173
    pathway (I) 143–165
    pathway (II) 167–182
    symptom 143–165
Desire and topology
    graph 1–16
Desire *x* object 71
Desired object 140
Detours and obstacles 42
Diachrony 76, 79
Dialectic of desire 144
Digraphs 23
The Divine Comedy 84
Discontinuity 57–58
Dora's truth 78
Doubtless 81, 114
Drive (I) 205–222
    deconstruction 209
Drive (II) 225–234
    partial 230–231
    sado-masochistic 226
Dual organization 83
Duo desire-demand 91

Duo need-demand 91
Duplicity 120

Ego
    function 118
    functioning dynamic 120
    fundamental property 33
    ideal 103
    ideal–ideal ego 104
    ideal primary identification 114
    identification 118
    network of cathected
        [invested] neurones 15
    signification 126, 164
The Ego and the Id 35
Ego-psychology 38
Envelopment-development-
    conjunction-disjunction 154
Euler 2
    work 12
Evanescent 158–159
Exhibitionism 227
Eyolf's Lady of the Rats 81

Fading 111, 159, 171
    moment of 172
Fantasmatic scenes 227
    axiom 184–185
    imaginary configuration
        of 157
Fantasme 143–165, 181
    determinant 176
    formula of 171, 183–203,
        213–214, 227
    frame of 189
    function of 185, 190
    fundamental function
        of 157–158
    fundamental use of 157
    inversion in formula of 214
    logic of 172

machine 173
maneuver 167
pathway 143–165
signification 160
strong scopic determination 191
vampire's 203
French
    code 54
    negation 55
Freud 15
    analytic cure 112
    clinical practice 144
    de-negation 34
    discovery 56
    The Ego and the Id 35
    four types of perversion 227
    function of the ideal 125
    His Majesty the Baby 110
    human structure 25
    I, the Majesty 110
    limit of castration 125
    negation 34
    ovum schema 231
    possibility of conceiving 128
    primary identification 155
    project for a scientific
        psychology 24
    Rat Man case 78–79
    switch-words 50
    "truth-values" 20
    case studies 144
    equation "penis-child" 269
    Father in the myth 239
    field 216–217
    formula 207
    fort-da 21
Freudian
    affirmation 215
    metaphor of determination
        153
    notion 110

paragraph 32
post 110, 144, 199, 209, 270
psychic life 207
schemata 29
sense 90–91
structure of schemata 28
subject 56
symbol for quantity 16
system 218
theory 8
topography 2, 89
unconscious 17, 45
Future anterior 114

Gisela's sterility 81
Graph 15
    direction 175
    dual structure as 96
    elementary cell 83, 96
    fundamental unity 83
    hole in interior circle 42
    Lacan's 11
    notion of chain in theory 29
    school 14
    structure 14, 30
Graph of desire 16, 34, 92–93
    hole in interior circle 42
    relational system 110
    structure of 45
Graph one 71–86
Graph three 74
    the question 125–140
Graph two 74
    ideal (I)—ego (M)—ideal (I)
        103–122
Graph theory
    function of connectivity in 22
    notion of chain in 29
    uniting topology and 39
*Group Psychology and Analysis
    of the Ego* 155

Hallucination 218
Halting points 120
Headless subjectivity 225
Hegel 177
Horizontal relations 195
Hospitalism 61
Hospitality relationships 38
The Human Condition 189
Human race
    origin of 37
    sexual relation 37
Hysterical symptom 147–148

Ibsen's Little 81
Ichspaltung 33
Idealization 126–127
Imaginary anticipation 76
Imaginary-Real-Symbolic 72
Impossibility 153, 168
    dissatisfaction and 165
    in mathematics 97
    of a metalanguage 172
    translating 136
Interior eight 32–35, 230–231
The Interpretation of Dreams 24, 29
Introduction of Narcissism 30
Introduction of the big Other 30
Introduction of the Ego 30, 33

Jakobson, Roman 7, 29, 46, 51–53
    notion of message 81
    words 55
St John's
    finger pointing upwards 162
Jordan closed curve 39
    cut on the torus 40–41
Jordan closed lines 40–41
Jouissance 9, 34, 165, 187, 217–218,
    225–227, 259–260, 262,
    267, 271, 276–278
    embody 269
    infinite 268

    interdiction of 277
    theory of 268
Jouissance and desire 235–252
Jouissance and desire (II) 253–264
Jouissance-demand-desire 89,
    272–273

Kasner 94–95
Kleinian school 157
Klein, Melanie 144, 195, 205–206
    group 196–197
Klein's bottle 8
Königsberg 14–15
    bridges of graph 11, 23, 27

Lacanian 1, 10
    algebra 71
    direction of the cure 7
    elaborations 99
    formulae 135, 170
    graph 11
    myth of the lamella 216
    notion of desire 260
    notion of the object 7
    notion 32
    "optical model" in
        Seminar I 17
    one 108
    orientation 238
    pathway 144
    proposal 3
    psychoanalysis 2, 6, 8, 130, 170
    psychoanalytical practice 2
    Seminar 7, 11
    Seminar 8, Transference 20
    signifying chain 21–22
    spatial metaphor in the
        optical model 3
    statement 191
    teaching 1, 7–8, 11
    text on linguistics 8
    theory 2, 37

translation 15
writing 152
Lacan's
abolishment 63
analytic cure 112
analytical practice 140
articulation between desire
    and dissatisfaction 169
battery 241
deconstruction of drive 209
diachrony and synchrony 76
diagnosis 205
doubtless 114
Ecrits 164
ego 118
elementary cell 74
elliptic speech 73
formula 139, 154, 202, 215
formulae of the
    fantasme 171, 226
function of punctuation 81
function of the full stop 81
graph 28, 31
ideas 255
indication 240
inexpressible 247
issue of identification 165
jouissance 250–251
letter in unconscious 146
lower-case letters 72
manoeuvre 259
mathematical development
    of time 248
moral condition of 122
nappie 133
nescience 137
No-Faith 238
notion changing 104, 106
notion of fiction 106
notion of homology 175
notions of continuous
    and discontinuous 25

omnipotent 130
other in 268
"partial drive" 231
petrifaction 117
position 125
proposal 30
psychoanalysis 122
psychoanalytic theory 208
reasonable 110
re-conceptualization 206
relationship between
    desire and *fantasme* 167
retroversion 114
S(A/) 241
schema 221
"sealed" interaction 77
self-quotation 156
Seminar 11, 205–206, 210
*Seminar 6: Desire and its
    interpretation* 184
*Seminar 7, The ethics
    of psychoanalysis* 41
*Seminar on "The Purloined
    Letter"* 21
*Seminar: Les non dupes
    errant* 191
signifying property 134
subject's message 81
subject-with-holes 215
subversion of the subject...
    46, 48, 53, 103, 182, 192,
    198–199, 214, 230, 241, 253,
    257, 261, 267, 272
times 46
translation 16
truth concerns reality 107
upper-case letters 72
with Hegel about desire 177
Lacan's teaching
    castration complex in 38, 51,
        75, 92, 108, 110, 140, 192,
        216, 240, 254, 267–278

Lacking consistency 250
Lacking object 220
Lagache, Daniel 144
    report 164
Lambda schema 120, 149
Language, structure of
    need, demand and desire 45–68
Lévi-Strauss, Claude 258
Linguistic code 50
Listener's discretional power 76
Localization 57
    real 58
    subject's 58

Magritte 189
Masochism 227
Mathematical graph theory 29–30
Mathematics and the Imagination
    94, 96, 245
Meta-language 173
Metamorphosis, natural 233
Metaphorical substitution 78
The metaphor of the subject 79
Metonymical character 148
Metonymy 122
Miller, Jacques-Alain 17, 44, 234
Mirror stage 4
Misrecognize myself 115
Möbius strip 7, 91, 218, 232,
    264, 270, 275
    structure 65
Modern linguistics
    culminating point 46
    dawn of 46
Moses's tomb 239
Mother tongue 60

Name-of-the Father 99–100
Narcissism 110–111
NASA schema 220
Natural metamorphosis 233
Necessary condition 65

Need 45–68
Need-demand-desire 89, 91, 129, 273
    context of the structure 272
    opposition 65
    principal articulations 67
    triad 67
Need's particularity 63
Nets
    ego 33
    mathematical graph 19
    theory 19–23
Neurosis-psychosis 59, 93, 100
    impossible 89–101
    negative of 213
    obsessional 172
    opposition 99
    significations in 173
    structural opposition 100
Neurotic eagerness 131
New psychical act 33
Newman 94–95
Non-Being 258–259
Non-contradiction, principle of 42
Non-relative sufficient condition 65
Notion, scholastic 106

Object a 19–42
    as a cut 42
    as a remainder 64
    cause of desire 66, 91
    different from 270
    functioning of 220
    in Seminar 11, 228
    localization of 93
    non-specularity of 270
    position 186
    subtraction of 189
    working as a trick 230
Obsessional symptom 148
Oedipus 74
    complex 98–99, 150, 180–181
Omnipotent 130

On narcissism 16
Optical model 3–4, 76
Ordered pair 154
Other's 232–233
  body 276
  demand 202, 222, 233
  desire 135, 214, 272
  discourse 135
  field of 232
  ideal 116
  man's desire 137–138
  of demand 178
  of the Other 237
  signification of 160
Overlapping 49
Over-determination 176
Ovum schema 28

Partial drive 230
Perversion 226
  formula of 213
  four types of 227
  inverted effect of fantasme 226
  structure of 226
Phallus
  signification of 271
Phantasy 157, 159, 161, 169,
  173, 179, 185, 187, 275–276
  fundamental 157
Phantom 129
Poe, Edgar Allan 21
Polysemy 17
Possibility of conceiving 128
Preconscious 2,
Presence-absence 90
Primordial repression 192
Psychical
  activity 200
  reality 47
  unity 47
Psychic energy
  notion of 217

Psychoanalysis 2, 25, 82, 125,
  150, 205–206, 256
  civilization's discontent 219
  discontinuous division 33
  ethics of 203
  fundamental series in 30
  Lacanian's 6
  notion of scene 187
  notion of the unconscious
    in 33
  psychoanalytical perspective
    of 206
  reality 107
  theoretical elaborations in 2
  topography in 2, 25
Psychoanalytic
  postulate 90
  question 125
  theory 115, 198, 239
Psychosis 59, 93, 100, 183, 198
  clinic of 99
  foreclosure in 100
  possible treatment of 98, 149
Psychotic structure
  clinical index of 100
Psychotic subject demand 85
The Purloined Letter 111

Quadrature of the circle 94–95
Quaternary topology 99
Quilting point 74, 76, 83
  virtue of stopping
    signification 77

Rat Man 144–145
  symptom 144
φ relation 26
Relation
  abolishment-offspring 67
  between "absolute condition"
    and "unconditional" 89–90
  between need and demand 90

envelopment-development-
    conjunction-disjunction 154
need-demand-desire 91
signifier-signified 91
Relative sufficient condition 65
Renversement 67
Repression proper 59
Retroversion 114
Returning point 161
Robert French dictionary 159
Rubber sheet 5

S(A/)
being, jouissance and
    desire 235–252
"being (Res), jouissance and
    desire" (II) 253–264
Sadism 227
Sadist's position 187
Satisfaction-object 6
Saussure's
    algorithm 245
    Course in General
        Linguistics 107
    elaborations 46
    notion of "linearity" 29
    reality 106–107
    teachings 47
Scene-shifter 156–157
School graph 13–14, 27
Screenplay 157
The Seminar, Book 9, 32
*Seminar 12, Crucial Problems
    of Psychoanalysis* 113
Sexual satisfaction 126
Sexuality 208–209, 255
Shifter 51, 53
Signification 121
    absolute 173
    metonymy of 133
The signification of the phallus 58
Signifier 34, 46, 110, 113, 241–242

all-powerful 154–155, 159
battery of 241
effect of 63
foreclosure of 99
functioning 134
isolating 108–109
legality of 208
locus of 182
master 109
Name-of-the-Father 243
nets of 208
nothingfication of 252
notion of 103
of the law 100
petrifaction under 117
phallic 164
pure speaking subject in 100
pure 57
quantity of 180
signifying elements 90
treasure of 80–81, 254
Signifying chain
    demand 66
    Lacan's notion of 30
    psychoanalytical notion of 29
Signifying-signifier 82, 85
Signorelli 255
Sophism 78
Sound-image 107
Spatial community 210
Spatial dimension 19
Spherical nature 37
Spherical subject 35
Stopping point 74
Stupefaction 149
Subject of desire 65
Subjectivity 255
Sublimation 126–127
Subversion of the subject... 71, 73,
    79, 86, 93, 99–100, 108, 113,
    128, 133, 144, 154, 160, 170–171,
    173, 181, 201, 235, 237

Lacan's 46, 48, 53, 103, 182, 192, 198–199, 214, 230, 241, 253, 257, 261, 267, 272
Sufficient condition 65
Super-ego 64
Symbol
  definition 37–38
  derivation 38
Symbolic
  connotation 82
  effect 93
  ideal's functioning 117
  order 61
  structure 93
Symptom, derivation 38
Synchronic reunion 80
Synchronic
  dimension 77
  structure 77
Synchrony 76

Telephony 50
Temporal
  dimension 20
  discordance 52
Temporal metaphor
  of the 'future anterior' 114
Three-element system (Imaginary-Real-Symbolic) 72
Three-leg biped 97
Topological game 96
Transitional object 133
Truth-Pretence, opposition 104

Unconscious 2, 6–8, 17–18, 20, 29, 35, 51, 53–55, 177–178, 184, 212
  act of speaking 237
  chain in 174, 181, 254

enunciation 200, 236–237, 242, 249, 251, 254
Freudian 17, 45
function of 180, 185, 212
in psychoanalysis 33
Lacan's theory of the topography of 2
language 58
level 200–201, 236
localization of the demand 202
localization 200
loops 254
of fantasme 185
of Seminar 11, 34
phantasy in Freud's 144
phantasy 144, 157
reality of 155, 193
signifying chain in 174
structure in 137, 207
structure of the subject of 28–29, 34, 46, 83, 92, 135–137, 200
topography of 2
Upholsterers call 74

Vertical relations 195
Vicious circle 230
Voice 34
Voyeurism 227

White figures-black figures 195
Winnicott's theory 134